The 'Holy Mother', Her Majesty Tzu Hsi, 1903

(The Mansell Collection)

The last
Great Empress
of China

by Charlotte
Haldane

人 夫 登 何

CONSTABLE LONDON

Constable & Co. Ltd
10-12 Orange Street
London WC2

First published 1965
© 1965 Charlotte Haldane

Reprinted January 1966

Printed in Great Britain by
The Garden City Press Limited
Letchworth, Hertfordshire

Contents

1   *The Dragon Throne*

In Peking, the northern capital of the Celestial Empire, there were three sections known as the Tartar, the Chinese, and the Imperial cities. Marco Polo, the first European to visit this jewel-city of the Far East, admired the exquisite symmetry of the plan —'arranged in squares like a chess-board, disposed in a manner so perfect and masterly. . . . '

In the very heart of this four-square vision of beauty lived *Nan Mien*—the Face which is turned towards the south—his Sacred and Imperial Majesty's—which few of his millions of subjects ever saw, nor dared to look upon.

The Imperial City was six and a half miles long, enclosed by walls plastered in red—the lucky colour. It lay between the northern, or Tartar, and the Chinese, or southern, sections.

Inside it was a citadel—the Forbidden City, enclosed in high purple walls, two and a quarter miles long. Access to this, 'The Great Within', was barred, as its name clearly indicated, to all but the privileged few granted admission to the Emperor's private domain.

The two great main gates to the Imperial City, with their brightly tiled watch-towers, were called the Gate of Spiritual

Valour, in the centre of the north wall, and the Meridian Gate, to the south. Within them the Gate of Supreme Harmony gave entrance to the Forbidden City and the huge State Halls — those of Supreme Harmony, Central Harmony, and Precious Harmony. To the north of these, reached through another gateway, the Gate of Heavenly Purity, lay smaller halls. For as one approached more closely to the Imperial apartments one entered a semi-heavenly realm. This gate led to the Palace of Heavenly Purity, the Hall of the Blending of Heaven and Earth, the Palace of Earthly Tranquillity and the Hall of Majestic Peace.

These magnificent buildings, glowing with colour, were reflected in the still waters of three artificial lakes, surrounded by flowering trees and shrubs. They all backed north, for according to immemorial tradition the Emperor must always face southwards, since 'All the stars in heaven salute the north'.

In the very centre of this vast rectangular design stood the magnificently carved and gilded Imperial Throne, inlaid with mother-of-pearl forming the shapes of writhing dragons.

The dragon symbol was everywhere—carved, sculptured and embroidered—for it was the sacred emblem of the semi-divine, semi-human Dragon, the Son of Heaven and Emperor of China. Dressed in heavy, richly adorned robes of yellow satin—the Imperial colour—the Emperor sat in silent, august majesty, whilst his assembled Court below worshipped him on their knees.

The Throne Hall was lit by great glowing lanterns, throwing up against the shadows the blaze of colour of the uniforms of those paying homage to their supreme master—master of the whole world.

There were the Imperial princes, his relatives, with their distinguishing red and yellow sashes; the ministers or mandarins, their round skull-caps topped by buttons of various jewels and hues denoting their rank, the highest being allowed the additional honour of a drooping peacock's feather.

Around the Dragon Throne stood the Imperial eunuchs; the dreaded Chief Eunuch and his principal assistants, gorgeously clothed in long-skirted, belted uniforms which hid their shame and denoted their respective ranks in that peculiar hierarchy.

The Dragon was sole undisputed ruler of the vast Middle Kingdom, the Celestial Empire and all its dependencies, stretching from the snow-capped mountains and bleak plains north-east and north-west to the sub-tropical China Sea that swept its immensely long southern coasts; containing eighteen provinces, protected on the north-east from savage invaders by the Great Wall. Within it lived more than four hundred million subjects of various races and religions.

For nearly three centuries the absolute master of this huge and mysterious realm was not, however, a Chinese, but a Manchu.

The Manchus were a virile race of hunters and warriors living beyond the Great Wall. They were rough and uncouth but hardy and daring; even their women enjoyed far greater freedom than those of the great rich country they were to possess.

In 1618 their leader, Nurhachu, declared war on the last Chinese Emperor of the Ming dynasty; defeated an army of 200,000 Chinese at Mukden, and made it his capital in 1625. In 1644 Peking fell through treachery, and the Emperor, after having killed all his family, hanged himself in shame.

The mighty Nurhachu died before he could consolidate his conquests. He was succeeded by his fourth son, Abkhai, for the Manchu succession did not always go by primogeniture. Abkhai called his dynasty the Ching, meaning Pure, and it was known from his day onwards as The Great Pure Dynasty.

When the Manchus became the undisputed rulers of the Chinese people, they adopted the Confucian ethic founded by the Great Sage in the sixth century B.C., and practised the Buddhist religion, taking both of these over from the highly civilized nation they had conquered.

The Emperor had a twofold mandate. In the religious sphere he was the Son of Heaven—his people's intermediary with the invisible powers on high, the gods and ancestors. On the secular plane his mandate from the spiritual realm was to rule the country justly. The Manchus also took over the highly perfected organization through which this was done : the mandarinate, a class of officials selected by public examination.

The religious duties of the Son of Heaven were complex and

arduous. In order that an Emperor-elect might be qualified to perform them, he must be chosen from the members of a lower generation than his predecessor. In consequence all Imperial princes of each generation were given the same Manchu prefix to their personal names. But an Emperor was far too sacred to be referred to so disrespectfully. Each occupant of the Dragon Throne was therefore given a symbolical reign-title by which he became known in the dynastic hierarchy.

Two Manchu Emperors became famous for their valour, rectitude, and learning. The first of these was the great Kang Hsi Emperor (1662–1723), whose reign-title meant Lasting Prosperity and who ruled China in the late seventeenth and early eighteenth centuries. He was a bold huntsman, a wise statesman, and a great scholar. Kang Hsi was succeeded by his fourth son, the Yung Chen or Harmonious Rectitude Emperor. But his reign was a brief one. In 1736, Kang Hsi's grandson, the second great Emperor, Chien Lung (1736–96), mounted the Dragon Throne, which he occupied for the following sixty years, the high peak of Manchu rule. His reign-title was Enduring Glory, and was no exaggeration, for he brought the administration to its highest state of perfection.

The reign-title of Chien Lung's son and successor was Chia Ching—High Felicity—a misnomer. For under his twenty-five years of rule the Chinese began the rebellions against the Manchu despots which in due course led to their overthrow.

In 1820 this feeble ruler was succeeded by his second son, known as the Tao Kuang Emperor—the Way of Splendour. But the splendours of the Manchu dynasty were already waning, and at the beginning of the next century they were to disappear for ever.

There was an ancient prophecy that one day a woman of the Manchu race would bring their heavenly mandate to an end.

Yet in the year 1835, when the Tao Kuang Emperor sat on the Dragon Throne, facing south in the very heart of his sumptuously beautiful Forbidden City, safely within its rose-red walls, this prophecy was not remembered.

In order that their racial purity should never be contaminated, the Manchu Emperors were forbidden to take Chinese wives or concubines; only girls of their own race were eligible. To emphasize the distinction between them, Chinese women were forbidden to wear the costumes and hair-styles reserved for Manchu ladies.

All Manchu women dressed according to prescribed rules. Their straight black hair was drawn back from the forehead and fastened in a bun. On this was pinned a square head-dress, shaped rather like a mortar-board, from which a tassel might hang on either side. This provided a severe background into which were pinned bright and colourful jewels and floral ornaments which matched the ladies' long pendant ear-rings. They were swathed from their necks to below their feet in long straight satin gowns fastened across the chest from the left to the right shoulder, with lavish embroidery on the sleeves (which covered their wrists), neckband, sideband and hem. This conventional garb allowed a great deal of latitude in the detail of its decoration.

The most important distinction, however, between Chinese and Manchu girls lay in their feet. For centuries the Chinese had inflicted the cruel custom of foot-binding on their female children. When a little girl was six to eight years of age, her mother would tightly wind strips of cotton around her daughter's toes and instep. These would remain for years, often causing the child acute pain. Gradually the toes, unable to grow freely, would atrophy, until in adolescence the girl possessed those tiny 'lily-feet' so greatly admired by Chinese men.

The girls of the hardy Northern conquerors were never subjected to this torture on aesthetic grounds. As their feet developed naturally from childhood onwards they learned to walk with incomparable grace, balancing the heavy decorated head-dresses on their straight slender necks.

In all Oriental countries it was the practice since time immemorial for the rulers, who at first were nearly always conquerors, to keep a harem of beautiful women as concubines.

In China this custom was not an Imperial prerogative. Every prosperous citizen usually had more than one wife and a concubine or two. But the Son of Heaven being the greatest and most powerful ruler on earth, his harem was also the largest and the most beautiful, filled with more entrancing young women than any other. And in order that their spotless purity might never even be threatened, no man, not even one of the Emperor's brothers or uncles, was ever allowed, under penalty of a horrid lingering death, to spend one night within the Forbidden City.

The Court was staffed by a regiment of more than three thousand eunuchs, headed by the all-powerful Chief Eunuch. They wore uniforms of different colours to denote their various grades. The higher and more gorgeously dressed were those closest to their Imperial master's person. But others performed every kind of service. There were highly skilled craftsmen among them, as well as cooks, clerks, gardeners and ordinary menials.

The eunuchs received free board and lodging, and in lieu of wages expected and were given emoluments such as tips and gratuities. All those who furnished supplies to the palaces or had business there—whether princes, statesmen, high officials or mere tradesmen supplying the kitchens, stables or kennels— had to deal with or through the eunuchs, who charged them the utmost 'squeeze' they could extort. The eunuch system was in fact a highly perfected protection racket.

Under all Chinese dynasties the eunuchs were regarded as an inevitable plague. After the fall of the Ming dynasty, which immediately preceded the Ching or Manchu, the depredations and corruption of the eunuchs were generally regarded as the cause of its ruin. The great Manchu Emperors, the Kang Hsi and Chien Lung, who were firm and wise rulers, managed to check this plague by stern measures, but ever since Chien Lung's time the eunuchs gradually succeeded in re-establishing their sinister power, and their nefarious system continued uninterruptedly until early in the twentieth century.

The Emperors, cut off as they were, with few exceptions, from all normal social intercourse with other men, imprisoned magnificently within the Forbidden City, condemned to spend most of their time in ornate but endless and exhausting ceremonial and ritual, were nevertheless human. Inevitably they turned to their chief eunuchs for companionship and often even for advice in their perplexities. No confessor of a Catholic king knew more royal secrets than the chief eunuchs of the later Manchu emperors, but whereas most of the former were saintly and virtuous men the latter were as unscrupulous as they were clever. A successful chief eunuch needed to have all the intelligence and astuteness of a brilliant statesman, and most of them also coupled this with the guile and greed of a ruthless criminal.

Those higher eunuchs who were in constant silent attendance, never speaking unless commanded to do so—the penalty for the slightest slip in the prescribed etiquette being a severe beating or possibly even beheading—probably became the most acute observers of human conduct the world has ever known. Their essential task was instantly to interpret the Imperial will, or even in advance to forestall it, to unravel the nuances and undertones, the frowns, sighs or smiles, the whims and vagaries of the semi-sacred individual on whom their lives literally depended from day to day.

By whispering gossip, slander or calumny into Imperial ears, a favourite eunuch was able frequently to bring about the disgrace or even death of anyone who had not taken the precaution of buying his benevolence. But perhaps the simplest and safest method of ingratiating himself with his lord was his ability immediately to satisfy his every caprice or vice. If the youthful Emperor as yet had no vices, it was to the eunuch's greatest personal advantage to provide him with them; to tempt him with gambling, drinking, opium-smoking or sexual incontinence.

In fairness to the eunuchs, it should be mentioned that they themselves were regarded with the greatest contempt and hatred by those normal males who considered the *castrato* as deeply inferior, ludicrous and despicable. Most of the young boys whose manhood was thus mutilated had no say in the matter. So the eunuchs, many of whom were men of considerable ability, formed a closed corporation with a permanent grievance against their employers and the world in general, and regarded their own

crimes and depredations as a justified means of avenging themselves for the outrage on their bodies and the ignominious status
to which this condemned them all life long.

Outside the Emperor's private apartments stood a small ivory
table. On this were placed jade tablets, engraved with the names
of the favourite concubines of the Son of Heaven. When His
Majesty retired to his Chamber of Divine Repose he would, if
the fancy took him, turn over the tablet on which was the name
of the wife or concubine with whom he would share his bed that
night.

A eunuch would be dispatched to the lucky young woman and
would carry her back in his arms through the silent courts and
long dimly-lit corridors of the Forbidden City, warmly wrapped
in a red silk gown, which in winter was padded with cotton wool.
She would then be undressed and laid naked at the foot of the
bed, to await the Dragon's embrace.

2 The Emperor Takes
a Concubine

On 3 November 1835, the wife of an obscure Manchu official gave birth to a baby girl. The child was not even born in Peking, but in the province of Anhui, where her father held an unimportant provincial inspectorship. Nor was there any particular rejoicing when a girl was born. In China, as in Europe or America, little girls were often given flower-names, and this one became known as Orchid.

In later years a crust of legend crystallized around Orchid's earlier life. According to one such story her father died at his provincial post and her mother, whose means were modest, decided to take Orchid and her younger sister to live with wealthy and influential relatives in Peking. They travelled in leisurely but pleasant manner by barge, along the Grand Canal, which linked the capital with the more important cities on the great Yangtze river. By mistake, a large sum of money being sent to a fellow-passenger, an important official, was delivered to the widow. When the error was discovered, the rightful owner of the sum, seeing how pretty was the widow's daughter, Orchid, allowed her to keep it. For the girl was a Manchu, and, all being well, would probably make a brilliant marriage. In that case he would be

17

more than repaid, he knew, for his timely help. Indeed, he was.

Among the Manchus two clans were as powerful as the clans of Scotland in feudal times. The direct descendants of the conqueror, Nurhachu, were members of the Imperial clan, and possessed many hereditary privileges, of which the outward insignia were the yellow or red girdles they wore. Having originally been the doughtiest warriors and bowmen, they were immensely proud of their tradition. As they became richer and more powerful their physical and mental prowess steadily declined. They were often very stupid, dissipated, and invariably intensely jealous of their rights, prerogatives, and emoluments.

The Yehonala were originally two separate clans—the Yeho and Nala—descendants of a Manchu prince, Yangkunu, whose daughter became consort to Nurhachu, the conqueror. And the Emperors continued to take girls of this clan as their wives and concubines. The little girl called Orchid was a member of this distinguished clan, and soon after her arrival in Peking, became known simply by this name.

The head of the Peking branch of the Yehonala was called Muyanga. He was an official holding an appointment in the Imperial Board of Works. The Muyanga family lived in the quarter of Peking known as the Tartar City, in Pewter Lane. Most streets in Chinese cities, like those in the cities of medieval Europe, were called after those who plied their trades or transacted their business there. Pewter Lane was the meeting-place of merchants and traders bringing pewter utensils from the faraway south-western province of Yunnan, for delivery to the vast Imperial stores.

Behind its non-committal walls the Muyanga home lay in a large garden where, in Chinese style, there were numerous one-storied pavilions in which members of the family lived with their retinue of servants, and in one or another of which there was always plenty of room to lodge relatives from the country. Orchid's family settled down there very happily—so much so that long after her brilliant daughter had left home to fulfil her dazzling and dramatic destiny, her mother, the Lady Niuhulu, continued to reside in Pewter Lane until the end of her life.

The Manchus had no objections to consanguinity; on the contrary, by the marriages of cousins, and especially members of the same clan, possessions and influence were all the more safely preserved and increased.

The young relative chosen to become Orchid's future husband was accordingly another Yehonala, a cousin whose name was Jung Lu. At what age they first met is uncertain, but it was not long after her arrival in Peking. It is also uncertain just how old she then was.

Jung Lu was to follow the military tradition of his clan, and in due course became an officer in the Eighth Banner corps. The Imperial Bannermen were so called because each of these regiments of Guards had a banner of different shape and colour. There were also eight Mongolian Banner regiments and a similar number for those native Chinese who took military service under the Manchus. But their own were the *élite*. A Commission in one of them was an hereditary perquisite, which Orchid's father, Captain Huei Cheng, also held by birthright, although he never seems to have been on active service. Peking was thronged with lazy Manchus in Banner uniforms who did little more than claim their pensions. But Jung Lu had a genuine military vocation. There is no doubt whatever that when the young cousins first met, Jung Lu fell deeply and permanently in love with Orchid.

Was this Yehonala girl beautiful or, at any rate, very pretty? Unquestionably she had exceptional charm. Today the word 'fascination' has almost lost its meaning; it seems positively Edwardian to describe any woman as fascinating. Yet this was precisely the mysterious quality she possessed to an almost magnetic degree, so that she could irresistibly impose her will on nearly everyone else. Her intelligence was undoubtedly exceptional, but her will-power was outstanding, outstripped only by her most unusual characteristic of all—boundless ambition. This was indeed remarkable in the daughter of an ineffectual small-time Manchu official and a mother who although admittedly charming and cultured was not in any other respect outstanding. There was definitely something enigmatic in Yehonala's personality that she did not inherit from either parent, a unique quality that was to set her apart from and above all other women in the world.

Orchid, now known as Yehonala, seemed even then exceptionally gifted. She was taught the arts practised by all daughters of good families, of which the principle were memorizing passages from the classics and much painting and calligraphy. These two were closely linked. Calligraphy was not merely 'writing' as Westerners practised it, but an art closely akin to painting, which over thousands of years had been perfected in order to produce with brush and ink the most graceful characters. For painting in the classical Chinese style Yehonala showed unusual talent ; throughout her life it remained one of her predominant interests. Yehonala undoubtedly possessed a quite exceptional memory. At the age of sixteen she had learnt at any rate the rudiments of the Five Classics of Confucius, which laid down the ethical code by which every literate Chinese was personally governed until the present century.

Yehonala's studies also included lighter literature, classical novels and plays, as well as much poetry.

During Yehonala's girlhood China was ruled by the Tao Kuang Emperor. He died — or, in the picturesque Chinese imagery, 'became Dragon-borne', wafted away to meet his illustrious ancestors on high — in 1850.

The succession passed to the Emperor's fourth son, a lad of nineteen, who was already a widower. He had been married to one of the Muyanga girls, whose name was Sakota, who died without giving birth to an heir. After her death a younger sister, Yehonala's cousin and playmate, was also called Sakota. She was as dull as Orchid was brilliant, as placid as Orchid was ambitious, as plain as Orchid was glamorous. They had nothing in common, yet their lives were thenceforward to be intimately and strangely linked.

The heir-apparent ascended the throne under the reign-title of Hsien Feng, or Universal Plenty. It was unfortunately chosen, for whilst he occupied the Dragon Throne, during the next eleven years, China knew troubles in plenty, but had few occasions for rejoicing.

The Empress Dowager, who ranked above the Emperor in dynastic precedence, retained the privilege of choosing her son's bride and concubines. She was naturally anxious that he should remarry in order to secure the direct succession. But his nuptials were forbidden by the Rites until after the expiry of the mourning period for his father, which lasted for twenty-seven months.

Hsien Feng's nuptial edict was published early in June 1852. It commanded district magistrates and other appropriate officials throughout the Empire to forward to the Forbidden City a detailed list of such Manchu girls in their localities as were considered eligible for selection as concubines. A minute investigation was then made of the claimants' pedigrees, dates of birth, upbringing and appearance. Since no decision of such vital importance was ever made without the advice of the Court astrologers, the exact time and date of birth were of paramount importance. The first draft of several hundred potentially suitable maidens was in due course thinned out, until only around sixteen or seventeen names remained on the list. Invitations were then sent to their lucky owners to attend at the Forbidden City to meet the Empress Dowager and the young Emperor. These summonses were delivered by hand. They were written on yellow paper and bore the Imperial seals. The colour, yellow, symbolizing gold, the sun, wealth, power, and magnificence, was exclusively reserved for Imperial usage. The messenger was received in humble deference, with the prescribed kowtows, by the fortunate young lady's father or other senior relative. And the entire neighbourhood was speedily aware of the momentously honourable occasion.

Such an Imperial summons immediately nullified any previous arrangement that a Manchu family might have made for the disposal of a daughter. None could aspire to so high an honour, so brilliant a match, as providing the Emperor with a concubine.

Amongst those who received this coveted command, Sakota, Muyanga's daughter, sister of Hsien Feng's late wife, stood high in the list of precedence. This also included her cousin Orchid, the Yehonala girl, who was already almost betrothed to the handsome young Bannerman, Jung Lu.

Some girls, deeply in love with a fiancé, might have been heartbroken at such an abrupt ending to a youthful romance and all dreams of requited love.

Yehonala may already have had a premonition of her high destiny. Possibly her horoscope revealed this to her. No one will ever know what were the secret thoughts of one of the most secretive minds of all time on that occasion, the very beginning of her amazing career. But it may be assumed that even at the age of sixteen Yehonala was a girl ruled by her head and not her heart.

Yehonala, with her highly developed artistic sense, had unerring taste and a faultless eye for delicate but harmonious colour schemes. For her first appearance in the Forbidden City she chose a gown of pale lilac, with carefully matched ornaments and embroideries. And like her rivals, according to the rule for all Manchu women excepting widows, she wore a dab of bright rouge on her lower lip.

On the appointed day the lovely Yehonala and the placid unimaginative Sakota, admired by their relatives, took their seats in the sedan-chairs that were to bear them for the first time into the Forbidden City. When all the maidens were assembled, the shy, giggling, pretty little candidates were ushered into a magnificent hall of the Empress Dowager's palace, filled with priceless works of art. Here they were in due course called up for presentation to Her Majesty, who regarded them with the cold and appraising eye of an experienced judge of human bloodstock. Beside her sat the pale, dissolute young Emperor. The girls' names were read out from his list by the Chief Eunuch, An-te-hai. Then tea was served to them, which provided their Majesties and the Court with a further opportunity to observe the candidates' deportment and manners.

According to her own later account, as soon as the young Emperor beheld the enchanting Orchid amongst her rivals at that very first tea-party, he paid her and only her the highest attention and honour. She was invited to take tea at the Imperial table, when for the first time His Imperial Majesty heard her speak. Perhaps the most powerful weapon in her armoury of fascination was an irresistibly attractive voice—a 'velvet' voice, as it was later described by her greatest British admirer, Sir Robert Hart. And it was obvious that she was highly intelligent, cultured, and practised in all the complicated arts of the decorum necessary to her new station.

The Imperial Concubines chosen by the Empress Dowager were divided into four classes or ranks. Her Majesty did not consider any of the aspirants before her worthy of being placed in the first class. Even Sakota — shortly to become Empress Consort—was only given the second rank. Yehonala was placed in the third class, *Kuei Jen,* meaning honourable person.

This appointment meant, of course, that her marriage to Jung Lu would never take place. Nor would she ever return home once she had entered the Imperial harem, but spend the rest of her life in strict seclusion in the Forbidden City.

It was said that Yehonala took the greatest care to ingratiate herself with the Empress Dowager. For so young a girl, and especially a Manchu, she was already unusually intellectual, and as soon as she became a member of the Imperial household she resumed her studies, reading the classics and the poets, and developing her talents as a painter. So she won Her Majesty's approval.

A different version of Yehonala's conquest of Hsien Feng, though less likely than the other, is more romantic.

In summer, when the dry hot winds from the north swept down on the rose-walled city, spraying it with clouds of irritating sand, the Court left Peking for the Summer Palace, the loveliest of all Imperial domains. Yehonala hated the Forbidden City all her life.

'It is so cold,' she complained even in her old age. 'There is nothing in it but vast buildings, empty save for echoes. Except for the Imperial Gardens there are no flowers, no fresh breezes. The place is cold. It has no heart.'

But this hatred was matched by an impassioned attachment to the Summer Palace. Its name was a misnomer, a considerable understatement to describe this exquisite creation, blending architecture with landscape-gardening to create the 'Bright

Round Garden', the perfect example of the Chinese genius for uniting the theory and practice of Confucian aesthetics in visual form. Great marble buildings, palaces, temples, were surrounded by flower-gardens of cunningly contrived colour-blending. Within these pleasances lay a huge artificial lake, Kun Ning, containing thousands of variegated goldfish sporting under vast stretches of lotus, the sacred Buddhist water-lily. From the earth that had been excavated by thousands of labourers to create it rose an artificial hill, and the various palatial residences surrounding it were artfully sited to create vistas and views of transcendent beauty from every angle.

So great was Yehonala's passion for the Summer Palace—greater than the emotion she felt for any human being—that it was later to influence her political policy in the most critical moment of her reign.

No more exquisite setting could be imagined for the first meeting between the concubine of the third rank and her all-powerful lord.

If their first meeting did in fact take place there, it was possibly not merely by accident that the bored young Emperor, casually passing by one of the little pavilions housing his concubines, with their tiny flower-filled gardens, should have heard a sweet voice singing an old song, caught a glimpse of the singer, the lovely girl known as Orchid, demurely in that garden plying her embroidery needle, fallen instantly in love with her, and commanded his eunuchs to bring her that very night to the Imperial bedchamber.

Almost from the moment of her arrival at Court, Yehonala, with her innate shrewdness and adaptability, realized the necessity of winning the favour of the Chief Eunuch and coming to a working understanding with him. One of the most marked characteristics of her cunning and realistic mind was the fact that —as if she had always been of the Blood Royal—she never forgot a faithful servant and rewarded all those loyal to her, whether viceroys or eunuchs, with the greatest generosity, so that they became her devoted and dependable henchmen. And if Hsien Feng did first behold the Orchid in the romantic setting of the Summer Palace, this could hardly have happened without the connivance of the Chief Eunuch or one of his assistants, and might well have been contrived by them.

Hsien Feng apparently first slept with Yehonala, the 'honourable person' with whom he had fallen in love, in 1855. This was the year in which the Empress Dowager, Tao Kuang's widow, died. Possibly at his mother's command, Hsien Feng had previously taken to his bed the uninteresting Muyanga girl, Sakota, whom he never loved. As soon as she became pregnant she was raised to the rank of Empress Consort. And when Yehonala also became with child, she was similarly promoted to the second rank, as *P'in* concubine.

It was then that for the first time this ambitious girl had a glimpse of the power that might one day be hers. Even if Sakota did produce the longed-for heir to the throne, Yehonala might still remain the Emperor's favourite. But if Sakota failed to do so, and she herself were to bear the son so desperately wanted by the Emperor, the Manchu hierarchy and the people of China, there might be no limit to her power.

Intelligence, genius even, can make little headway without luck. The birth of her son, heir to the Dragon Throne, was the luckiest event that ever befell Yehonala, the 'Open Sesame' to the absolute power she in due course achieved. It was merely by bad luck that the young Empress bore a sickly girl child, that very soon died, and, had she lived, would have been of no dynastic interest whatever. It was by the greatest good fortune that the concubine Yehonala gave birth to a healthy boy in the month of April 1856. She was thereupon immediately raised to the first rank, that of *Quei Fei Yi,* the last character meaning feminine virtue. This was the title under which she was known for a few years longer—the Yi Concubine.

But who did in fact father this male baby, who only a few years later became the ruler of the Celestial Empire? Hsien Feng was twenty-five at the time of becoming a parent, and already half paralysed, owing, it was said, to the life of debauchery he had been leading under the eunuchs' evil influence for the past ten years.

Very early in her career the Yi Concubine became the subject of malevolent gossip at Court, which her increasing interest in matters of State continued to fan. The southern provinces were more or less permanently inimical to the Manchus and many scurrilous versions of her private life were published and circulated there by those who had never, of course, come within hundreds of miles of their subject. One of these is almost too absurd to mention, let alone to believe. According to this invention Yehonala never gave birth to a child at all, but bought a male baby from an ordinary Chinese woman through the intermediary of the eunuchs and passed on this child as her own and Hsien Feng's. The silliness of this scandal is obvious when one recalls how jealously the Manchus guarded their racial purity. Had Yehonala and An-te-hai ever contemplated such a plot, the infant would certainly not have been a Chinese one.

There seems little doubt that Yehonala was the mother of the heir to the throne, and none at all that Hsien Feng was desperately anxious for one. It might not have been impossible to persuade him that he was the child's father, or to agree to allow the world to believe this to be so, if he knew himself by then to be impotent as well as unpopular as a ruler.

Could the father of this important infant have been Jung Lu, Yehonala's former fiancé?

Jung Lu was an officer in one of the Banner regiments—the Imperial Guards — and therefore in close proximity to the Throne. He never lost touch with his beloved, even after she had entered the Great Within. According to Court gossip, maliciously spread by the Yi Concubine's enemies and slanderers, Jung Lu, who was never to be her husband, became her lover. Their assignations were arranged by the Chief Eunuch, An-te-hai, who thus made himself more than ever indispensable to his young mistress. Although the discovery of such an intrigue would have made the lovers subject to the death penalty—the man first suffering indescribable tortures—it would not have been the first of its kind in the melodramatic annals of Chinese Court history.

Whether or not Jung Lu was Yehonala's lover, and possibly the father of the heir to the Dragon Throne, whether or not their love was consummated, or sublimated into a life-long attachment on both sides, it is a fact that Jung Lu was the only man—since eunuchs did not count as such—who until his death retained his influence over Yehonala; the only one who dared to speak his mind openly to her when he thought it necessary, although even he did not succeed in avoiding periods of disfavour and the dangerous consequences of incurring her anger.

3   *The Red Barbarians*

A great politician, like a great artist, is born, not made. At the age of three Mozart was already picking out little tunes on the harpsichord; at the age of twenty-one the Yi Concubine was the most influential individual in the Celestial Empire. To have discovered her extraordinary flair Hsien Feng could not have been quite such a fool as his detractors made out. In his desperately difficult and lonely situation she must have seemed to him a blessing from heaven: no mere concubine but almost the only dependable partner and adviser he had. For this girl, so different from the stupid Empress Consort, and indeed from every other woman he had hitherto known, was a natural politician, avidly interested in affairs of State in all their complexity. She was soon reading the confidential State papers presented to the Emperor, and when he gave audience to his ministers would be eagerly listening behind the magnificent brocaded silk curtains that hung behind the Dragon Throne and hid her from their sight.

Shortly after the birth of Hsien Feng's heir, the Imperial troops had some success in repelling and containing the rebel armies. Such an omen might not be ignored; it seemed clear to the astrologers and therefore to everyone else that the heavenly Emperor as well as Hsien Feng's sacred ancestors now dwelling with him were benevolently inclined towards the Son of Heaven. But this was an over-optimistic view.

At that crucial period the Hsien Feng Emperor was possibly already too ailing to deal personally and effectively with State business. But one of the principal grievances his officials and ministers had against him was that in contrast to his illustrious ancestors he was lazy and uncultured. Even more offensive to these scholarly critics was the undeniable fact that in matters of high policy he no longer relied on their experience and advice, but more and more on Yehonala's—the Yi Concubine, a young girl of twenty-one who painted, sang, and recited poetry quite nicely, but was—and indeed how could it be otherwise?—utterly ignorant of world affairs, the complications of the military arts, and the tricky business of commerce with foreigners. Yehonala, moreover, was a Manchu, to whom the welfare of China and of the Emperor's millions of subjects was in every way subordinate to the continued power and glory of their conquerors—the Great Pure Dynasty.

Yet for a short period nobody at Court, neither the Imperial princes, members of the Council nor the Censorate, would have risked the disgrace and possibly even death that might have resulted had they at that point challenged her power over the Emperor. The situation was unparalleled, and inevitably unstable.

During the reigns of the great Manchu Emperors, Kang Hsi and Chien Lung, there were strong hands at the helm. But their successors were unable to stem the constantly rising tide of rebellion throughout the Empire.

In 1833, during the reign of the Tao Kuang Emperor (Hsien Feng's father), an intelligent and ambitious young Cantonese student called Hung Hsiu-chuan failed to get a first-class degree in the civil service examinations. In 1837, when he was twenty-four, he tried again, and again failed to reach the top standard. Such frustrated intellectuals were always potential leaders of revolt. At that moment young Hung happened to read some

Christian tracts. In his disturbed psychological condition he there-upon had a series of revelations which convinced him that he himself was the Brother of Christ and was destined to free his countrymen from their Manchu oppressors.

Hung soon collected adherents in greater and greater numbers, became a powerful leader, and, pursuing his dreams of grandeur, founded a new Chinese dynasty of his own, which he called the Heavenly Peace or Taiping dynasty. His followers publicly pro-claimed their defiance of Manchu rule by refusing to shave their frontal hair and to wear the remainder in a queue. The Manchus contemptuously called them the long-haired rebels.

The movement spread so rapidly and successfully that by 1853 Hsien Feng, the young Emperor, was faced with a colossal rebellion, which was not finally suppressed until twelve years later. The Taipings swept through province after province, taking one stronghold after another along the great Yangtze river. By March 1853 they gained control of Nanking, the second greatest city in the Empire, which they captured in ten days, after killing all its Manchu inhabitants, numbering around twenty thousand.

Hung Hsiu-chuan, the former obscure student, there pro-claimed himself Emperor and Nanking his Imperial city, to the delirious applause of his victorious followers. The Taiping momentum did not, however, stop there. In 1855 their armies were threatening Tientsin, the last stronghold between the rebels and the capital, only eighty miles away. But at that point they were at last thwarted and repelled by an army under the com-mand of Tseng Kuo-fan, in the Manchu Emperor's service.

Tseng Kuo-fan was a great strategist and also a learned Confucian scholar. Rumour credited his appointment as Commander-in-Chief of the Imperial troops to Yehonala. The story went that this great man had been enthusiastically recom-mended to His Majesty by his beloved counsellor, the Yi Concubine.

Whether this was true or not, throughout her life Yehonala did show one of the most essential characteristics of a successful ruler : like Louis XIV of France, she had an undeniable flair for appointing and promoting the most able statesmen and soldiers of her time. This was not, however, infallible; feminine intuition rarely is. She by no means always learned to estimate correctly the abilities of those who served her—and lived to rue the day when she allowed herself to be influenced by unscrupulous opportunists.

When it came to dealing with an entirely different and much more serious problem than internal government, Yehonala was completely astray. Never in her life did she have a glimpse of the vast ocean that washed southern Chinese shores; nor, for very many years, did she see those foreign barbarians who came in warships to despoil her country, rob her people, and wreck her palaces. In the seclusion of the Forbidden City the young Yi Concubine was almost certainly ignorant of the threat to China from European sea-power and those whom it brought to those Far Eastern coasts.

The magnificent halls of State and reception-rooms in the Imperial palaces contained a vast collection of priceless treasures. Most of these were gifts or tributes brought to the Emperors by the heads of vassal States. Among them were a large number of European clocks. Had Yehonala inquired how they came to be there, she might have learned that they were brought to the Court of the last Ming Emperor, in 1601, by a remarkable Italian Jesuit, Father Matteo Ricci, who hoped to convert the slit-eyed heathens to Christianity.

Whilst the first Manchu Emperor, Shun Chih, did not adopt this strange foreign faith, he permitted Ricci, who was also a remarkable mathematician, to remain and to help the Chinese to learn a little of European science. They were particularly fascinated by the European clockwork system and the clocks which the Emperor received with much gratification. During this Emperor's term of office, Dutch and Russian envoys also arrived in Peking.

The Kang Hsi Emperor raised no objections to missionary activities, and during the seventeenth century the conversion of the Chinese made considerable headway. It might have been even more successful had this new religion not conflicted with the deeply-rooted Chinese custom of ancestor-veneration, amounting to worship. The Jesuits petitioned His Holiness the Pope in far-away Rome for a ruling which might enable them to overcome this obstacle. But the Pontiff considered that such idolatrous practices were incompatible with the true religion, and in 1716 Kang Hsi, finding the missionaries were becoming increasingly troublesome, banished them. In due course, however, the Imperial authorities were obliged, under duress, to re-admit them. And the Catholics were followed by missionaries from every other Christian denomination, with unfortunate consequences for themselves and the Chinese people throughout the nineteenth century.

But the Europeans were not lured to this exotic Far Eastern Empire in order to save the souls of its millions. They were more excited and attracted by accounts of its untold riches, and by the hope of illimitable and profitable trade, and exploitation of its resources. The Portuguese, the great mariners, arrived in 1514, and by the 1550s had established their base at Macao. They were very soon followed by the Dutch, French, and British, who became increasingly predominant. By the middle of the eighteenth century the British East India Company had obtained a monopoly of the Cantonese trade, even though it was conducted under all manner of tiresome restrictions imposed by the deeply suspicious local authorities.

Europe became more and more avid for Chinese silk, porcelain, lacquer, and especially the new fashionable drink that Samuel Pepys called 'tee'. But excepting money, the British could offer no sufficiently attractive inducements in return to an ancient nation well satisfied with its own commodities. In 1834 the monopoly of the East India Company was abolished, and the British merchants, although resorting to heavy bribery and corruption of the Cantonese officials, were confined to a minute portion of Chinese soil under constant harassment.

Yet the British did not neglect to attempt to establish more friendly relations by diplomatic overtures.

In the last year of the mighty Chien Lung Emperor's reign, 1793, a first British embassy, headed by Lord Macartney, arrived in China. But according to the tenets of the Celestial Empire it was quite ridiculous for the Son of Heaven to receive envoys from a foreign barbarian, a petty monarch thousands of miles across the ocean, on terms of equality. This was intimated to King George III's representative. Certainly an ambassador might come as a tribute-bearer on his master's behalf. The ruler of the Celestial Empire was well accustomed to receiving such emissaries, who acknowledged the supremacy of the world's overlord by entering the presence on their knees and performing the kowtow. This was an elaborate ritual of nine—thrice three—bows, the symbol of respectful subjection.

The British, shocked by such unbelievable arrogance, would not fall in with these disdainful terms. They would kneel to no man save their own king. After much diplomatic manoeuvring and parleying, as they had come so very far, Chien Lung agreed to receive Lord Macartney and his suite informally, at his hunting palace of Jehol, a magnificent residence in the mountains outside the Great Wall, about a hundred miles from Peking, where the earlier and hardier Manchu Emperors delighted in all field-sports and the chase after wild and dangerous beasts. Protocol being at last satisfied and simplified in order that the visitors should not too greatly lose face, Lord Macartney and his entourage were received with all the generosity of traditional Manchu hospitality; dazzled by the riches and splendours of the Imperial Court and especially by His Majesty. But the practical results of this first embassy were nil.

Even more unsuccessful was a second diplomatic mission in 1816. This was headed by Lord Amherst, who arrived in Peking during the reign of Chia Ching, meaning High Felicity, the Chien Lung Emperor's son. Again the visit was bedevilled by the demand that the envoys should perform the kowtow. Lord Amherst really had very bad luck indeed. For when the situation had dragged on for some time and a summons to Court was at last received, the splendid uniforms of the Ambassador and his suite had not yet arrived, nor the all-important presents in lieu of tribute, so that, being unable to appear before the Emperor suitably dressed and equipped, Lord Amherst never met him at all.

The misunderstanding was complete. The Emperor was convinced that these red-faced men were tribute-bearers from King George III. With true Chinese politeness he acknowledged that vassal's good intentions, at the same time administering to him a sharp rebuke.

'I fully recognize,' his Edict ran, 'the spirit of reverent submission which animated you. . . . ' But it pointed out that as this king lived so very far away, he was requested not to send any more missions. They were a waste of time; His Majesty 'attached no value to products from abroad'. Moreover, the envoys were wholly ignorant of Chinese ceremonial procedure, and the bickering which followed their arrival was highly displeasing to the Imperial ear.

Commercial relations at Canton continued to deteriorate. They became beyond repair when the foreign merchants, having no legitimate goods with which to tempt the Chinese in return for those luxuries which they so keenly wished to acquire, began illictly to import opium into China with the connivance of corrupt local officials.

The vice of opium-smoking was already strictly forbidden by the authorities and in 1839 the Tao Kuang Emperor made a determined effort to stamp out this nefarious trade. He appointed a powerful mandarin as Viceroy of the huge southern province of Kuangtung and sent him to Canton. Commissioner Lin, as he was known, immediately took stringent steps, ordering the foreign merchants to surrender to the authorities their stocks of opium. When they made a show of resistance they were put under house-arrest; their victuals were withdrawn and their servants ordered to leave them.

The British at Hong Kong appointed Captain Charles Elliot to take up the matter on behalf of their subjects. Although Great Britain has ever since been under the stigma of the consequences, Captain Elliot did in fact attempt to co-operate with the Chinese authorities. He assured the British merchants of compensation, whereupon the huge number of 20,291 chests of opium were handed over, and destroyed by Commissioner Lin. Far from this terminating the incident, however, further difficulties followed, culminating in the famous—or infamous—Opium War of 1839–42. Twice a British naval force attacked and destroyed the Bogue forts protecting the Canton river; thousands of Chinese and Manchus were killed.

A first peace treaty was arranged in 1841, but this the Emperor indignantly refused to ratify; and it was not until a British fleet was threatening Nanking in 1842 that at last a valid treaty, known as the Treaty of Nanking, was signed. This laid down the pattern for all subsequent treaties between China and the foreign powers, exacting the heaviest penalties from the defeated. Hong Kong was ceded to Britain. All the great ports on China's southern coastline were to be opened to foreign trade, and at Shanghai, in particular, British subjects were conceded extra-territoriality, no longer under Chinese jurisdiction but only responsible to their own officials. The huge indemnity of five million pounds was also extracted from the Chinese Government.

Although Tao Kuang was forced into accepting these ignominious conditions it is hardly surprising that it was with certain secret reservations that he did so. And when, on his death in 1850, the young Hsien Feng Emperor mounted the Dragon Throne, his reign already bedevilled by the Taiping Rebellion, he inherited also the consequences of the foreign aggression.

In 1856 another disastrous war for the Chinese broke out at Canton. There was lying there a small Chinese vessel, the *Arrow*, which had been licensed at Hong Kong, and in consequence was flying the British flag. The enormously fat Viceroy, Governor Yeh, arrested some Chinese sailors in this ship and ordered the flag to be hauled down. Various grave disturbances, riots and attacks on foreigners in defiance of the Nanking Treaty, led to increasing conflict, which became known as the *Arrow* war. Towards the end of 1857 the British, joined by the French, led by Lord Elgin and Baron Gros, attacked Canton and took Viceroy Yeh prisoner. They banished him to Calcutta, where he died.

Lord Elgin and his expeditionary force then proceeded northwards and in 1858 captured the vital stronghold, the Taku Forts at at the mouth of the Peiho river, protecting the city of Tientsin, and uncomfortably close to Peking. The Emperor then sent a special envoy, Chi Ying, to negotiate with Lord Elgin. He failed in his mission, and, apparently at the Yi Concubine's suggestion, was 'presented with the silken cord of self-dispatch, as a mark of the Throne's benevolent leniency'.

Yehonala may have advised Hsien Feng to pass this sentence. But it was only according to tradition that an unsuccessful envoy was beheaded or, as a favour, allowed to commit suicide. Both before and after this incident, the practice was followed; often diplomats and generals, unable to bear the shame of failure, killed themselves voluntarily.

A treaty was, however, signed with Lord Elgin on 26 June, by which the British and French further opened up the country for their trade, and won the right to have resident diplomatic representatives in Peking. His lordship, presumably never having heard of Yehonala, the Yi Concubine, and unaware of the fact that his principal opponent in this game of war and diplomacy was a mere ignorant Manchu girl, went away satisfied.

The Manchus had signed all these treaties forced upon them by the invaders under compulsion, with strong reservations. Hsien Feng, or possibly Yehonala, when realizing how harsh were the terms, refused point-blank to carry them out or to honour the agreement made by the Imperial representatives. And on this occasion a great many of the scholars and high officials were on Yehonala's side, for they were following the precepts of the Great Sage Confucius himself. The spirits, he taught, did not recognize an oath made under duress.

Hsien Feng and Yehonala were acting in the best tradition of their own faith. But it was unlikely that the British or any other Christian foreigners, who rarely troubled to study the Chinese point of view, would accept the consequences.

A year later, when it became clear to the British Government that the Chinese Government had no intention of implementing the terms of the treaty Lord Elgin was ordered back, and another Anglo-French force appeared at the mouth of the Peiho. The Chinese, however, had by then taken their precautions. The Taku forts were found to be strongly fortified and the invaders were repelled with severe losses.

The defeat inflicted on the foreign devils provided Hsien Feng and Yehonala with a sweet but short-lived triumph. It was of course utterly unacceptable to the Anglo-French forces. In August 1860 an army of 13,000 British, 7,000 French, and 2,500 Cantonese coolies — the Cantonese traditionally hating the Manchus and happy to fight against them even under European command—captured Tientsin from the landward side, where it was less adequately defended. According to the Manchu rules of the game this was regarded as a very unfair move. Plenipotentiaries were then hastily sent from Peking to negotiate with Lord Elgin, but were, not unnaturally, received with suspicion and did not succeed in stemming the invaders, who moved still nearer to the capital, to Tungchow, a mere dozen miles away.

On 6 September the Hsien Feng Emperor published an Edict. Certain European historians considered that Yehonala was responsible for the drafting of it, or at any rate had inspired it. The general tone of this document was one of high moral and not altogether unjustified indignation. It began in traditional fashion —'Swaying the wide world . . . '—whether or not the Emperor still believed this to be the case. It then pointed out that he had never forbidden England and France to trade with China; referred to the capture and banishment of Viceroy Yeh at Canton, and even agreed that by his harsh measures against the foreigners he had brought this on himself. It next referred to Elgin's unsuccessful attack on the Taku forts, then burst into a spate of reproachful oratory, and concluded :

> These barbarians live in the remote parts of the earth—whensoever the British and French repent of their evil ways and return to their allegiance, we shall be pleased to permit them to trade again. . . . But should they persist in their wicked violation of every right principle, our armies must mightily smite them. . . .

To Western minds it might well appear incredible that more than half-way through the nineteenth century this Edict should have referred to the 'allegiance' of the British and French to the Dragon Throne, as if their respective rulers were in a state of vassalage to the Manchu Emperor. Yet in his utter ignorance of conditions outside the Celestial Empire, the Son of Heaven, like Yehonala, apparently still believed this to be the case. The proffered forgiveness was framed in terms similar to those used to repentant rebels, when they were to be re-admitted, crawling, to Imperial favour. And the Edict condemned as shocking and scandalous the mere suggestion that Lord Elgin, the plenipotentiary of her Majesty Queen Victoria, should be received by the Emperor on any basis of equality between them.

But the British and French were more than shocked, really horrified, by the ensuing violation by the Chinese of that international law of which these ignorant Orientals, most unfortunately for all concerned, knew nothing. In due course arrangements were made for the discussion of an armistice. The negotiators on the European side—thirty-eight British and French officers, together with their interpreters—arrived at the agreed meeting-place, bearing, according to the rules of international warfare, a flag of truce. The Chinese showed no respect whatever for this hallowed emblem. They immediately seized and bound the envoys, carting them off like trussed pigs to the grounds of the famous Summer Palace, where they were horribly tortured according to the traditional Chinese mode of dealing with captured enemies. Half of them died of their injuries. The rest returned in due course with appalling wounds and mutilations.

From the European point of view this was the culminating act of treachery to the rules of civilized warfare committed by the Chinese. Yet the retaliation for this black and cruel deed was hardly civilized either.

The foreign troops now advanced on Peking. Physically ailing and mentally vacillating, Hsien Feng panicked, and with him many of his ministers. But on this occasion Yehonala for the first time showed her mettle. As brave as Joan of Arc, she remained firm and implacable towards the enemy. Her tremendous courage was described by a Chinese official and diarist. 'Certain Princes and Ministers besought the Yi Concubine to induce the Emperor

to leave on a tour—to save his face the Emperor's proposed flight
from the enemy was described as a tour of inspection of his realm.
'His Majesty was only too anxious to start at once, but the
Concubine Yi persuaded two of the Grand Secretaries to
memorialize against his doing so and . . . a Decree was issued
stating that under no circumstances would the Emperor leave
his capital. Another Decree was put out by Concubine Yi offering
large rewards to any who would slay the barbarians.'

'I cannot understand,' the diarist remarked, 'why His Majesty
was allowed to leave.' Later events revealed that already there
were princes and others at Court who had every reason to wish
for his departure from Peking. 'Up to the very last moment the
Yi Concubine begged him to remain in his Palace, as his presence
there could not fail to awe the barbarians. . . . How, she said,
could the barbarians be expected to spare the city if the Sacred
Chariot'—a euphemism referring to the Son of Heaven—'had
fled, leaving unprotected the tutelary shrines and the altars of the
gods?'

It appeared that the Court was in fact at that moment at the
Summer Palace, about fifteen miles distant from the capital,
where there was no immediate danger to the Emperor's person.
Nevertheless, Yehonala was overruled and His Sacred Majesty,
'attended by all his concubines, the Princes, Ministers and Dukes,
and all the officers of the household, left . . . in a desperate rout
and disorder unspeakable. . . .'

In the confusion of the flight the Yi Concubine, her heroic
advice having been rejected or ignored, must have clearly
realized, as she rode in her closed palanquin along the bumpy
roads to safety, that her power over the Emperor was waning.
She knew that certain Princes very close to him were her implacable enemies. For some time it had been rumoured at Court
that she was falling from favour. Her rapid rise was due to the
fact that she had been lucky enough to give Hsien Feng an heir.
Her child was the most precious asset remaining to her. But
where, at that moment of crisis and confusion, was the four-
year-old boy? She had to find him immediately.

Through the eunuchs, no doubt, Yehonala made inquiries all

along the straggling line of chariots, palanquins, and carts taking the fleeing Son of Heaven and his Court to Jehol. Yehonala's anxiety for the little prince's safety and perhaps even more for her own was ended for the time being when it was reported to her that the boy was travelling in the palanquin of Sakota, the Empress Consort. Until then she had never been a rival. She lacked all interest in high affairs of State; she was a simple woman, whose greatest sorrow was that she had no children. And so whilst the Yi Concubine listened so eagerly to the debates of the Imperial Council and acquired the immense hold she for a short time possessed over the Emperor, the Muyanga cousin whose high rank brought her no marital or maternal satisfaction devoted her affection to Yehonala's child.

During the three-day journey to Jehol, with frequent halts at resting-places and wayside temples along the mountainous roads, Yehonala had much to think about, and little that was pleasant.

Everyone knew that, although so young still, the Emperor was a sick man, who might not live to return to Peking. And if he did not do so, would she?

One grain of comfort did, however, remain to Yehonala. Amongst the hundreds of horsemen accompanying the Sacred Chariot was Jung Lu, in command of a strong detachment of troops of the Yehonala clan that formed part of the Imperial bodyguard.

4 Villainy in High Places

Western thriller-writers and their readers often delighted in sinister Chinese villains, crafty and sadistic criminals. And however deplorable it may be that for too long this was the popular image of a Chinese mandarin in Western eyes, even more deplorable was the fact that too many such characters did in fact exist and thrive. One of these full-blooded scoundrels was the Assistant Secretary, Su Shun, whose plotting caused Yehonala to lose her power over Hsien Feng and very nearly her life as well.

Su Shun was also a Manchu, of no more aristocratic birth than the Yi Concubine. He was, however, the foster-brother of Tuan Hua, Prince Cheng, one of the Imperial princes descended from Nurhachu's line, and by whom Su was introduced into the Imperial entourage.

During Hsien Feng's youth Su Shun had been one of his boon companions in debauchery. At first he held only an obscure post in the Board of Revenue, but his promotion was rapid. For one with his ambitions it was necessary to accumulate a vast fortune, and this he did very easily, by the simple method of having the richest bankers and merchants in Peking arrested on some charge or another and holding them in jail until they paid up the huge sums in blackmail he mercilessly squeezed out of them. By such direct and brutal expedients Su Shun in a comparatively short time acquired more than twenty million pounds in bullion, jewels and other property.

Hsien Feng's devotion to the Yi Concubine after the birth of his heir unavoidably won her the bitter enmity of this ambitious scoundrel. Their mutual antagonism and rivalry in due course came to an open clash. Su Shun, determined to oust the Grand Secretary, Po Sui, and usurp his powerful position, demanded that the Emperor should order his superior's execution on trumped-up charges of bribery and corruption. Yehonala dared to plead with Hsien Feng to spare the life of this elder statesman. The first open sign that the Yi Concubine's influence over the Emperor was waning was seen when he refused this plea of hers for leniency—a sign that was noted with distress at Court, where Su Shun was feared and detested by everyone except the Imperial princes who continued to protect him.

Su Shun was firmly abetted by his foster-brother, Prince Cheng, as well as by another of the Imperial princes, Tsai Yuan, Prince Yi. These three conspirators noted that Hsien Feng's health was rapidly failing; his heir was still a small child. If the boy could be taken from his mother, their power would be all the greater; better still, to murder the Yi Concubine would be to eliminate their stubbornest opponent. So long, however, as the Emperor was living in the Forbidden City, such a scheme seemed to them impracticable.

The panic that ensued at Court when the barbarians were approaching Peking was artificially inflated by Su Shun and the two princes, and when the disorderly cavalcade left for Jehol they remained as close as possible to the Sacred Chariot. They were confident that on arrival at Jehol it would be possible for them to persuade Hsien Feng to banish his former favourite concubine to the Cold Palace, a sinister name for a sinister residence where concubines who had fallen from Imperial favour were relegated, and once she was imprisoned there they would find means to ensure that she did not escape.

On arrival at Jehol, Hsien Feng was gravely ill, no longer sexually viable or susceptible to his former favourite's charms, and the conspirators were soon successful in hardening the Emperor's heart against the Yi Concubine, whom he refused to see.

Su Shun must have been very sure of himself at this stage. The two princes played their parts with equal impudence. The plotters won a considerable victory when they induced the Emperor to consent to the heir apparent being removed from his mother's care and placed in charge of Prince Yi's wife. They had managed so to arrange matters that none of the honest ministers and advisers had accompanied the Court on its flight.

Nevertheless, in spite of his cunning at Jehol, Su Shun there made the two capital mistakes for which he was in due course to pay with his life. He had overlooked the fact that Jung Lu, whose fortunes were so intimately linked with Yehonala's, was in charge of the Imperial Guard, and, even more recklessly, that whoever else he had taken the precaution of eliminating from the immediate Imperial entourage, the eunuchs still remained in closest proximity to their master. They never spoke, but as usual watched, listened, and when the appropriate moment came, acted. It was through An-te-hai that Yehonala was kept fully informed of every move being made by her enemies; it was through him that she played the master-stroke that defeated them.

The conspiracy dragged on for months, during which the unhappy Hsien Feng lay slowly dying. On the day before his thirtieth birthday the Court Astrologers presented him with a Memorial which should have given him some encouragement, since it announced that the stars showed several good omens for his future. But the Decree he published in reply to this was a pathetic piece of evidence that he himself knew better—or rather, worse.

When, on the following morning, the Court assembled in one of the splendid reception halls of the palace to pay its respectful birthday congratulations to the Son of Heaven, no one failed to notice the absence of the Yi Concubine—the final sign of her disgrace. From that day until he died, some weeks later, Hsien

Feng made no more appearances in public. And even on his death-bed he did not send for the girl whom he had once so madly loved.

By then the ambitious plotters had come close to success. The young heir apparent was already in their hands; but in order that no opponents should stand in their way, they drew up an Imperial Edict ordering the imprisonment of the Emperor's brothers, and appointing the Princes Cheng and Yi as Regents during the infant Emperor's minority.

In order, however, that an Imperial Decree that proclaimed a new reign should be legally valid, it was necessary to affix to it the Imperial seal, the characters on which stated that this vital State paper was issued 'by Lawfully Transmitted Authority'. The State Seal, the actual instrument of legal power, was the Emperor's own private possession. But on Hsien Feng's death this precious seal had apparently vanished, much to Prince Yi's and Su Shun's consternation. To have searched for it too openly would have been almost an acknowledgement of their conspiracy. They decided to trust to luck that the Decree might nevertheless be accepted, once they had disposed of the Emperor's brothers in Peking, the Princes Kung and Chun, who would certainly challenge it.

During his last illness Hsien Feng was nursed by a young eunuch called Li Lien-ying, an adept masseur, whose physiotherapy helped to relieve the Emperor's pain. When he was on his death-bed the two treacherous princes had ordered everyone to leave the Imperial apartment and had then, apparently, obtained the dying man's signature to their Decree. At that moment only one person might have told them what had become of the Imperial Seal, but with good reason he remained silent. Li Lien-ying's stupendous career began with the death of Hsien Feng.

One chronicler unhesitatingly stated that Hsien Feng had been poisoned by Yehonala, although for months before his death she had been denied an audience with him. Yet the suggestion was not without some substance, since the Chief Eunuch was her devoted henchman, and this highest of all positions to which a

eunuch might attain was in due course filled by Li Lien-ying.
Unlike Su Shun, the eunuchs seldom underestimated their
enemies, or their patrons.

Wasting no further time in search for the Imperial Seal, immediately on Hsien Feng having 'mounted the Dragon' that was
to carry him to join his heavenly ancestors, the princes issued the
proclamation of the boy Emperor, for whom they chose the reign-
title Chi Hsiang, meaning Good Omen—ironically enough from
their point of view. Tsai Yuan became Chief Regent, with the title
of Chien Kuo, to which he had no lawful right, since under the
dynastic law it could only be used by the reigning Emperor's
brothers or uncles; in this case, the Princes Kung and Chun.
And inevitably the self-styled Regents were obliged by protocol
to issue on the following day a further Decree raising the
Imperial Consort, Sakota, and the little Emperor's mother,
Yehonala, to the rank of Empresses Dowager.

They were known from that time onwards as, respectively, the
Eastern and the Western Empress, after the siting of the palaces
in which they dwelt. At that moment there seemed perhaps no
immediate danger in the eyes of the conspirators in conferring
those titles on Hsien Feng's two widows according to the dynastic
rule, since the Eastern Empress was of no account, and in any
case a house-law of the Great Pure Dynasty had hitherto forbidden an Empress to become head of the government.

Immediately after Hsien Feng's death, however, Yehonala
was in greater danger than ever. Su Shun repeatedly urged the
two princes to have her killed, and had they felt themselves strong
enough to do so at that moment they would certainly have done
so. But they feared the vengeance of the Yehonala clan and
above all the Yehonala Bannermen, who at Jehol outnumbered
their own bodyguard. They therefore decided to postpone her
demise until after the Court's return to Peking, to which Su Shun
was obliged very reluctantly to consent.

One false step, and Yehonala would never have seen the
Forbidden City again. But with her usual unfaltering courage
and illimitable cunning, she took good care not to make one.
Outwardly as composed, charming and deferential as ever

towards her enemies, no bereaved concubine mourning her late lord could have appeared more sweetly innocent. She knew, too, that her kinsmen were all around her, and no doubt this gave her confidence; but she took the greatest care to have no direct communication whatever with Jung Lu, nor did she need to do so, since An-te-hai was their go-between. And it was also through the Chief Eunuch that in the greatest secrecy Yehonala was able to send an urgent message to Prince Kung in Peking, informing him of the conspiracy against the Imperial family and urging him to take immediate steps to defeat it. Before doing this, the Western Empress took the precaution of obtaining the Eastern Empress's agreement that this very secret message to their brother-in-law should be delivered in their joint names. And how Yehonala obtained Sakota's consent to this move revealed to the full her genius for intrigue and her swiftness at seizing an opportunity. All her life she was largely to owe her success to this unique capacity for timing.

The Co-Empresses were invariably surrounded by a cohort of ladies-in-waiting and Court ladies, among whom the wives of Prince Yi and Prince Cheng were constantly present; Su Shun's wife also acted as her husband's spy on them. Even out of doors there was no guarantee of secrecy. Yehonala's problem at that point was to arrange to be quite alone with Sakota, if only for a few minutes, in some place where their whispered conversation might not be overheard. When the propitious moment occurred, she instantly seized upon it.

The Empresses and the Court ladies were walking one afternoon in the lovely gardens surrounding the Jehol palaces. And there, at the end of a narrow path, where only two persons might walk abreast (and inevitably the first two in the procession of laughing, chattering women were the Co-Empresses) was an ornamental pond, containing lotus-blossoms and goldfish. Yehonala and Sakota now bent over the water, seemingly admiring the flowers and fish, to all appearances a pair of guileless Imperial sisters enjoying this innocent pleasure. There, in a hurried whisper, Yehonala told Sakota of her plan and won the Eastern Empress's agreement to it. By the time the next pair of ladies appeared, they were able to observe only the delighted smiles of their mistresses. Yehonala's may well have held a tinge of triumphant malice.

Meanwhile, news of the death of the Emperor and the Edict proclaiming the boy Emperor's reign and the appointment of the Regency reached Peking, causing a storm of protest in the capital.

At the very moment when the Western Empress was in such great peril, fortune took a turn in her favour. Whilst the Franco-British force was still advancing on Peking, General Tseng Kuo-fan soundly defeated the Taiping rebels in the province of Anhui and captured the important city of An-ching from them.

Yehonala's supporters in Peking promptly noted this heavenly signal. Memorials from the Censorate and other government offices were dispatched to the little Emperor at Jehol, begging him to appoint the two Empresses as Co-Regents, 'to administer the Government with suspended curtain', a Chinese term referring to the fact that at audiences these sacred female visages were hidden from the kneeling ministers by a light yellow silk curtain that hung down in front of the Imperial dais (and through which the attendant eunuchs relentlessly peeped, missing no word or gesture of those on the other side of it).

Nothing in China ever happened quickly; again and again the Europeans having official or business dealings with the Chinese would be infuriated by the procrastinations, delays, rituals, empty politeness, compliments, smiling and bowing, tea-drinking and fan-fluttering that ineluctably took place before, in the English idiom, 'coming down to brass tacks'. Never, apparently, could they realize that in Confucian China protocol, ceremonial, and ritual were part of the basic fabric of belief, outlook, and behaviour. To omit the least detail of these activities, laid down since time immemorial, would seem to a Manchu or Chinese as ill-bred, as blasphemous, as it would seem to an Englishman to keep on his hat in church, or to remain seated during the playing of the National Anthem.

And such long-drawn-out discipline, to which a well-bred, well-educated Chinese was innured from childhood, was the basis of all character training. It required the keeping-up of an inscrutable front. But behind the smooth forehead, the veiled eyes, the expressionless mask, the ready smile—best of all defence mechanisms—the brain was free to pursue its unspoken activities. And in due course the plan thus formed would come to fruition.

In Court circles these gestures and posturings, these ritualistic forms of behaviour, attained their highest pitch, were observed with fanatical punctiliousness, and served to hide the deepest guile. All her life Yehonala was a stickler for the strictest observance of etiquette, practising it herself as an example to her inferiors, no doubt, but above all as the most subtle instrument of her power. Like a snake, her will might lie coiled for hours, weeks, years; but when it sprang its strike was deadly.

The tension during those last weeks in Jehol, whilst the late Emperor's corpse was being prepared for its final conveying to the tomb-palace in the Western hills, must have been terrific. But now it was chiefly Su Shun and the usurping princes who were beginning to feel the strain.

Not a single detail of the Rites might be omitted, and when the preliminary ceremonies at Jehol were completed, the body was placed on an enormous 'domed pavilion, curtained with yellow satin, embroidered in gold. It was borne shoulder-high, on a network of poles, lacquered in crimson and gold. The secondary poles crossed and recrossed each other as the weight was divided up among the bearers [one hundred and sixty strong men]. Unless the transport was effected with infinite precautions, the oscillations might have tossed the coffin in the air. The bearers, keeping time under orders from their chief, had to advance three steps, then stop during three beats (struck on a musical wooden gong), then advance three steps, and again stop during three beats without moving—and so on, for a hundred and fifty miles. At each halt the bearers were changed, and at each resting-place (every fifteen miles) temporary pavilions had been erected, to shelter the dead Emperor and his suite.'

It was obligatory for the Regents to accompany, at this snail's pace, the body of their late Imperial master. They had, therefore, plenty of time to reflect on the situation they had created for themselves, and to take their dispositions for the future. The outlook was not propitious. For they knew that ahead of them travelled at all possible speed the two Dowager Empresses, whose official duty it was to precede the funeral cortège in order to be waiting at the gates of Peking to receive it according to the Rites.

5   Sweets of Power

Jung Lu and the Yehonala Bannermen had been ordered to accompany the Imperial remains, whilst Prince Yi's own guard had been detailed to escort the Empresses. At Ku-pei Kou, a pass where the road led from the mountains into the plain, the Western Empress was to be assassinated.

The resting-places along the road, where the Imperial bier was lowered to the ground for the night, were known as the 'mat-shed palaces'. On arrival at the first of these the mourners, headed by the new Regents, reverently knelt down according to protocol, as the coffin was lowered to its temporary resting-place, and all their suite did the same, not daring to move or even to raise their eyes until the permitted moment.

And it was then that Jung Lu, with faultless timing giving the signal to his Bannermen to follow him, leapt into the saddle and rushed into the night, galloping to the rescue of his beloved. Pursuit was impossible. Nor was there either interference or resistance from her escort when Yehonala's dashing lover rode up to her palankeen. As the guard of her own clansmen closed around her to protect her for the remainder of the journey, Yehonala, with the Imperial seal safely in her custody, perhaps gave a small sigh of relief and a grateful smile to her beloved.

The slow, magnificent and grotesque procession far behind her now resumed its patient crawl to the capital. It never for a moment occurred to the princely conspirators to attempt to evade the fate that they now knew awaited them on arrival in Peking. A grim touch of irony was added to the situation by the Western Empress, who took care to send back messages of gratitude to Tsai Yuan for the assiduity with which he was attending the late Emperor's last journey; these he acknowledged with equally correct formality. Nor did Yehonala neglect to send a large tip, a thousand taels, to the self-appointed Regent, to be distributed to the bearers. This he also punctiliously acknowledged.

Su Shun was the only one of the three who showed signs of the appalling nervous strain they were enduring. He, the plotter-in-chief, Yehonala's admitted enemy, had warned them over and over again that this cunning female must be got rid of if their great plans were to succeed. They had feared to strike at her in Peking; intended to do so at Jehol, but on one pretext or another had postponed the decisive moment until it was too late. The trick Jung Lu played on them finally defeated them.

To add to their troubles the progress of the procession was considerably delayed by torrential rainfall, which turned the sanded roads into muddy gulleys.

Immediately on their arrival the Dowager Empresses held a secret council with the late Emperor's brothers and those ministers of State who had remained loyal to them, as the result of which it was decided to postpone all drastic measures until the prescribed ceremonies were completed. Yehonala well knew that now she could afford to wait. Apart from the shocking effect any deviation from the prescribed Rites would have had throughout the Empire, any untoward incident would have been an unpropitious omen for the new reign. Precautions were nevertheless taken.

On the evening before the funeral cortège was expected in Peking, Prince Kung posted a large 'guard of honour' at the north-western gate, where it would enter the city. As the catafalque appeared, the child Emperor, accompanied by his mother, the Western Empress, the Eastern Empress, widow-in-chief, the Imperial Princes and all the notables and ministers, awaited it with the pomp and reverence the occasion required.

No doubt the accompanying self-appointed Regents summed up out of the corners of their eyes the strength of the guard of honour and saw that it was, in fact, a military force of sufficient size to cope with any attempted *coup de main* on their part.

A large marquee had been set up just inside the gates, and to this the parties now adjourned, in order that Prince Yi might report to the little Emperor his faithful service in bringing his late father's remains to their last resting-place.

There they faced one another: the six-year-old boy in his stiff long silken gown and button-topped cap, with his mother and her Co-Empress at his sides, his uncles and chief ministers behind him; the two self-appointed Regents with Su Shun, the arch-plotter, listening with bowed heads and assumed reverence as the girl whose life they had so stupidly spared stepped forward to thank them on behalf of her son for the successful fulfilment of their onerous task. Su Shun's thoughts were probably the bitterest: how near and yet in these circumstances how impossibly far he was from the enormous wealth with which he had hoped to bribe his way out of this dilemma, had fate not so inexorably led him straight into the enemy's camp.

Su Shun's fury at that moment overwhelmed him, and turning to his fellow-conspirators he exclaimed in venomous tones: 'Had you listened to me when I first proposed to do away with this woman, we should not have come to such a pass!'

But Yehonala was now in complete control of the situation. Prince Yi knew as well as his opponents that, lacking the authority of the Imperial Seal, the Edicts he had induced the dying Hsien Feng to sign were legally inoperative. Perhaps it was because he had nothing more to lose, perhaps because he was goaded to do so by Su Shun's anger, or simply with that obdurate stubbornness characteristic of Manchu and Chinese alike, he now put these Decrees forward, maintaining his claim that he and his fellow-Regent were the sole authorities appointed by their late master during his heir's minority, and that the Empress of the Western Palace had no right to be present at an audience except by their consent.

The final touch of drama was supplied by Prince Kung, who held out the Edicts, stamped with the Seal of Lawfully Transmitted Authority, appointing the Co-Empresses as Regents during the little Emperor's minority. The Western Empress gave the sign to the guards, who summarily arrested the three conspirators. The meeting, or audience, was over.

There followed the next stage in the prescribed ritual. The Imperial Family proceeded with all speed to the principal gate of the Forbidden City, where once again they knelt to receive the catafalque as it was carried into the Great Within. The arrested Princes and Su Shun followed, under military escort.

Yehonala had already composed the Decree which she now immediately issued in her son's name. It was a long one, the first of many she was to promulgate during the following years, and must have given her a delicious sense of power. The Edict ended with an announcement:

> A Memorial was presented to us . . . in which it was asked that the Empresses Dowager should for the time being and during our minority administer the Government. . . .

'We therefore,' the Decree continued,

> authorised Tsai Yuan to issue a Decree concurring in the Censor's proposals; but he and his colleagues, while pretending to comply with our wishes, issued a Decree quite different from that which we had ordered, and promulgated it in our name. . . . Their behaviour displays monstrous ingratitude for his late Majesty's favours, and any further leniency on our part would be a just cause of offence to the memory of the departed sovereign, and an insult to the intelligence of the Chinese people. Tsai Yuan, Su Shun and Tuan Hua are hereby removed from their posts.

Their principal supporters were at the same time removed from the Grand Council.

No one imagined, of course, that this lengthy and subtle indictment of his mother's enemies had been drawn up or signed by a child of six. It merely proved that the situation had already been accepted by all the Emperor's relatives and ministers and that the Western Empress was now in full and official control of affairs of State. It also bore the stamp of the Imperial Seal and therefore ineluctable validity: the seal that Yehonala had received in Jehol from her devoted eunuch, Li Lien-ying, and which she had guarded day and night, in peril of her life, in anticipation of this glorious moment.

With their traditionalism and erudition the Chinese were always the masters and disciples of proverbial proceedings. So, knowing the wisdom of striking whilst the iron was hot, Yehonala issued a second Decree, in her own name this time, with no beating about the bush, in reply to the outrageous claim made earlier in the day by Prince Yi.

Their audacity in questioning our right [the plural referred to herself and her sleeping partner, the Eastern Empress, but merely for form's sake] to give audience to Prince Kung this morning shows a degree of wickedness inconceivable, and convicts them of the darkest designs. The punishment meted out to them is totally inadequate to the depth of their guilt.

This punishment, stripping the Princes of their rank and titles, was a mere preliminary to their executions that were shortly to follow.

As for Su Shun, Yehonala honoured him by a special Decree in which she at last avenged herself for all the perils and disgrace his machinations had inflicted on her at Jehol. Nor did she forget his wife, who, secure in her husband's ascendancy at the time, had openly shown her scorn for the deposed Yi Concubine. This Decree was a blend of personal vindictiveness and political argument, in which equal emphasis was laid on Su Shun's crimes (which no one disputed) and his alleged violations of precedent and propriety, the traditional code of which Yehonala made herself the high priestess, and which time and again was invoked to cloak her own illicit activities.

Yehonala, with the rapaciousness that she showed throughout her life—and which might be accounted for by the very modest beginnings from which she had risen to her present dazzling position—had already decided that Su Shun's vast fortune was to be channelled into the Imperial coffers. A further Decree, issued on the following day, carried a warning to those who might be tempted to take a cut of it on the way to the Imperial treasury.

This Decree, although no doubt generally approved of, did not restore to Su Shun's former victims the sums he had so ruthlessly extracted from them. But it is always a slight satisfaction to see an arch-villain receive his deserts, and there was no pity for Su Shun now that his turn had come.

6 Slicing the Melon

The temporary success of the Tsai Yuan Conspiracy, as it was later called, was due to the fact that when the Hsien Feng Emperor left so hastily for Jehol, he appointed Prince Kung, his brother, as plenipotentiary to come to terms with the British and French invaders at Peking. This Prince was born in 1833, and had he succeeded to the Dragon Throne the history of the Great Pure Dynasty might have taken a more successful turn, for Kung was a statesman of considerable ability. He had no particular love for the Yi Concubine, but was pushed into an unwilling alliance with her, owing to the bitter personal enmity between himself and his cousin, Prince Yi, as well as his loathing of Su Shun, whose intrigues, he well knew, were directed against himself as well as against Yehonala. But at the time of the Court's flight to Jehol he was powerless to thwart them.

Prince Kung had been given no easy task by his brother.

The Allied troops were at that time encamped close to the Summer Palace, the Bright Round Garden. When their emissaries were captured by the Chinese, Lord Elgin and the French Commander, General de Montauban, were horrified and infuriated by the condition of those envoys who, having had the luck to survive their abominable treatment, were returned to them in a pitiable state. They had been tortured and horribly mutilated.

Hsien Feng was in residence at the Summer Palace at the time of this outrage, and the British and French commanders therefore assumed that it was committed by his orders. Lord Elgin, after the capture of Peking, resolved to take drastic reprisals for it : to burn to the ground and utterly destroy the Emperor's most cherished private domain. Admitting that the provocation Elgin had endured was very great, this act of vandalism shocked even one of his own officers, young Captain Charles George Gordon, who afterwards, as 'Chinese' Gordon, became famous throughout the British Empire.

'Owing to the ill-treatment the prisoners experienced at the Summer Palace,' he wrote to his mother from the British encampment,

> the General ordered it to be destroyed, and stuck up a proclamation to say why it was so ordered. We accordingly went out and, after pillaging it, burned the whole place, destroying in a Vandal-like manner most valuable property which could not be replaced for four millions. We got upwards of forty-eight pounds apiece prize money before we went out here; and although I have not as much as many, I have done well. Imagine D. . . giving sixteen shillings for a string of pearls, which he sold the next day for five hundred pounds ! . . .
>
> You can scarcely imagine the beauty and magnificence of the places we burnt. It was wretchedly demoralizing work for an army. Everybody was wild for plunder.

The orders for this sadistic revenge came from Lord Elgin; his French colleague, Baron Gros, refrained from signing them, but did not restrain his own troops from participating in the looting, and a French historian, La Gorce, was in agreement with Lord Elgin's policy :

> With Asiatic peoples, nothing convinces more than mere brutal strength; nothing succeeds like the *fait accompli*. . . .

When news of this appalling act of vandalism reached Jehol,

the Emperor was even more favourably impressed than ever by Su Shun's advice that all foreigners should be ruthlessly exterminated. It was, however, utterly futile. Although a Decree was published forbidding Prince Kung to spare the lives of any captured barbarians upon any pretext whatever, the Emperor's brother, whose personal resentment was no doubt equally bitter, had the political shrewdness to ignore it, realizing that shutting the stable door too late was no realistic policy for a good Confucian.

The invaders certainly seemed justified in their claim that the only thing the Chinese understood was force. In due course Prince Kung managed to obtain from his brother an Edict confirming the Peking Convention he concluded with the British and French. Their terms were, as was only to be expected, harsh. This Convention re-affirmed the previous Treaties of Tientsin, as well as those of 1842–44, and extended still further the privileges then exacted by the foreigners. There was to be an exchange of diplomatic representatives between the Manchu Court and the European powers. In addition to the ports already open to foreign control, this was extended to the provinces of Manchuria, Chefoo, Taiwan, Swatow, and Hainan. The great Yangtze river, with its important cities for trade and commerce, was to be opened to foreign navigation, and foreigners—especially missionaries—were to be given the right to reside and carry on their vocations in the interior. The Treaties of Tientsin (1858) and the Peking Convention even imposed on the Chinese the obligation to permit their own nationals freely to become Christians and to protect them and their alien religion. As usual, the Chinese were obliged to pay heavy indemnities, of which a certain proportion was allocated by the Western governments to missionaries and missions.

Prince Kung, bearing in mind that the Taiping Rebellion was not yet stamped out and might still bring about the downfall of the Great Pure Dynasty, accepted these harsh terms, which remained the basis of all diplomatic negotiations between China and the Western Powers until well into the next century. And in order to facilitate future dealings with the foreign Powers he founded the first Board or Office through which these would in future be conducted, the Tsungli Yamen.

Throughout the second half of the nineteenth century foreign aggression against China continued almost uninterruptedly. The rival Great Powers saw this vast and almost defenceless country as a luscious melon, from which, as the Chinese put it with bitter sarcasm, they felt free to help themselves to juicy slices. The British were not the only depredators. Before the sacking of the Summer Palace the Russians had annexed huge tracts of land north of the Amur river, and in 1871 they occupied another large area in Chinese Turkestan. In 1880 they generously returned this —or part of it—to China for a huge indemnity. The French, between 1867 and 1887, made themselves masters of Annam, Cochin-China and Cambodia, vassal states which they united into a new colony called French Indo-China. And finally, the rising young Far Eastern Power, Japan, also took a hand in this ruthless aggression.

The final concession wrung from the Chinese, which was a constant source of annoyance and irritation to all classes, was the right of Christian missionaries to establish themselves and to preach anywhere in the Empire. Throughout the Empress Dowager's life this situation was as infuriating to her as to everyone throughout her vast country—excepting that relatively tiny minority of her people who accepted the alien faith and were contemptuously referred to as 'rice-Christians'. For in the constantly recurring famines the missionaries took good care to feed their own converts.

In matters of religion the Chinese always showed the most admirable toleration. But the Christians were as intransigent as the Chinese were broadminded. Any compromise between their own dogmatism and the Chinese religious and ethical outlook was utterly unacceptable to them. Undoubtedly, according to their own principles they did, or attempted to do, a great deal of good. Many missionaries became martyrs to their faith. There were anti-Christian riots all over China, some of them very serious indeed. From 1862 to 1870 incidents of various degrees of savagery occurred in the provinces of Kiangsu, Chihli, Szechwan and Kweichow.

In every instance the Treaty Powers used these as pretexts for obtaining further concessions, and brought pressure to bear on the Manchu authorities to suppress the agitation among the people.

The worst of these outbreaks took place in Tientsin in 1870, when a Roman Catholic church was burnt down, priests and nuns were massacred, and the French retaliated by gun-fire on the Chinese. Once again the Government was forced to pay the foreigners an indemnity amounting to 460,000 taels and to send an official to France to apologise for the incident.

To the credit of the British people, a number of their leaders did not support such forcible methods of conversion.

On 9 March 1869 Lord Clarendon stated in the House of Lords that, 'Missionaries require to be protected against themselves, and they are a constant menace to British interests.'

The Duke of Somerset asked, 'What right have we to be trying to convert the Chinese in the middle of their country?' And many others held their view. But in Victorian England, where the missionary organizations were a very strong pressure group, this was not a majority opinion.

The Manchu régime was by then largely dependent on foreign and especially British aid for its survival. This symbiotic relationship between the Manchu dynasty and Government on the one hand, and the British politicians and traders on the other, culminated, in 1864, in the appointment of a remarkable Irishman, Sir Robert Hart, as Inspector-General of the Imperial Maritime Customs. Hart, who was born in the same year as Yehonala, had gone to China as a student-interpreter in the consular service. A man of outstanding financial ability and strong personality, he was one of those rare Britons who actually *liked* the Chinese. When Hart first became Inspector-General the revenues from the customs duties at the treaty ports were eight million taels, and the customs staff numbered two hundred. By 1901 he had increased the former to twenty-seven million taels, and the staff to five thousand one hundred and thirty-four.

In 1865 Hart moved from Shanghai to Peking. He soon became the most influential foreigner in China—so much so that the imperial princes, ministers, viceroys of the Empire, and lower officials constantly sought his advice. He was equally closely in touch with the foreign diplomats and envoys and played a more and more political role. The Manchus were delighted by the enormous increase in the revenues he procured for them; the Chinese, however, were more critical, and probably with reason. The statesman Li Hung Chang, who himself amassed a colossal fortune whilst serving his country's interests, wrote of him in 1876: 'We know that Robert Hart is malicious at heart, yet driven by lust for money he is quite willing to serve us. . . .'

The truth was, probably, that Hart was quite sincere in his affection for the country of his adoption; that he did not neglect his own interests, but, finding himself in a position of such enormous power, did not over-abuse it as a Chinese of that period would almost certainly have done.

7   *Motherly and Auspicious Rule*

As soon as the Co-Empresses took over the Regency the little Emperor's title was altered to Tung Chih, meaning United Rule or All-pervading Tranquillity. But this was no more an accurate description of his brief reign than the title formerly chosen for it.

An Edict soon followed the proclamation announcing this change, in which with the hypocritical modesty convention demanded, the Dowager Empresses referred to their acceptance of the burden thrust upon them.

At the same time both Empresses received honorific titles. Sakota, the senior, and Eastern Empress, became Tzu An, the Motherly and Restful; Yehonala, the Western Empress, was to be known as Tzu Hsi, the Motherly and Auspicious. Each title carried with it an annual income of 100,000 taels, roughly 20,000 pounds, a trifling sum, even in comparison with the incomes of European queens, and of course only a small proportion of the immense personal fortunes of the Empresses.

When Yehonala gave birth to the heir to the throne, Sakota knew that she would never regain the favour of the Hsien Feng Emperor. She was so bitterly disappointed that she refrained even from paying the usual courtesy call on the young mother and baby, her excuse for this lapse from etiquette being that her own birth-date was astrologically inimical to the child's and that such a visit might harm him. But when the little boy was able to do so he clearly showed his preference for the Eastern Empress, in whose palanquin he had been found on the flight to Jehol.

During Hsien Feng's lifetime, even although Yehonala had fallen from favour during his last months, Sakota knew that she dared not openly show her antagonism to her rival. The Emperor had doted on her, and, if he recovered, might again do so. After his death their mutual peril had united them against the conspirators. But as soon as they returned to Peking and assumed joint power there was no longer any need for the Eastern Empress to conceal her feelings. Yehonala, the Western Empress, with good reason did so, and took care to pay Sakota all the deference and respect due to her position as senior Dowager. She could well afford this empty gesture, for in every way she had and intended to retain the upper hand.

Sakota made no secret, either, of her personal antagonism to An-te-hai, the Chief Eunuch, who had thrown in his lot unreservedly in the service of the Western Empress. Tzu An also watched with the keen eyes of the thwarted the promotion of Jung Lu as Councillor of State in succession to the decapitated Su Shun.

The Tung Chih Emperor was a lively and healthy little boy, on whom his mother apparently doted.

At the age of four, according to custom, the Emperor's training for his future tasks began. He was given a tutor, chosen by his mother, who kept a wary eye on both master and pupil.

From his infancy Tung Chih was used to the deep reverence paid to the Son of Heaven from every lesser mortal with whom he came in contact, and he soon learned that to all, with one exception, his whims were law. His mother, fortunately for herself, enjoyed that dynastic precedence over his own that enabled her to exercise some discipline in handling him. But even she could not prevent the eunuchs from exerting their usual sinister influence on her son. During his childhood all those of higher rank privileged to wait on him, from An-te-hai downwards, strove tirelessly to amuse, entertain, and spoil their young Imperial master.

Like the late Hsien Feng Emperor, as he grew older Tung Chih took little interest in art, letters, or philosophy. But in his Manchu blood was a long tradition of expert horsemanship and archery. From the time when he was big enough to be lifted on to a shaggy little pony, the boy Emperor was passionately devoted to horses and riding. And his riding-master and instructor in archery was the new Imperial Councillor, the handsome Banner-man and favourite of his mother, Jung Lu. It was noted at Court that Jung Lu adored the little Emperor as lovingly as if he had been his own son, although it would have been as much as any-one's life was worth to have put such an impression into words. But as Jung Lu spent whole days at a time riding and shooting and playing with the boy, it was almost unavoidable that he should be seeing a good deal of his mother.

Until Tung Chih was big enough to be seated on the enormous Dragon Throne, and with his little legs under their stiff silken gown dangling down from this exalted height give audiences to his princes and ministers, the Co-Empresses carried out this duty on his behalf, veiled from the sight of the kneeling officials by the yellow curtain. Later, a bamboo screen, through which one might peep, stood behind the throne, and through this the Western Empress whispered to her son the answers or orders he should give to the councillors in front of him.

Imperial audiences were invariably held at sunrise—considered the most auspicious hour for them. Before they began, the ministers-in-attendance and other officials, viceroys, governors of provinces, tribute-paying princes or their representatives, had to be at their appointed places in the throne-room, to which the eunuchs led them. They were obliged to kneel, sometimes for hours on end, on the hard cold floor; no easy position for the elderly, who fastened little cushions round their knees, under-neath their stiff and heavy gowns, to ease the strain. In this sub-servient position they listened to the voice of the Western Empress, emerging from behind the yellow curtain like that of some Oriental oracle or sphinx, and later to Tung Chih, repeat·

ing her instructions. Even the Imperial Princes, even Prince Kung, whose political rank was equivalent to that of a prime minister, had to follow this ritual; the only difference being that the position on the floor marked out for them was in the front row, closer to the curtains.

Her Imperial Majesty the Empress Dowager proceeded in state to the Audience Hall from her private palace in the grounds. Eight eunuchs in gorgeously coloured robes bore her chair-of-state; the two principal eunuchs walked on either side of it, steadying it with their hands. In front walked four eunuchs of the fifth rank, and behind, twelve more of the sixth rank.

When this procession arrived and Her Majesty entered the Audience Hall to the unanimous kowtowing of all those assembled before the Peacock Throne, the session was open.

The great Taiping Rising lasted from 1851 to 1864. Yehonala had gained considerable credit by her support of General Tseng Kuo-fan, Commander-in-Chief of the Imperial Forces. Tseng kept the Empress Dowager informed of his successes in a series of detailed dispatches. The Decree issued in 1864 jointly by the Empresses, in the name of the child Emperor, Tung Chih, was attributed by her subjects to the Western Empress. It ended by stating that

This glorious victory is entirely due to the bountiful protection of Heaven, to the ever-present help of our Ancestors, and to the foresight and wisdom of the Empresses Regent. . . .

The Decree could hardly have been expected to emphasize that had not the British seconded 'Chinese' Gordon to the staff of Li Hung Chang (Tseng's deputy) and the command of the 'Ever Victorious Army', the Taipings might never have been defeated, and few of her subjects would have dissented from the back-handed compliments Yehonala paid herself on this auspicious occasion.

Tseng Kuo-fan was given the title of Senior Guardian of the Throne, a marquisate of the first rank, hereditary in perpetuity, and the decoration of the double-eyed peacock's feather.

It was four years later that this victorious general was appointed Viceroy of Chihli province. His way to his new post lay through the capital, and on this occasion he was summoned to an audience with his Imperial mistresses. The Grand Secretary and Senior Guardian of the Throne was paid the highest honours. When he was conducted into the Audience Chamber by one of the Imperial Princes, he found the young Emperor (now eight years old) seated on a throne facing west. At this period the Empress Dowager still conducted her interviews with her subordinates from behind the yellow curtain; Tzu Hsi sat there, on the Emperor's right hand, Tzu An on his left, but, as usual, nobody paid her any attention and Yehonala was her son's mouthpiece. The following account of this and later audiences given to Tseng Kuo-fan was stated to be a verbatim record of the proceedings by a Chinese scribe in attendance:

Upon entering the Throne Room Tseng fell upon his knees as in duty bound, and in that position advanced a few feet, saying 'Your servant Tseng Kuo-fan respectfully inquires after Your Majesties' health.' Then, removing his hat and performing the kowtow, he humbly returned thanks for Imperial favours bestowed on him. These preliminaries completed, he rose and advanced a few steps to kneel on the cushion prepared for him below the dais. The following dialogue then took place:

Her Majesty Tzu Hsi:	When you left Nanking, was all your official work completed?
Tseng:	Yes, quite completed.
Tzu Hsi:	Have the irregular troops and braves all been disbanded?
Tseng:	Yes, all.
Tzu Hsi:	How many in all?
Tseng:	I have disbanded over twenty thousand irregulars and have enrolled thirty thousand regulars.

This was the formula for an Imperial audience which never varied: short, sharp, and to the point. When Tzu Hsi had asked the questions, and the answers had been given, there was a pause. If she asked no further question, the silence from behind the yellow curtain was the only indication to the favoured one kneeling on the cushion in front of the Imperial thrones that the audience was at an end. He then kowtowed again and withdrew.

It was in 1870, whilst Tseng was Viceroy, that there occurred at Tientsin, within his administration, the terrible massacre of the French missionaries and their converts, for which the French demanded compensation and retribution. In Nanking, meanwhile, matters had not gone well either, and when Tseng's successor was murdered, the Empress decided to recall him from his post in the north and re-appoint him to the scene of his greatest triumph. Li Hung Chang was sent as Viceroy to Chihli.

Such able and devoted servants of the Manchu dynasty as Tseng and Li were not so numerous as their Empress might have wished. To these men she showed the greatest generosity and gratitude, almost overwhelming them with the number and magnificence of her presents.

Her generosity was, however, more than equalled by her demands on those honoured to be in her highest service. Tseng was no longer in robust health and already blind in one eye, no doubt due to cataract. He felt more than reluctant at that advanced age to undertake the long journey to the south again and to pick up the heavy burden of office that awaited him in Nanking. But Tzu Hsi would not hear of his retirement. To disobey the Imperial command was an impossibility, and only death could free the Empress's highest officials, like the commonest slaves, from her thrall. So the ageing and ailing old warhorse had no choice but to set out again. On his way south he was accorded another audience with her Majesty, reported by the scribe who had been present at his previous meetings with her, and, even more clearly this time, revealing the mastery and clearsightedness with which she followed matters of State, as well as her reactions to the activities of the foreign missionaries who were increasingly bedevilling her reign :

Tzu Hsi: When did you leave Tientsin ?

Tseng: On the 23rd.

Tzu Hsi: Have the ringleaders in the massacre of foreigners been executed yet?

Tseng: Not yet. The Consul told me that the Russian Minister was coming to Tientsin and that the French Minister was sending a deputy to witness the executions, so that the decapitations could not be summarily carried out.

Before resuming her inquiries, the Empress, who from behind the yellow curtain had been closely watching her Viceroy, now asked him:

Tzu Hsi: Have you quite lost the sight of your right eye?

Tseng: Yes, it is quite blind; but I can still see with the left.

Tzu Hsi: Have you entirely recovered from your other maladies?

Tseng: Yes, I think I can say that I have.

Tzu Hsi: You appear to kneel, and to rise from that posture quite briskly and freely, as if your physique were still pretty good?

Tseng: No, it is not what it used to be.

This the Empress would not bring herself to admit, since she was determined still to make use of this faithful servant. She therefore resumed the political theme:

Tzu Hsi: It would be a fine thing if we could secure ourselves properly against invasion. The missionary complications are perpetually creating trouble for us.

Tseng: That is true. Of late the missionaries have created much trouble everywhere. The native converts are given to oppressing those who will not embrace Christianity.

[The phrase used by Tseng, literally translated, was 'eat the religion', possibly in reference to the ceremony of the sacrament.]

Tseng: And the missionaries always screen the converts, whilst the Consuls protect the missionaries. Next year, when the time comes for revising the French Treaty, we must take particular pains to reconsider carefully the whole question of religious propaganda.

Two years later, this loyal and faithful servant died at his post in Nanking.

In a special Decree commemorating his death, the Empress referred to him as 'the very backbone of the Throne'. But much as she undoubtedly regretted him, she showed no remorse at having so ruthlessly used 'this good and loyal man' until his end. Nor, as Li Hung Chang in his turn discovered, did she refrain from working his colleagues and successors to death in the interests of the State and the dynasty.

Prince Kung had been confident that the Empresses Regent would leave all matters of policy, and therefore the real power, in his hands. But, like many others both before and after him, the Prince underestimated Yehonala's ambition, the motive-spring that ruled her life.

The first round in the struggle for supremacy between them occurred at an audience in April 1865. The statesman-prince may merely have had cramp in his knees or been irked beyond further endurance by the physical and political situation in which he found himself. But the strain proved too much, and before the Imperial voice became silent—this being the only official intimation that the audience was at an end—Prince Kung rose to his feet.

Whether it was An-te-hai for whom Prince Kung in due course developed a hatred that put an end to the Chief Eunuch and his machinations, or another, who, peeping through the curtain, witnessed this disgraceful act of disrespect, the Prince's scandalous breach of etiquette was instantly reported to Her Majesty. She gave a rapid order, the audience was immediately suspended, and her brother-in-law was forthwith seized by the eunuchs on duty on his side of the curtain, and hustled out of the Throne Room. Nor was this all.

The Empress issued an Imperial Edict, informing the world that Prince Kung had been guilty of this act of gross disrespect to the Throne and—this was the crux of the matter—had dared to usurp the power to which he was not entitled. No doubt was left as to who was, and intended to remain, master. For good measure he was also accused of favouritism in distributing certain appointments, an accusation that was usually brought against a disgraced statesman or official and could always be made to stick. For these offences the Imperial Prince was deprived of his offices, including the direction of the Tsungli Yamen, the Foreign Office, which he himself had founded.

The Empress was, however, sufficiently realistic to know that she could not permanently clip the Prince's nose—metaphorically, in this instance—without spiting her own face. Having no option, he made suitable, tearful apologies, and shortly afterwards was reinstated in his former authority. But the lesson had been a sharp one.

Yehonala had real intelligence and intuitive gifts that occasionally seemed almost to amount to second sight. But, like patriotism, these were not enough to cope with the increasingly difficult internal and external problems of the realm, and particularly with the foreigners who were now in China to stay, it seemed, for all time.

The traditional Confucianist attitude to them, which the Empress Dowager fully shared, was clearly expressed in a Memorial presented to the Dragon Throne by one of the most learned and distinguished Censors, Wu Ko-tu. From documents such as this one the Manchu Empress, the Motherly and Auspicious, gained her impressions of the barbarians who were residing in her country :

. . . I have seen with my own eyes the foreigners who live in

Peking walking abroad, preceded by the females of their household either on foot or in sedan-chairs; the menfolk following meekly in their rear, like servants—all unashamed. They have made some scores of treaties with China. . . . Is there a word in any one of them concerning reverence for parents, or the cultivation of virtue and respect for the nine canons of rightful conduct? No! Is there one word in any one of them as to the observance of ceremony, as to duty, integrity, and a proper sense of shame, the four cardinal principles of our nation? Again, no! All that they speak of is material profit . . . and with the meretricious hope of profit they beguile the Chinese people. . . . They know not the Heaven-ordained relationship between Sovereign and Minister, between father and son, husband and wife, elder and younger brother, friend and friend— yet we propose to require them to conform to the five principles of duty! It seems to me that one might as well bring together dogs and horses, goats and pigs, in a public hall and compel these creatures to perform the evolutions of the dance! . . . I have heard that in their dispatches and treaties, the puny hobgoblins or petty monsters whom they have the audacity to call 'Emperors' are placed on a level of equality with His Sacred Majesty.

This Memorial from an acknowledged Confucian authority dealt with the difficult question of the procedure to be adopted when the Emperor received foreign ambassadors. Two British embassies, that of Lord Macartney to the great Chien Lung Emperor in 1793, and that of Lord Amherst to the Chia Ching Emperor in 1816, had been bedevilled by this crucial matter of protocol, the inflexible ruling that *everyone*, whether Manchu, Chinese or foreigner, *must* kowtow on such occasions. The point had, however, arrived, when the Manchu rulers were anxious to find some way out of the deadlock, since the British, who were becoming more and more indispensable to the Chinese need for 'material profit', refused resolutely to perform the kowtow, and a solution had to be found without loss of face. Wu Ko-tu ingeniously suggested it, for, since these barbarian envoys were already so low, it was surely beneath the Imperial dignity to accept their genuflexions before the Dragon Throne?

In reply the Empress stated,

We have perused this Memorial and find it not lacking in point. The foreign ministers are hereby permitted to appear at Audiences and to act thereat in accordance with their own national Court ceremonies. Thus the Throne will display its benevolent indulgence to the strangers from afar and make a proper distinction between Chinese and barbarians.

8   A Court Scandal

The Censors constantly sent in memorials protesting against the fantastic extravagance that prevailed at Court, and against the favouritism shown by Her Majesty to her eunuchs. These were condescendingly acknowledged—approved even—but everything went on exactly as before.

The Privy Purse was nevertheless beginning to feel the strain of all this enormous expenditure. And this was the alleged pretext for an unprecedented step taken by the Empress, one of her very few mistakes of judgment.

It was an inexorable rule that on pain of death no eunuch might ever leave the city of Peking to travel in other parts of the Empire. But, whether or not for his own greedy ends, An-te-hai obtained the consent of Tzu Hsi to do precisely this. The ostensible reason for his departure was a mission to collect tribute from the Governor of Shantung. In 1869 he set out in great magnificence, sure of his protectress's power to save him from any unpleasant consequences of this violation of the dynastic law. This was the opportunity which Prince Kung had been awaiting to avenge himself for the slights the Empress had inflicted on him, and, with even greater pleasure, to punish the intolerable insolence shown to himself and all the Imperial Princes by her favourite.

The governor of Shantung province, Ting Pao-chen, one of the most honest and efficient administrators of the Empire, scandalized by the Chief Eunuch's presumption, sent a secret and express messenger to Prince Kung, reporting fully on An-te-hai's outrageous behaviour, and asking for instructions. On receiving this message, Prince Kung, with artful timing, hastened to visit Tzu An, the Eastern Empress, whilst the Western Empress was pleasurably engaged in amateur theatricals, unaware of the threatening storm. Tzu An listened willingly to the Prince; she, also, had her grievances and longing for vengeance. He had already drawn up an Edict for her to sign, for both Empresses possessed the authority independently to issue such proclamations. Tzu An shrank a little when she read it. Timid and retiring though she was, she had a shrewd foreboding of the consequences to herself of publishing such a decree. 'The Western Empress will assuredly kill me for this,' she sighed. But her sense of duty and her longing for revenge prevailed; picking up her brush, she put her name to it, and out it went.

Ten days later Prince Kung had the satisfaction of presenting her Eastern Majesty Tzu An with a second Edict for signature:

Ting Pao-chen now reports that the eunuch An was arrested in the Ti An prefecture and has been summarily beheaded. Our dynasty's house-law is most strict in regard to the proper discipline of eunuchs and provides severe punishment for any offences which they may commit. They have always been sternly forbidden to make expeditions to the provinces, or to create trouble. Nevertheless, An-te-hai actually had the brazen effrontery to violate this law, and for his crimes his execution is only a fitting reward.

Strange as it may seem, no warning whispers of An-te-hai's danger, of his arrest or execution, reached Tzu Hsi's ears until the eunuch's head had rolled. Several of those who had accompanied him on his regal progress down the Imperial Canal were also killed. Six escaped, but five of them were caught and put to death by strangling. An-te-hai's family were sent as slaves to the north-western frontier guards—a worse fate, possibly, than his own. One only of the lesser eunuchs managed to save his life and succeeded in returning to Peking.

During An-te-hai's absence, his place in Yehonala's intimate councils was filled by Li Lien-ying, the eunuch who, by stealing the Imperial seal in Jehol, had frustrated the conspiracy of Su Shun, and thus indirectly raised her to the Throne. Ever since, Li had been the recognized successor to An-te-hai, but even he could not have hoped so soon to become the most powerful eunuch— and, in due course, the second most powerful individual—in the land. He could not have felt a great deal of pity when the subordinate who alone escaped the fate of his colleagues now secretly informed him of this sad event. The secrecy surrounding the matter was possibly due to the fact that, as everyone knew, the Western Empress herself was finally responsible for allowing An-te-hai to defy her house-laws so impudently that the two Edicts published by her colleague entailed clearly implied criticism of her own conduct, and a loss of face all the more galling since she had not the slightest grounds for rescinding them. The risk of breaking this shocking news to her could only be taken by Li Lien-ying, who did so, no doubt, with well-simulated horror. Officially Tzu Hsi was completely checkmated by Prince Kung and Tzu An. All the greater for that reason was her fury at the trick they had played on her.

Until now Yehonala had always succeeded in masking her own real feelings. She had observed a punctilious attitude towards her despised colleague and rival; in her antagonism to Prince Kung she herself had made use of protocol and house-law to chasten him. Since she had been the real power behind the little Emperor's throne no one had dared to challenge her authority, and for this reason, perhaps, she had become over-confident and lax in observing the rules outwardly, whilst turning them to her own advantage.

At first she refused to believe the news Li Lien-ying brought her. Undoubtedly she keenly felt the loss of An-te-hai, though little guilt at her own responsibility for his fate. The loss of face was another far more important matter. It seemed incredible to her that Tzu An would have dared to act so decisively behind her powerful colleague's back. She instantly realized how seriously she had underestimated the possible danger to her own despotism from the sudden dramatic intervention of this dim female in her personal and administrative affairs. She knew that she could and should have foreseen that Prince Kung would only await the right moment to strike at her, and it was she herself who had given him this delightful opportunity.

Publicly she was obliged to accept the situation. But privately she could not and did not do so.

As soon as Li Lien-ying acquainted the Western Empress with the fate of his predecessor, she marched off to the palace of Benevolent Peace, her colleague's private residence in the Forbidden City, to demand a full explanation. Throughout her life, whenever danger threatened, Yehonala followed the maxim that the best form of defence is attack. Nor did she ever forgive or forget an injury, whether real or imagined.

This appears to have been one of the occasions when Tzu Hsi gave vent to her ungovernable rage, which was truly imperial.

Even her most devoted enemies had to admit how great was the charm, the fascination, she exerted whenever she chose. But the reverse side of her nature was even more effective. Imperial Princes and statesmen wilted and paled under the lash of her tongue.

Poor Tzu An crumpled at the first vitriolic words of her accuser. Feebly she tried to exculpate herself—though no excuse was needed for the entirely lawful punishment to which she had condemned An-te-hai—by attempting to shift the blame for the Edict on to Prince Kung. There was no need to draw Tzu Hsi's attention to that statesman's responsibility for it; their mutual enmity was by then common knowledge at Court. She left Tzu An after threatening to avenge herself on both of them, and although she could not do so immediately, the Eastern Empress knew only too well that her Western sister's threats were not idle ones.

Li Lien-ying stepped into the Chief Eunuch's shoes. His nickname was Pi Siao Li—Cobbler's Wax Li. He was the son of a very poor peasant somewhere in the north and in his teens had run away from home and made his way to Peking. There, submerged amongst the poorest and humblest townsfolk, Li just managed to keep body and soul together by doing various odd jobs, and, when he was given the opportunity, by cobbling. He was semi-starved, permanently hungry, friendless and unwanted. He was also unusually ugly, for his face was badly disfigured by pock-marks, although he had a strong and healthy body.

One day, in the street called Nan Chi Tzu, near the gates of the Forbidden City, there was a rush of colour and a tremendous clattering and shouting. Li, who was as curious as all Chinese, pushed his way through the crowd in order to see the cause of this commotion. He beheld a procession of splendidly dressed and accoutred horsemen, whose long whips lashed at the people to force a way through for their chief. When Li inquired who this magnificent personage might be, he was told that it was the 'Lord of Nine Thousand Years', His Majesty's Chief Eunuch, An-te-hai, who had no right to assume this title, which was only one degree lower than that of the Son of Heaven, but no matter.

In the Confucian world, family ties were the strongest of all bonds, as Li knew. A beggar who could claim kinship with a prince had the right, willy-nilly, to that great man's protection and help. Li became thoughtful. If only he could find some such connecting link of relationship, however remote, he might perhaps enter the Forbidden City, wear such splendid uniform, and eat his fill as often as he liked. Riches and power might be his one day. Many others as poor and insignificant might have such dreams, but Li was no mere dreamer.

There was but one obstacle to making his dreams come true : the fact that Li was not a eunuch but a normal male. With remarkable will-power and impressive courage the young cobbler thereupon decided to perform a very painful operation on himself. When he had done so, and, after weeks of suffering, recovered from it, he presented himself at the Forbidden City, with the story he had meanwhile prepared, claiming that he was a young relative of the Chief Eunuch's. An-te-hai thereupon received Li and enrolled him on the staff of the three thousand *castrati* who served His Imperial Majesty. At first the young recruit was obliged, like all the rest, to perform menial tasks and to receive his share of the kicks, cuffings and beatings that were their daily portion. But, with his unusual intelligence and powers of intrigue and ingratiation, Li's promotion was rapid.

Whether the story of his origins was fact or legend, Li Lien-ying did have an unparalleled career. But his memories of early poverty, his physical suffering on account of his self-mutilation—or possibly mutilation by another hand—caused him to become a misogynist who hated the entire human race except for one person only : his Imperial Mistress.

9 *The Emperor's 'Good Fortune'*

The boy Emperor was his mother's greatest treasure, a kind of living sceptre which she guarded with the greatest vigilance. She herself chose his tutors both for their scholarship and their reliability, and kept a sharp eye on them as well as their Imperial pupil. Throughout his childhood Her Majesty continued to shape Tung Chih into the docile instrument he was to be for the transmission of her own orders and sole control of the State in his name.

Tung Chih, however, was an observant, precocious boy. When he entered his teens it was not long before he began to assert himself, becoming more and more difficult for his mother to handle. He was acutely aware of his own rights and power, and anxious to exercise them.

Unfortunately, however, he soon began to go down the slippery path that had wrecked the health of his predecessor. Like the former Emperor, he was not an intellectual. He had, however, been a healthy lad, fond of horses, hunting and field-sports, in the honourable Manchu tradition. Yet in a very few years it became apparent that Tung Chih's reign might be an even briefer one than Hsien Feng's. And as Su Shun had been a boon companion to Hsien Feng in that Emperor's dissolute youth, so now two evil counsellors encouraged and abetted Tung Chih in all his vices. These, two, Wen Hsi and Kuei Pao, were members of the Empress Dowager's clique. She was therefore well aware of her son's scandalous behaviour, yet did nothing whatever to alter it.

Everyone in the Forbidden City and even in the lowest purlieus of Peking knew about it. Under cover of darkness and some kind of disguise, accompanied by his favourite eunuch, the young Emperor would sneak out from his Imperial palace to sow his wild oats in the rowdiest and most sordid brothels and opium dens in the city. When it was time to hold the Imperial audiences at sunrise, he had often still not returned from his nights of orgy.

Even in the licentious and corrupt ambience that surrounded him, however, there remained one or two conscientious and brave officials who endeavoured to save the Son of Heaven from this systematic debauchery. One of them, Kuei Ching, even took the drastic step of decapitating a few of the most disreputable eunuchs—but not, of course, their chief. He received small thanks for his zeal, for the Emperor promptly dismissed him and continued to invite disaster, which was not long in setting in. Tung Chih became ill, but, whatever his disease on that occasion, he temporarily recovered.

The Empress Dowager's attested indifference to her son's outrageous behaviour and its consequences was not so much due, perhaps, to resentment at his open disrespect and even defiance, as to genuine and justified fear for her own future. The time was quickly coming near when he would assume power. She would then be compelled to relinquish it. The outlook was not a pleasant one. By this time Tzu Hsi had incurred the open enmity of Tzu An and all the Imperial Princes, headed by Prince Kung. Her only firm ally was Li Lien-ying, whose destiny was entirely dependent on hers. Had Tzu Hsi herself for a moment considered it either safe or desirable to give up the Regency, Li Lien-ying would have fought like the tiger he was to maintain her in it. If she herself showed any maternal reluctance to abandon her son to his vices, to preserve his health and dignity, Li had no such scruples. Her Majesty saw no immediate prospect of retaining power directly. But one possibility still remained of exercising at least indirect control over the Emperor. The time had come for Tung Chih to take an Empress and three or four concubines. If his mother could persuade him to accept as First Consort a girl of her own choice, she might use her as an instrument of her will and plans.

Jung Lu, who remained in highest favour with the Empress Dowager, had a friend, Feng Hua, with a daughter who seemed to Tzu Hsi fitted for this high rank. But so had the Imperial Tutor, Chung Chi. His daughter's name was A-lu-te, and she was both intelligent and beautiful. The rivalry between the Empresses Regent once again produced a clash, for the mere fact that Tzu Hsi favoured Feng Hua's daughter inevitably meant that Tzu An gave her support to A-lu-te. And in the last resort the Emperor himself made his choice. A-lu-te became First Wife, and the daughter of Feng Hua only a concubine.

This was a serious setback for the Empress Dowager, his mother, since it was clear that A-lu-te would not become the malleable tool for whom she had hoped. But the Western Empress never accepted defeat—which was one of the secrets of her power. One never has to accept defeat if one is sufficiently ruthless to balk at nothing : even the death of one's only son. If that son were so unfilial as to prefer his own choice to his mother's, he would have to bear the consequences. And for Tung Chih they were tragic.

The astrologers having decided on a favourable and appropriate date, the Regency ended on 15 November 1872, and the seventeen-year-old Emperor entered into the administration of his realm. The Decree which closed Tzu Hsi's and Tzu An's Regency pointed out that :

His Majesty assumes today the control of the Government, and our joy at this auspicious event is in some degree blended with feelings of anxiety as to the possible results of this change; but we bear in mind the fact that his sacred Ancestors have all feared the Almighty, and endeavoured to follow in the sacred traditions of their predecessors.

In this Decree Her Majesty made no secrets of her misgivings regarding her son's abilities, nor did she seem to expect that he would now settle down to devote himself to his exalted task. Yet oddly enough that did apparently seem to be his intention, for which A-lu-te appeared chiefly responsible. For, like Yehonala before her, the new young Empress Consort showed considerable interest in matters of State, or, possibly, a desire that her husband and she herself should assert their new authority unmistakably.

Their first act of rebellion against the Matriarch was Tung Chih's firm refusal to allow the Empress Dowager, the former Regent, to read the official documents awaiting his signature before he himself did so, and occasionally to see them at all. The antagonism between the young couple and Tzu Hsi was plainly visible to all at Court.

This loss of face was completely intolerable to Yehonala. At thirty-seven, after twelve years of uninterrupted power, the Empress Dowager was being firmly placed on the political shelf. And worse might shortly happen. In spite of his marriage, Tung Chih did not reform his dissolute habits; his health was already undermined. If A-lu-te produced an heir to the Throne, she herself would become Empress Dowager in the event of Tung Chih's death. For Yehonala the outlook was an increasingly grim one, especially when it became known that the Empress Consort was pregnant. Only if by some strange coincidence the Emperor and young Empress were to die before the birth of their heir would it be possible for the Regency to be resumed, a highly unlikely contingency unless fate might be assisted in bringing it about.

In December 1874, the Tung Chih Emperor published an unusual Decree: 'We have had the good fortune,' it began, 'this month to contract smallpox . . .'

This odd turn of phrase was due to a Chinese belief that smallpox was a lucky disease—presumably, to have endured and recovered from. It was similar to the belief prevailing in the West that all children who contracted measles, chicken-pox, whooping-cough or mumps might as well get them over with : so much so that the healthy members of a family were often placed with the

sick one to make sure of catching the infection. But was Tung
Chih's good luck on this occasion encouraged by someone in
whose interest it lay that the Emperor's horrible disease should
end his life?

Tung Chih might easily have caught his small-pox in one of
the brothels and opium dens he visited during his nocturnal
escapades into Peking. This could neither be proved nor dis-
proved. But the outward symptom of this virulent infection is
an eruption of running pustules all over the sufferer's face and
body.

A Chinese meal, eaten with chopsticks, consists of a large
variety of dishes and courses: those served by the eunuchs at the
Imperial table were never fewer than one hundred, and often
more. Table-napkins were not used in China; instead, small
square towels sterilized in steam were passed to the diners, who,
between each course, wiped their faces as well as their lips with
them. This was an agreeable and normally more hygienic practice
than the use of a dry table-napkin. But it could be, and on certain
authenticated occasions was, turned to a deadly purpose. If the
hot, steaming little towel were first rubbed on the face of a smallpox sufferer, covered in highly infectious running pustules, and
then passed over the features of an intended victim . . . ? A
master, and above all the Son of Heaven, would never himself
wipe his face. This menial task would be performed by a reveren-
tially attendant eunuch under the supervision of the Chief
Eunuch in person. It might be a simple and devilishly effective
method of assassination.

Whether or not Tung Chih was thus disposed of will never be
known. What is certain is that he was dead within little more
than a fortnight after his good fortune had befallen him. His
Decree announcing his illness continued:

Their Majesties, The Empresses Dowager, have shown the
greatest possible tenderness in their care for our person. They
have also consented to peruse all Memorials and State papers on
our behalf, and to carry on the business of the State, for which
we are deeply grateful. We feel bound to confer upon their

Majesties additional titles of honour, so as to make some return, however small, for their infinite goodness.

It had taken the Motherly and Auspicious Empress less than two years to return to power, with the reins of government firmly in her hands again, and no intention of relinquishing them. A-lu-te and her unborn child still remained alive. But as both Empresses Dowager, all the Princes and ministers, and other mourners gathered around the late Tung Chih Emperor's funereal bed, Her Majesty's plans for the succession were already well advanced.

Tung Chih's tragic end had been foreseen and even predicted by Kuei Ching. He would never have dared to suggest that the two Ministers of the Household whom he had accused of systematically debauching the late Emperor had done so with his Imperial mother's approval or even connivance. But, knowing that such rumours were prevalent at Court, the Empress Dowager dismissed the pair forthwith. If they had in fact been her tools, they had served their purpose. Tzu Hsi even expressed her gratitude for Kuei Ching's devotion to the Throne by offering to reinstate him. That honest servant, however, declined this honour for reasons which may have been obvious to his Imperial mistress, since she did not press it upon him.

10   *A New Lease of Power*

The Emperor being no mere temporal ruler but the Son of Heaven—the only semi-human, semi-divine link between the millions inhabiting the Celestial Empire on earth and the heavenly regions, the only intermediary between them qualified to perform the requisite Rites—the Dragon Throne might never be left without an occupant. As Tung Chih had died before producing an heir solely competent to perform these religious duties, it was—in the Empress Regent's view, at any rate—an immediate necessity to provide him with a successor. The speed and ruthless efficiency with which Tzu Hsi now set about to fill the gap were calculated to undermine all opposition to her implacable will.

Although until then she had apparently achieved her supremacy by sheer strength of personality, she and others in the Imperial household realized quite clearly that her power largely rested on the military support of her own Yehonala clansmen headed by Jung Lu, who controlled the Imperial bodyguard.

So, before summoning the Imperial Council to appoint a successor to the Son of Heaven, Her Majesty did not neglect to take the necessary precautions to cope with any difficulties that might ensue. Jung Lu was on special duty with his Bannermen within the Forbidden City, and another of her loyal supporters, Li Hung Chang, who had distinguished himself in the defeat of the Taiping Rebellion, and been rewarded with the Viceroyalty of Chihli, at her request sent reliable troops, who were stationed at other strategic points.

Very fortunately for the Empress's scheme, the Imperial Princes did not see eye to eye in the selection of a suitable successor to Tung Chih. These princes were above all anxious to resist any further strengthening of the power of the Yehonala clan. The appropriate candidate should also be one of a younger generation than the late Emperor's, as such duties could not be performed by a member of his own generation.

The obvious candidate from this point of view was a great-grandson of the Tao Kuang Emperor, a child called Pu Lun. But Prince Kung also had a son who might be chosen for this exalted task, and for this reason there was a certain amount of conflict between the electors.

The Empress Dowager was well aware of this, but in any case her own mind was already made up. Some years previously she had arranged a match between her own younger sister (another Yehonala, of course) and Prince Chun, who was the seventh son of the Tao Kuang Emperor, and younger brother of the late Hsien Feng and Prince Kung. This child was therefore a first cousin of the Tung Chih Emperor, of the same generation, and ineligible to perform the required Rites for the peace of his spirit. He was then about four years old.

Having carefully made her preparations, Tzu Hsi summoned the Imperial Princes in conclave with herself, Tzu An, and the officials who were also entitled to be present, such as members of the Imperial Council, of whom only five were Chinese. In addition to the troops, Li Lien-ying had posted trusted eunuchs of his own selection at strategic points in the Forbidden City. In this setting, perfectly prepared for a *coup d'état,* the Council took place in the ornate, lacquered and gilded Palace of Mind Nurture. Only one member of the Imperial family was excluded from this gathering, Tung Chih's widow, A-lu-te, by the express command of the Empress Dowager Tzu Hsi.

All present kowtowed as the Co-Empresses entered the Council Chamber. Tzu Hsi wore the full ceremonial Yellow Dragon robe reserved for formal occasions; on her head was a sable hat encircled by a coronet of jade and pearls; her long necklace of three hundred perfectly matched pearls hung down to her knees; and her square bootees were also pearl-embroidered. In spite of her platform heels she was a tiny figure, but so imbued with authority and majesty that not one man in that vast cold hall did not fear her.

Tzu An, the Eastern Empress, was also gorgeously dressed, but looked as stiff and expressionless as a doll.

From the outset, Tzu Hsi took charge of the proceedings. With her usual imperturbability she went straight to the point. She opened her attack with the firm statement that it was imperative to elect a new Emperor immediately, since the Dragon Throne might not indefinitely remain unoccupied on the assumption that the late Emperor's widow would in due course bear him an heir.

Prince Kung, as spokesman for the Imperial Princes, was in a delicate position, since his own son was a possible choice. He tactfully suggested that it might still be possible to postpone the announcement of the late Emperor's departure on high until A-lu-te's child was born. If it were a boy, the succession would then be assured; if a girl, the matter could be raised again. His Imperial relatives supported this proposal.

But Her Majesty immediately countered it by placing the problem on a wider basis. Her statesmanship always adroitly supported her intrigues and secret plans, and now she pointed out that there were still rebellions in the south, and that as soon as it became known that the Throne was vacant, these might lead to an attempt to overthrow the dynasty: a contingency that all those present, as well she knew, were as anxious to avoid as herself. And, like the best Chinese scholar-statesmen, she was never at a loss for a picturesque parable with which to press home her point: 'When the nest is destroyed, how many eggs will remain unbroken?'

This astute political reference found instant support from the three councillors representing the southern provinces and also the other statesmen present. The situation could well be exploited by the remnants of the Taiping rebels who, only recently subdued, might at such a favourable moment return to the attack.

Now Tzu An ventured to put in a word for her ally, Prince Kung, whose son was the candidate she proposed. In accordance with protocol, Prince Kung thereupon kowtowed, refusing such honour for his own family, and proposing the alternative Imperial candidate, the young Pu Lun, in the direct line of descent from the Emperor Tao-Kung. Her Majesty's counter-argument to this proposal had been well prepared.

When Pu Lun's father, in his turn, made the customary refusal, on the pretext (which he himself did not, of course, believe) that his son was also unworthy of such high honour, she once again resorted to precedent. 'That has nothing to do with the case,' she informed him tartly; 'but as you yourself are only the adopted son of Yi Wei, what precedent can any of you show for placing on the throne the heir of an adopted son?'

Astutely the Empress then asked Prince Kung's view in this matter, and the Prince did find a precedent from the Ming Dynasty in the fifteenth century.

'But that is a bad precedent,' Her Majesty immediately retorted. 'The Emperor Ying-Tsung was not really the son of his predecessor, but was palmed off on the Emperor by one of the Imperial concubines. His reign was a period of disaster; he was for a time in captivity under the Mongols, and afterwards lived in retirement in Peking for eight years, his brother having ascended the Throne.'

The moment had now arrived when the Empress thought it appropriate to name the candidate she had previously chosen: her own nephew, a child of four. By the accession of this little boy her Regency would be safeguarded for at least another ten or eleven years.

'As for me,' she said, turning to her colleague, the Eastern Empress, 'I propose as the heir to the Throne Tsai Tien, the son of Yi Huan, and advise you all that we lose no time.'

Time was, in fact, the essence of the matter. Prince Kung, not daring directly to thwart her Imperial Majesty, did, however, turn to his younger brother and furiously inquire from him whether the right of primogeniture was to be completely ignored. For the choice of Prince Chun's child was flauntingly in disregard of all traditional procedure.

But wasting no further words in discussion, Her Majesty at once proceeded to put the onus on the Imperial Council. Under her implacable gaze the princes and councillors voted. Only the Imperial Princes dared openly to defy the Empress Dowager's will : three of them voted for Prince Kung's son, and seven for Pu Lun, who, had precedent been followed, must have been chosen. The ministers and councillors, not surprisingly, all backed the candidate proposed by the Western Empress.

Victory for Tzu Hsi by fifteen to ten.

She had been so sure of gaining her way as usual, although her choice was glaringly and outrageously against all precedent and protocol, that her plans had been laid well in advance down to the smallest detail.

Night had fallen. It was bitterly cold in Peking, swept by one of those needle-sharp wind-storms that covered the whole city with a layer of gritty yellow dust. The Forbidden City was well guarded by Jung Lu's troops. The Western Empress now ordered Prince Kung to betake himself to the lying-in-state of the late Emperor, to preside over it, and he had no alternative but to obey her command. As soon as he was thus disposed of, Tzu Hsi ordered a guard of household cavalry to accompany the Imperial Yellow palanquin and its bearers and attendants to Prince Chun's palace, and to bring the Emperor-elect forthwith to the Forbidden City. The child's mother, her own sister, was no doubt informed in advance of her powerful senior's intentions.

The poor little boy was awakened in the middle of the night, wrapped in padded silk quilts and swathed in furs, and carried to the Imperial Chair, crying bitterly, as if he already had a premonition of the dire consequences that would follow his summary delivery into the power of his terrible aunt. His mother and nurses accompanied him. He was not put to bed immediately on arrival in the stormy darkness (which all present regarded as a

bad omen for his future reign), but taken in solemn state to the
death-bed of his predecessor : a frightening scene for a tiny boy
to witness at such an hour. There he was made to kowtow to the
inert corpse, sumptuously arrayed in its ceremonial robes pre-
paratory to departure on the Dragon's back to the celestial
regions.

A strange macabre scene by the light of the lanterns swaying
in the draught : the kneeling child; the weeping widow, bearing
in her womb the infant now destined never to succeed, her own
life in imminent danger; and the impotently furious Prince
Kung, father of the legitimate but rejected alternative heir;
surrounded by crowds of sumptuously dressed, observant
eunuchs, Li Lien-ying's henchmen.

The Decree now issued by Tzu Hsi, also signed by the cowed
Tzu An, was one of her most daring edicts. The Empresses
Regent, it stated, 'were absolutely compelled to select Tsai Tien
[the new little Emperor's personal name] for the Throne.' He
became heir by adoption to his uncle, Hsien Feng; but it was
intended that 'as soon as he should have begotten a son,
the Emperor Tung Chih would at once be provided with an
heir.'

This statement was a challenge to all orthodox precedent with
regard to the Rites that were obligatory on an Emperor's death.
For Tsai Tien, whose reign-name was to be Kuang Hsu, or
'Brilliant Succession', was totally unqualified by the laws and
customs of lineal descendence to offer the sacrifices for the late
Emperor's soul that would enable it to rest in peace. It was thus
condemned to a kind of limbo until the gods should be appeased
on its behalf. This violation of the code of ancestor-veneration in
due course aroused bitter opposition throughout the whole
Empire : a storm of protest with a dramatic climax to it that
would have swept from power any less ruthlessly successful despot
than the Empress Dowager.

There still remained one danger, although now considerably
lessened by her *coup d'état,* for the Western Empress to face.
So long as A-lu-te lived, so long as there remained a chance that
the infant in her womb might be born and be a son, the Empress

Dowager's position was not impregnable. But a few months' respite remained.

As soon as the Council had approved the choice of the new Emperor, the princes and ministers, putting the best possible face on it, presented a petition to the Regents asking them to resume their responsibilities during the child ruler's minority. This was, of course, the focal point of the Western Empress's plan. Tzu Hsi's Edicts and Decrees were as formally and correctly constructed as her stiff, magnificent ceremonial robes. But underneath those robes, those layers of enveloping silk, there was a human being, and underneath or between the lines of her official utterances there was often a sardonic Oriental humour, a fine appreciation of life's irony. When she took her writing-brush in hand to draw them up, her tongue may well have been curling round her cheek.

Not so very long ago she had accepted her first Regency in similarly modest and reluctant terms. Their Majesties were given 'dutiful thanks for this virtuous act'—the assumption of the burdens of government laid upon the two august ladies by fate— in the child Emperor's name, and thus all the required gestures of protocol were completed.

The Empress Dowager now had leisure to turn her attention to the problem of A-lu-te.

Tung Chih's widow was awarded an honorary title in her turn —a hollow one indeed in the tragic circumstances. Her deep grief at her late husband's death was not mitigated by it. Perhaps this was because Time, the alleged healer of all sorrows, was not given the leisure to bring her the balm dispensed to others. For on 27 March 1876—just three months later than Tung Chih—she died. It was sad, very sad indeed, that in her inconsolable unhappiness at his loss, A-lu-te, it was officially announced, had committed suicide.

There is no precise evidence as to the manner in which this convenient tragedy occurred. Malicious gossip murmured that the Western Empress, the Motherly and Auspicious, had pointed out the young widow's tragic duty to her, although she had taken no more active steps than that to encourage her to it. But Her

Majesty's enemies did not hesitate to accuse her of having taken more direct measures to end A-lu-te's life and that of her unborn child. And what, from the Empress's point of view, could have been more desirable than the death of that foetus, which could not, unfortunately, be brought about without his mother's demise, whether by her own pathetic hand or by adroitly administered poison—in dispensing which Li Lien-ying was an expert?

When the Empress imposed her own choice—her nephew, now the little Kuang Hsu Emperor—on the dynasty and the country, she was well aware of the risks she was taking, determined to take them nevertheless, and confident of overcoming all opposition. She knew that this would crystallize around the thorny problem of providing the late Tung Chih with a spiritual heir, and in her Decree announcing the new Emperor's accession she stressed that 'as soon as he should have begotten a son, the Emperor Tung Chih would at once be provided with an heir'. But it was obvious to all who read it that this child of four would be unable to fulfil that obligation for at least another eleven or twelve years. It was less obvious, except to those in the know, that the likelihood of his ever doing so was even more remote.

Although the Imperial Princes and other members of the Grand Council had been compelled much against their will to accept the predetermined choice of their indomitable mistress, their resentment was unappeased. It was first expressed officially in a Memorial from a Manchu member of the Grand Secretariat, which, in veiled and guarded terms, and, as was customary, quoting many historical precedents, was a direct attack on the Empress Dowager, as was obvious to everyone who could read between the lines.

The Memorialist then proceeded to examine in detail and point out all the defects in the procedure which had been taken, as well as the promises for future rectification of the situation by the Empress Dowager. And he also voiced the general alarm that the unappeased shade of the late Emperor, the anger of the sacred ancestors of the dynasty and the gods on high, might cause inevitable and terrible disaster to fall upon the realm.

As Her Majesty's knowledge of historical and dynastic precedent was equal to the learning of any of her advisers, she knew only too well that this Memorial was a daring slap in the face, a challenge to her authority. Moreover, in spite of its guarded phrasing, the Memorial clearly expressed the anxiety of the Imperial Princes regarding the succession. The boy Emperor was only a member of their clan on the paternal side; his mother was a Yehonala. The Memorialist was asking, even demanding, a valid document guaranteeing that the Empress Dowager's clan, already half in possession of the Throne, should not in due course usurp it.

In her reply, Her Majesty made no secret at all of her feelings, of her extreme anger, and her words conveyed a clear warning to any who might be encouraged to provoke her further. She repeated that:

> We have already issued an absolutely clear Decree on this subject, providing for an heir to the late Emperor, and this Decree has been published all over the Empire. The Memorialist's present request gives evidence of unspeakable audacity and an inveterate habit of fault-finding, which has greatly enraged us, so that we hereby convey to him a stern rebuke.

In the matter of audacity the Empress Dowager neither had nor ever intended to have any rival. And this Decree she expected to discourage any other member of the mandarinate from further incurring Her Majesty's wrath and retribution.

But for once her expectation was thwarted by the ultimate sacrifice a conscientious official might make, and which was now made by a man who in consequence was to be remembered in Chinese history as the arch-type of the heroically devoted servant.

The censor, Wu Ko-tu, determined to offer his own life on his late Emperor's behalf, hoping thereby to placate the wrath of the gods and to save his country from their catastrophic vengeance. He first took a strong dose of opium and then hanged himself in a little temple close to the sacred Imperial Tomb of his late master, Tung Chih. Nor did he even forget to apologize in a humble posthumous letter to the little temple's priest for so defiling his sacred precincts.

Wu Ko-tu's suicide caused an enormous sensation throughout the whole of China. Before killing himself he wrote a very long Memorial which was in due course presented to the Empresses Dowager, in which he set out in full detail and noble terms his reasons for this act of self-sacrifice on behalf of the dynasty and nation. His motives were solely and profoundly ethical.

In a farewell letter to his son he pointed out that their family tree went back for more than five hundred years, that for two centuries there were members of their clan among the Imperial concubines, and that for three hundred years they had devoted themselves to husbandry and scholarship.

The most remarkable paragraph in his Memorial, from some points of view, was the final one, relating to foreign innovations. For when he sacrificed his life for the ancient traditions, the ancestor-worship and sanctity of which the Emperor was the living symbol, Wu was aware that already the Middle Kingdom, the Celestial Empire, was set on a new path. The centre of the world it traditionally was, would remain. But Europe and America had already fastened their tentacles on it and would never let go until they were rudely shaken off, almost a century after his death.

There seems little evidence that the Empress was a religious woman. As was necessary in her position, she paid her respects to the Buddha, and punctiliously observed all the ritual laid down by Confucianism on the appropriate occasions—when it suited her to do so. But she was, and for this there is ample evidence throughout her life, incorrigibly superstitious : as superstitious as Catherine de Medici. She seldom undertook any activities— even the most trivial daily items of behaviour—without first consulting the Court Astrologers and a kind of pocket Chinese *Old Moore's Almanack* which she always kept close to hand. She was no less deeply moved—even shaken—by Wu's suicide than all her subjects. And to the end of her life she secretly believed with them that the disasters that befell China in the latter half of the nineteenth century were traceable to the wrath of the gods on behalf of the slighted ghost of the Tung Chih Emperor.

11 Disgrace of a Lover –
Death of a Rival

Whilst Tzu An had always refrained from interference in matters of State and took no interest in the recurring crises in China's relations with the foreign Powers, she was always very keenly concerned with the rules governing the dynastic tradition and palace protocol. She gradually recovered from the shock she felt when, after signing the Decree liquidating the Chief Eunuch An-te-hai at Prince Kung's prompting, her Imperial Sister had descended on her like an avenging fury. So much so that she had risked incurring Tzu Hsi's further enmity by supporting the Tung Chih Emperor's choice of A-lu-te as Empress Consort, and the candidature of her ally Prince Kung's son as his successor. When Tzu Hsi imposed her nephew on the Council and nation instead, the rift between the Co-Regents widened still further. For throughout his life Kuang Hsu felt nothing but resentment for his terrifying Aunt, and in his childhood, like his predecessor, gave all his affection to the genuinely motherly Eastern Empress, Tzu An. At a very early stage in this Emperor's upbringing he became the focal point of much wrangling and dissension between the Imperial Sisters, who squabbled bitterly about his diet and companions.

In argument the Empress of the Eastern Palace was no match for her Co-Regent. But the Western Empress, preoccupied with matters of State, did not waste her time supervising every meal and every snack between meals given to the little Emperor. As soon as her back was turned his kindly protectress would continue to spoil him.

With two recent examples of the sinister influence of the eunuchs on the child-Emperors in mind, the Western Empress forbade Kuang Hsu to play with the little eunuchs, whose official functions were similar to those of pages at European Courts. She informed her Sister that they were 'an evil-minded lot', despite the fact that they were eunuchs—or for that very reason. She correctly pointed out that they would teach the child things he should not know. Nevertheless, the Eastern Empress allowed the boy to keep this bad company, with consequences she might have foreseen had she had her Sister's foresight.

Inevitably Li Lien-ying was already taking a hand in this situation, as in all Court intrigues. The games he played with Kuang Hsu were of a different calibre from those of his subordinates; his mischievous teasing led to Imperial tears. Naturally enough, the little Emperor ran to his protectress, Tzu An, with complaints against the Chief Eunuch. And with her usual clumsiness the Eastern Empress reported the matter to Li Lien-ying's mistress, demanding that he should be severely punished for his presumption. The Western Empress thereupon sent for the Chief Eunuch, wishing to know whether or not he had behaved improperly towards His Imperial Majesty. Li Lien-ying's emphatic denial that he had ever done anything of the kind was promptly accepted.

Such incidents during his childhood may well have been the origin of the permanent mutual antipathy, in due course deepening into hatred, between the Emperor and the Dowager's henchman. Like his Imperial Mistress, Li had a long memory. He also had unusual patience. When his opportunity to avenge himself in due course came, he took it with his usual sadistic delight.

Only Tzu An, whose natural obstinacy was as great as her lack of subtlety and endearing modesty, refused to accept the fact of the Chief Eunuch's enormous influence with her Co-Regent.

The simmering antagonism between the two Empresses suddenly erupted again in 1880. One of the most important religious ceremonials laid upon them was the pilgrimage to the tombs of defunct Emperors. The observances and rites to be performed there were all dictated by precedent, and in their performance precedence was of capital importance. An open clash occurred in that year, when the Imperial widows proceeded to the tomb of their joint spouse, the late Hsien Feng Emperor.

Sakota was entirely within her rights in claiming the central place on this occasion, since, childless and unloved though she had been, she was nevertheless First Consort, and, as such, fully entitled to it. Yehonala, however, was unwilling to accord this precedence to the woman whom she had so completely supplanted in every other way both during and after Hsien Feng's lifetime. To the alarm and shame of the entire Court, compelled to witness this appalling breach of manners in silent horror, the Imperial ladies openly quarrelled. Tzu An was indeed rash when she dared to remind Tzu Hsi that at the time of the Emperor's death she had still been a mere Imperial concubine, and had only been elevated to the highest rank after his demise. Whether or not Tzu Hsi so far forgot herself on this inauspicious occasion as to elbow her rival out of the place Tzu An was trying to deprive her of, she nevertheless immediately occupied it.

Although Tzu Hsi never hesitated to ignore or defy Imperial protocol when it suited her purpose, as it did now, she was far too well versed in such matters not to realize the exceedingly bad impression this incident created on those who witnessed it. The momentary triumph was no compensation for the fact that Tzu An had so deeply outraged her pride, and, by compelling her to assert herself so firmly on so solemn an occasion, caused her to commit so awful a breach of manners.

And as if this were not enough a much more serious personal crisis occurred in her relationship with Jung Lu very soon afterwards.

Yehonala was now forty-five years old. Until then Jung Lu

had been the most important man in her life. By this time rumour and gossip had assumed without question that he was her lover. Ever since the perilous days at Jehol and after her return to the Forbidden City, Jung Lu had watched over and guarded the Empress with perfect devotion. In every crisis it was he who furnished the reliable cohorts to protect her against any move by her enemies. There is little reason to doubt that he had indeed loved Yehonala as he loved no other woman, and that as far as she herself was capable of sexual passion, it was for Jung Lu that she felt it. She had showered honours and promotion on him. If she had needed a pretext for keeping him close to her person at times when the presence in the Forbidden City of any normal male save the Son of Heaven was rigorously forbidden, she had found a perfectly good reason for making this possible in his case by appointing Jung Lu Comptroller of her Household.

Whether or not their liaison had come to an end in 1880 is uncertain. But even if Yehonala might have conceded—which was more than improbable—that her feminine charms had ceased to fascinate Jung Lu as in the past, it was inconceivable that he should so much as glance at another woman within the Forbidden City itself. Since Jung Lu was a strong, healthy, handsome man of normal instincts, it might be taken for granted that he had occasionally allowed himself the amusement of an intrigue with a pretty girl; but if he did so, Yehonala was unaware of it. Certainly he must have been very rash or very much in love to have an affair with one of the ladies who had been a concubine of the late Tung Chih Emperor.

Although the Empress had very little affection for the young Emperor, she supervised his education as carefully as his predecessor's. According to custom, the little boy was provided with a tutor when he was five years old. This post was one of very great influence in the Forbidden City, and Her Majesty had selected a brilliant scholar to fill it—Weng Tung-ho, whose native province, Kiangsu, was traditionally the most famous centre of learning in the Empire.

Like all the Court officials, the Imperial tutor took care to cultivate in his small pupil the deepest respect for the Matriarch.

He found other ways of ingratiating himself personally with her. By what means he did so—and it must have been a very delicate undertaking indeed—Weng now conveyed to the Empress the news that was already known to most of those in high places at Court: that Jung Lu was having an illicit liaison with a certain lady, and that in the course of it the Comptroller of the Empress Dowager's household had taken advantage of his privilege to remain in the Forbidden City at night—a very grave offence indeed. It was also generally believed that the Eastern Empress was aware of this scandal, and that instead of denouncing the lovers she had actually protected them. If this were true it would have been a natural enough reaction, but could only increase the Western Empress's hatred for her.

As usual, Yehonala moved with ruthless speed. This defection on Jung Lu's part must have been the severest blow her feminine vanity ever suffered. But the steps she took on learning of it were both thorough and discreet. Refusing to believe any evidence but that of her own eyes, she found means of discovering the lovers together. In any other case the culprits would no doubt have been put to death. Whether in view of the close and tender bonds that had for so many years existed between herself and Jung Lu, whether in gratitude for the steadfast loyalty with which he had helped her to power and maintained her in it, Yehonala seems to have carried out her sentence on him with maximum discretion. Inevitably he was banished from Court and from her sight. But when she sent her former lover into exile at Sianfu, he was given an important and face-saving military post there. Seven years elapsed before Jung Lu was recalled to Peking, when once again he was to save his Mistress from danger, and be fully restored to her favour.

If Tzu An had indeed condoned Jung Lu's infidelity, her satisfaction at depriving Tzu Hsi of his personal and official services did not last long.

In March 1881 the Eastern Empress with almost incredible rashness renewed her complaints against the Chief Eunuch, Li Lien-ying. By then he was in such high favour with the Western Empress that he behaved towards her colleague with intolerable insolence. His own subordinates naturally followed his line, and even Tzu An's own eunuchs were encouraged to treat her with the greatest disrespect. And like An-te-hai before him, Li had arrogated to himself the title of 'Lord of Nine Thousand Years' : an impudence which was quite unpardonable, since by using it he placed himself only one stage lower than the Emperor's sacred person. But Tzu An was not to repeat her success in disposing of Li's predecessor. Her attempt to break his power was a futile one, and it cost the Eastern Empress her life.

It was said that the Western Empress indeed permitted Li Lien-ying unusual liberties. She encouraged him to speak his mind freely, without waiting until he was first spoken to. In later years, when referring to Her Majesty, he would use the term *Tsa-men,* meaning 'we two', as if he were either a member of the Imperial family or her social equal.

Li's hold over Her Majesty was due to several causes. She never liked to confide in women, since from girlhood she regarded them as potentially dangerous rivals. She was too intelligent to take pleasure in their trivial gossip. She was suspicious of all men save Jung Lu, and him she had lost owing to his foolish infidelity and the deep wound this had inflicted on her feminine vanity. Li was intelligent, tactful, an adroit flatterer and entertaining companion, and their personal ambitions—for enormous wealth and autocratic power—were complementary. But over and above all these considerations was the paramount necessity for the Empress to have always at hand a willing and able instrument to carry out her more sinister plans. From the day when Li, still an inconspicuous but already ruthless young eunuch, had stolen the Imperial seal at Jehol she relied on him in every one of the dramatic crises in her life, and he never failed her. The Empress Dowager was no Lady Macbeth; she never sullied her small hands with their long, pointed finger-nails, of which she was so proud. Whenever she needed a reliable spy, inquisitor, or executioner, Li was available.

Only a few months after the last bitter quarrel between the Empresses, Tzu An fell ill. Her indisposition appeared at first a natural one, and not particularly serious. One account of her end seems, to say the least, far-fetched, for it is hard to believe that, as is claimed, the Eastern Empress was poisoned by her own hatred of her colleague. She took to her bed, and never again left it.

The historians, whether genuine or pseudo, claimed that Tzu An died after eating some poisoned cakes sent her during her illness by her Sister. As no autopsy was performed, the evidence that she was murdered at Li Lien-ying's or his Mistress's command, will for ever remain indecisive. Yet that they found her death extremely convenient cannot be denied. Perspicacious readers may find a sinister as well as gentle irony in the Valedictory Decree Tzu An dictated on her death-bed : ●

> In spite of the arduous duties of the State, which have fully occupied my time, I was naturally of robust constitution and had therefore fully expected to attain to a good old age and to enjoy the Emperor's dutiful ministrations. Yesterday, however, I was suddenly stricken with a slight illness and His Majesty thereupon commanded his physician to attend me. . . . And now, most unexpectedly, I have had a most dangerous relapse. At 7 p.m. this evening I became completely confused in mind and now all hope of my recovery appears to be vain. I am forty-five years of age and for close on twenty years have held the high position of a Regent of the Empire. Many honorific titles and ceremonies of congratulation have been bestowed on me : what cause have I therefore for regret?

Those touchingly dignified lines do not give the impression of having been dictated by a woman dying of rage. Reading between them, one feels that this noble lady of 'naturally robust constitution' may well have suspected the cause of her sudden and unexpected relapse. Yet there is also an impression of relief, as if in spite of herself Tzu An was almost thankful to have reached the point of no return in the long and unequal struggle between herself and Tzu Hsi.

12 *Imperial Marriage*

Another six years remained until, at the age of seventeen, the Emperor would assume his Imperial responsibilities : six years during which the Empress Dowager was at last the sole and unchallenged ruler of the Celestial Empire. At the beginning of this period of autocratic power she was still plagued by the recriminations Tzu An was no longer there to make, but which, like an avenging legacy, were taken up by others. The Censors did not cease to take advantage of their rights to memorialize the Throne on the increasing extravagance and corruption at Court. But Her Majesty felt herself in a sufficiently strong position either to ignore these Memorials or to reject them contemptuously.

Only one person remained sufficiently strong to oppose her effectively, one whom she knew to have been more than Tzu An's ally : Prince Kung, who had persuaded the Eastern Empress to sign An-te-hai's death warrant, who for years had been the only one of the Imperial Princes sufficiently powerful to contradict Her Majesty when he found it necessary to do so, whom on several previous occasions she had severely reprimanded but never yet dared to dismiss finally from his high position as Prime Minister and head of the Grand Council of Ministers.

The Son of Heaven was growing up, and the Empress was obliged to realize that her autocratic reign as Regent must, inevitably, soon come to an end. But although the Emperor would shortly become the acting Head of State, the Empress Dowager was already making plans to remain as ever, if no longer the power on the Throne, the guiding spirit and autocrat behind it. Weng Tung-ho, the Imperial tutor, had served her well, and as a reward for the personal service he had given her, she appointed him President of the Board of Works and a Member of the Grand Council. The leader of this Council was Prince Kung; the Grand Secretary was an old and eminent statesman, Pao Yun.

Prince Kung never made any secret of his detestation of the Chief Eunuch, Li Lien-ying. The Empress suspected the Prince of having encouraged the Censors in presenting a series of Memorials reproving her for the extravagance and depravity they claimed existed at Court. Had she for a moment been willing to grant that such a state of affairs did exist, the Empress would hardly have been able to deny that the responsibility for it was chiefly Li's. Of course, she did nothing of the kind, but proceeded instead to turn the tables on her Imperial brother-in-law and his colleagues. It was clearly necessary to destroy Prince Kung's authority before the young Emperor took over the affairs of State.

The tremendous power wielded at this time by Her Majesty— her autocratic rule, her pride and strength of will, and her genius for political manoeuvring—are superbly exemplified in the Decree she issued in 1884, dismissing from their high offices Prince Kung and all the other members of the Grand Council.

This Decree began by stating that, 'Our Country has not yet returned to its wonted stability, and its affairs are still in a critical state.'

This was an oblique reference to the trouble with France, a dispute over the territory of Tongking, which Chinese resistance was impotent to prevent the French from annexing—another slice of melon lost to the foreign devils.

'There is,' the Decree continued, 'chaos in the Government, and a feeling of insecurity amongst the people.'

It is, therefore, of the utmost importance that there should be competent statesmen at the head of affairs, and that our Grand Council should be an efficient pivot and centre of administration.

Prince Kung, at the outset of his career, was wont to render us most zealous assistance; but this attitude became modified, as time went by, to one of self-confident and callous contentment with the sweets of office; and of late he has become unduly inflated with his pride of place, displaying nepotism and slothful inefficiency.

In view of the *coup d'état* by which the Empress had placed her own infant nephew on the Throne, defying the Manchu dynastic house-laws and leaving the shade of Tung Chih without an heir, this charge of nepotism has a breath-taking audacity.

And, striking back as usual, firm in her policy that the best course of defence was attack, the Empress, so constantly criticized for her own conduct, continued :

The House-Laws of our Dynasty are most severe, and if there were any truth in the accusations of treason that have been made against Prince Kung, we should not hesitate for a single moment to inflict upon him the extreme penalty of the law.

It had almost certainly occurred to her to do so, and to rid herself of Tzu An's chief prompter as she had disposed of his tool, the Eastern Empress. Her reasons for refraining from this extreme measure were probably political rather than personal. Even when she was most displeased with the Prince, as now, and as she had been with Jung Lu, the Empress was too shrewd and farseeing a ruler to deprive herself so drastically of those servants of the Throne whom she might need to use in future. Because her emotions—hatred, desire for revenge, or mere spite—were at all times under the control of her calculating mind and will, she was actually to achieve a reputation among her subjects and the foreign diplomats in her capital for feminine magnanimity and generosity :

As a mark of our Imperial clemency we have decided to permit Prince Kung to retain his hereditary Princedom, together with all the emoluments thereof, but he is hereby deprived of all his offices, and the double salary which he has hitherto enjoyed is withdrawn. He is permitted to retire into private life and attend to the care of his health.

Two other members of the Council were dismissed at the same time, 'to be employed in lower positions hereafter'.

The scene, when this Decree was read out to Prince Kung and his colleagues, must have been very gratifying to Li Lien-ying. There they were, in the vast Audience Chamber, on their knees, their stiff ornate robes spread out around them, not daring even once to raise their eyes to the Peacock Throne on which their Imperial Mistress sat, looking down on them. The days when the Empress Dowager had ruled from behind the bamboo or yellow curtains were past; now she sat enthroned in all her splendour, looking down on those who, however high their rank, had no more power to thwart any of her schemes than the meanest coolie.

Prince Kung was thus put into cold storage, and his retirement lasted for ten years, at the end of which time the dramatic events which had meanwhile intervened must have caused the Empress to congratulate herself on her foresight in 1884; for when she again found herself in need of his services, these were still available to her.

She now, however, replaced him on the Grand Council by another Imperial Prince, Li, whom she had no difficulty in handling.

But at this time, with her own approaching compulsory retirement in view, the Empress was concerned above all in strengthening the power of her clan, so that when she went, the young Emperor would be well under the control of the Yehonala faction. Jung Lu was still in banishment. The Son of Heaven's earthly father, who had married her younger sister, was Prince Chun, who now, although apparently much against his will, was promoted to the position of Adviser to the Council.

Ever since Her Majesty had chosen his son to succeed her own son as Emperor, Prince Chun had foreseen the very delicate position in which this would place him personally, and with more foresight than ambition had declined the great honours which, as the Emperor's father, he might have claimed.

His promotion in 1884 to a post which was in fact far more than merely advisory and an even more exalted one than the position until then held by Prince Kung, aroused another storm of protest from Imperial Clansmen and Censors. The Empress's promise, after the death of her son, that she would provide him in due course with a posthumous heir, was still not fulfilled. It appeared, therefore, that the succession might now be altered in favour of the Yehonala clan. Prince Chun, as the Kuang Hsu Emperor's father, could, if he wished, persuade him to appoint a successor from their own family, thus putting an end to the claims of the former reigning House.

As was customary, the Memorialists drew on historical and dynastic precedents to strengthen their case. But the Empress could quote precedents as glibly as anyone. After having once again made a bow of hypocritcal obeisance to it, she proceeded calmly on the course upon which she was determined.

And then, once again taking the attack to her attackers, Her Majesty—an indignant Imperial Matriarch plagued by the teasing of her unruly children—informed them that,

> You cannot possibly realize how great and numerous are the problems with which I have to deal single-handed. As to the Grand Council, let them beware of making Prince Chun's position an excuse for shirking their responsibilities. In conclusion, I wish that my Ministers would for the future pay more respect to the motives which actuate their Sovereign's actions, and abstain from troubling me with their querulous criticisms. The Memorialist's requests are hereby absolutely refused.

Once again it was made unmistakably clear to all that the word of one person and one person only was Law: the word of

Tzu Hsi, the Motherly and Auspicious ruler of the Celestial Empire.

And for good measure the Empress Dowager tightened the screws still further, proceeding, as the last and final gesture of her Regency, to marry her nephew, the Kuang Hsu Emperor, to her niece, his first cousin, the daughter of her younger brother, Duke Kuei Hsiang—yet another Yehonala.

The Kuang Hsu Emperor, the little Tsai Tien (his personal name), was a delicate child. When he was first brought into the Forbidden City, sharp-eyed observers in his immediate entourage, such as his eunuchs, noted that he had some defect of the genitalia that made it unlikely that he would in due course produce an heir. As he was her own sister's child, the Empress must have known this since his infancy, and for that very reason, probably, so hastily raised the little boy to the Throne. But although he was handicapped from a genealogical point of view, Kuang Hsu grew up otherwise quite normally, and the time arrived in due course for him to take over his Imperial duties.

When Tung Chih had to be provided with a bride, the Empresses Dowager shared the privilege of selecting a suitable young woman. In allowing A-lu-te to be married to him Tzu Hsi had made one of her rare mistakes, and this time she was determined not to repeat such an error. She was in any case in a much stronger position now, since she was no longer obliged to contend with the despised but occasionally very obstinate Tzu An. Moreover, the Kuang Hsu Emperor, on the verge of seventeen, although no fool, was a nervous and shy youth, who had been conditioned since his infancy to respect and fear his dynastic superior, and to regard her word as Law.

By making this match between the Emperor and her niece, the Empress intended to establish the Yehonala clan in power more firmly than ever. The girl, moreover, was as pliant a tool in Her Majesty's interests as she could wish to find. The fact that the young cousins loathed each other from childhood was no obstacle to her plans, but an asset. For when, as was shortly to happen, Her Majesty would be obliged to hand over the government to Kuang Hsu, she would leave at his side a spy, all the more willing to report his every move to the Empress Dowager in retaliation for the slights he inflicted on his unloved First Wife.

The young Empress was given the title of Lung Yu, meaning Honorific Abundance—which was cruelly ironical, since the marriage would obviously be more honorific than real and the opposite of abundant in offspring.

In spite of his natural timidity and dread of Tzu Hsi, the Emperor dared to show his dislike for his Consort quite openly.

On the night before the marriage ceremonies began a minor disaster occurred, when the canopies under which they were to take place were burned down, and some of the surrounding buildings also caught fire. The damage was quickly made good by the eunuchs, but, as if even the heavens were on the unfortunate bridegroom's side, the weather on the wedding day was appalling:

> It was a dreary day, raining, and the wedding candles would not burn; Kuang Hsu would not look at his wife; and the young Empress would not look at Kuang Hsu—they hated each other from the very first . . . and with the ill-fated wedding of her nephew and niece, Tzu Hsi began to hate Kuang Hsu—a hatred that became a terrible relentless hatred, souring her life, Kuang Hsu's life, and making the young Empress the most unhappy woman at the Court.

But the Empress Dowager's hatred for her nephew was not solely due to his antipathy to his First Wife. Whether because of his physical handicap, which was no secret to her, or his timid, unprepossessing personality, she always despised her nephew. And her genuine hatred for him later on was largely due to Kuang Hsu's own conduct, which fanned this contempt into a harsh and bitter flame.

The marriage was presumably never consummated; certainly there was no heir. And the unfortunate little First Wife's misery was increased by the fact that her Imperial husband-in-name made no secret of his warm and genuine affection for her rival, the lovely Pearl Concubine.

When the Empress Dowager arranged the match between the Emperor and her niece, her aim was not only to strengthen the Yehonala faction at Court, but to forestall any future attempt by an ambitious young Empress to follow the imprudent example of the late A-lu-te in opposing Her Majesty. But although in this she was successful, she lapsed in vigilance on appointing the Emperor's two concubines. These were sisters, the two young daughters of the Viceroy of Canton. By some odd freak of time or fate, one of them was fat and stupid and disliked by the Emperor as much as Hsien Feng had disliked the similarly placid and dull Sakota; but the other was the most beautiful girl who had appeared at Court since those far-away days when the lovely Orchid, Lan Kuei, now the all-powerful Empress Dowager, had been chosen by Hsien Feng as his beloved. The Pearl Concubine (her sister was known as the Lustrous Concubine) very soon incurred Her Majesty's displeasure, which was no doubt fanned by the young Empress's hatred of her rival. And in due course this lovely girl's fate was an even more horrible one than that of Tung Chih's widow.

The marriage ceremonies over, there was no longer any possibility of prolonging the Regency indefinitely. Two years later Kuang Hsu, nineteen years old, became Emperor in fact as well as in name, and the Empress Dowager, in great state and magnificence, betook herself to the rebuilt and redecorated Summer Palace, where she was to live in retirement for, it appeared, the remainder of her life.

13   Old Buddha

In 1889, at the age of fifty-four, the Empress Dowager Tzu Hsi, having on several occasions previously expressed her keen anxiety to lay down the burden of her second Regency, was compelled to keep her word and do so. In fact the Emperor should have taken over the government two years previously, when he came of age, but Tzu Hsi had managed to postpone this evil moment until after his marriage.

By virtue of dynastic law, the Empress Dowager was still able to retain considerable power. For her seniority, both in age and rank, placed her above the Emperor in the dynastic hierarchy and gave her the right at her own will and in her own time to overrule him permanently or temporarily. In any real crisis, therefore, she might still be the power above the Throne. And whilst Her Majesty knelt to no man under the sun, even the Son of Heaven was obliged to pay her the respect of the ritual kowtow.

Although no longer directly governing the Empire, Tzu Hsi was empowered further at any time to enforce her will by keeping control both of the councils and affairs of the Imperial Family and the appointment or dismissal of the leading ministers and other officials. The custom, on retirement, was for the hitherto ruling monarch to change residence in the Forbidden City as a symbol of the change in régime. So now Her Majesty moved from the Palace of Kindliness and Tranquillity to the Palace of Tranquil Old Age. This was not, however, her ultimate destination.

From the time when, nearly forty years previously, Yehonala had been chosen as concubine to the Hsien Feng Emperor, she had hated the formal, cold halls and palaces in the Forbidden City. And now that she was free to do so, she was delighted to spend her retirement at the Summer Palace. On this vast and glorious domain, with its marble residences nestling in groves of flowering trees and shrubs, its great lake covered with lotus blossom, its pools, rivulets, canals, and fairy-like circular bridges mirroring their beauty, the Empress and Li Lien-ying lavished enormous sums, not for a moment hesitating to steal even from the Imperial Treasury the monies earmarked for the equipment of the national Navy—with, in due course, disastrous results. With her usual caution, however, she provided herself with documentary evidence that the Emperor, and not she, was responsible for this change of residence.

EDICT BY THE EMPRESS DOWAGER

From the time when I first lowered the curtain and attended to State affairs, I have been filled day and night with fear and awe, as though I were travelling along the edge of a chasm. Although the Empire is now fairly peaceful, this is no time for leisurely relaxation or for any diminution of strenuous endeavour. . . .

I am, however, aware that the Emperor's desire to restore the palace in the West springs from his laudable concern for my welfare, and for this reason I cannot bear to meet his well-meaning petition with a blunt refusal.

Moreover, the costs of construction have all been provided for out of the surplus funds accumulated as the result of rigid economies in the past. The funds under the control of the Board of Revenue will not be touched, and no harm will be done to the national finances.

The Empress's Edict, in which she thus attempted to repudiate the accusations against her, ended with three paragraphs admonishing the Emperor and all servants of the State to be 'loyal, diligent and strenuous, and to beware of wasting their substance on frivolity and extravagance'.

And having published this masterpiece of hypocrisy by Her Majesty, the Emperor concluded his Edict by announcing that

> We have respectfully selected by divination the tenth day of the fourth moon of this year (1889) as the date upon which We will reverently escort Her August Majesty's equipage to her new residence.

It was around this time that, in connection with the disaster of a great drought—one of the recurring climatic plagues of China —the Empress Dowager received from Li Lien-ying the nickname by which she became affectionately known to all her people for the rest of her life. During such periods of trial and sorrow it was usual—as it is in Christian churches—to pray for rain, and such prayers, with much incense-burning, chanting and other ritual, were offered up to Buddha. On this occasion, Her Majesty's prayers were granted, and rain fell in abundance on the third day of the ceremonies and offerings :

> Li Lien-ying was so excited and happy that he could not forbear the opportunity to compliment Tzu Hsi.
> 'Rain has come,' he said, 'Your Majesty is great! See how Buddha answers her prayers! It is almost as though she were Buddha herself!'

And from that day onwards Li devotedly and reverently addressed his Imperial Mistress as 'Old Buddha'. Very soon she became known, first to the Court, then to her subjects, and finally to posterity, by this highly complimentary nickname, which she gladly acknowledged. For the prefix 'old' was equivalent to 'venerable' and 'wise', similar to the English 'Venerable Bede' or 'Grand Old Man'. Some English authorities in fact referred to the Empress Dowager as the Venerable Buddha. But

Old Buddha seems to have more intimately affectionate over-tones, even with a hint of humour.

There was a traditional ritual governing the seasons when the hundreds of varieties of blooms in the gardens of the Summer Palace were to be brought to perfection—peach, plum, almond and cherry blossom in the spring, lotus and peonies in summer, chrysanthemums in autumn and winter. Old Buddha would rise before dawn to embark in her enormous marble barge, propelled by a crowd of eunuchs, on the lake Kun Ning, to watch the opening of the lotus buds at sunrise, gradually unfolding their delicate pink petals to the morning light. But equally keenly she watched the eunuchs, wading knee-deep in the water, cutting and transplanting the sacred water-lilies.

'Nothing of the lotus is lost,' she explained to Der Ling, her lady-in-waiting, like any thrifty housewife. 'The roots, stems and leaves are used in medicine. Our people use the leaves, which are cleaner than paper in which to wrap food. The blossom and the young shoots may be eaten.'

Her Majesty knew the name of every variety of chrysanthe-mum grown in her gardens, and there were more than one hundred varieties and ten thousand boxes of them—all as dazzlingly lovely as their names, such as Purple-Phoenix-rejoicing-at-the-Sun; Dragon's Whiskers, which was a huge white one as large as a dinner-plate; another tightly folded white one appropriately called Snowball (which she ate); Golden Bells; the Rainbow; a litany of beauty. Sometimes she herself would tend and prune them with a pair of golden scissors. Yet with all her power and authority even she could not impress her will on Nature as she did on human beings; all her efforts to raise a green chrysanthemum failed.

And woe betide any gardener found wanting. Her Majesty's daily walks through the Summer Palace gardens ineluctably call to mind those of the Queen of Hearts in *Alice in Wonderland*. The eunuch-gardeners watched her approach in fear and trembl-ing, for at the slightest sign of neglect or incompetence on their part—a wilting petal, a drooping leaf—any one of them might, like the Queen's gardeners, hear the dreaded sentence, 'Off with his head!'

Flowers were symbolically connected with many of the seasonal festivals that Old Buddha had full leisure to celebrate now. The ritualistic titles of these festivals were often as poetic as the names of the chrysanthemums—the Beginning of Spring; the Feast of the Lanterns; the Excited Insects; the Corn Rain; the Dragon Boat Festival; the Sprouting Seeds; the Feast of Heavenly Gifts; the White Dew; the Frost's Descent; the Great Snow. Old Buddha particularly loved the snow and the fairy-like transformation of the gardens by hoar-frost.

The elaborate and expensive theatricals in which the Empress still often took part were provided by her troop of resident actors in a vast and specially constructed theatre containing her private suite and dressing-rooms. She also enjoyed playing various games of skill—some of her own invention—with her ladies-in-waiting, which they tactfully nearly always allowed her to win. She continued to paint, to read poetry and history; oversaw all the details of production in her private silkworm nurseries, silk-spinning and dyeing factories and embroidery workshops; concocted simples and complexion creams; collected more and more jewels and jades of colossal value; and was never for one moment of the day or night alone save at her own express command.

When she retired, after her four strong middle-aged serving-women had bathed and massaged her, a lady-in-waiting was on duty in her bedroom throughout the night; an alert eunuch stood outside, and at every door and in every corridor guards and sentries were stationed.

During the day-time, the Empress, who was a great walker and very fond of exercise, would be followed wherever she went by the ladies-in-waiting and crowds of eunuchs carrying anything and everything—from snacks to stools—that she might suddenly have a capricious fancy to use. When she went on the lake in her royal barge, her 'picnic' meals were served hot, on gold plate, by a snake-like file of eunuchs who passed the dishes from hand to hand, from attendant kitchen barges. Yet this woman, more pampered and luxuriously served than any other Empress in history—whether Eastern or Western—remained not only sacred and mysterious to her subjects, but intrinsically lonely.

Her Majesty had a little summer-house built on a small eminence near the wall of the Summer Palace grounds, at a spot that overlooked the road to Peking. And there she would often sit, like any common housewife at her window, watching the traffic to and from the city going by.

Sitting in her little summer-house, almost as completely cut off from the everyday world as a walled nun, the Empress at times appeared almost greedy for some visual contact with it. Her thoughts at those times were her own. But it might not be too rash an assumption to suggest that during her retirement at the Summer Palace—an earthly paradise if ever there was one—with every whim gratified, Old Buddha was often restless, intensely bored, and quite unreconciled to her loss of supreme power.

At the age of fifty-five, in any case a difficult age, she was becoming more and more hardened and embittered.

Within a few years of her retirement, however, the Empress, abetted as usual by Li Lien-ying, found an excellent temporary distraction. In 1894 she would celebrate her sixtieth birthday, a highly auspicious event in Chinese estimation, since the average life-span was a far shorter one, even if death ensued from natural causes. Old Buddha had a remarkable constitution, which matched and was no doubt the mainspring of her steely will. She had hardly known a day's illness, and her zest for life was as great as ever. If she no longer ruled her immense country, she was the richest woman in China and intended to become still richer.

Her sixtieth birthday was to be the occasion for such superlative celebrations as the capital had never yet known, but the cost of which was not to come out of the Imperial privy purse. In view of the great distances involved, all the leading provincial officials, Viceroys, Governors and lesser bureaucrats, were invited in plenty of time to Peking to pay their homage to their Imperial Mistress on this auspicious occasion. Many of them must have groaned on being honoured with these summonses. For they were each expected to contribute to the Empress's birthday present no less than one quarter—twenty-five per cent—of their annual salary. The many millions of taels thus impressed would partly pay for the festivities and partly find their way into the Empress's treasury, of course via the slippery fingers of Li Lien-ying and his subordinates. In addition to these contributions in coin, there were now endless processions wending their way over mountains and through gorges, along roads and canals, bearing gifts in kind —such treasures as only China could bestow on her Empress : priceless jewels, ornaments and services of pure gold, jewel-encrusted screens, furniture of the finest and most exquisitely carved wood, porcelain vases so heavy that several men were required to carry them, carpets in hues of delicate softness that teams of weavers had laboured over for years, silks and em-broideries of gossamer lightness . . . .

Nothing gave Old Buddha, with her highly developed aesthetic sense and appreciation of sumptuous display, greater pleasure than planning such festivities as were due to take place. And nothing could have been a more bitter disappointment to her than their cancellation. Her reason for taking this desolating step was given in a Decree which aroused general admiration and doleful respect :

> The auspicious occasion of my sixtieth birthday, occurring in the tenth Moon of this year, was to have been a joyful event, in which the whole nation would unite in paying to me loyal and dutiful homage. . . . I was not disposed to be unduly obstinate and to refuse these honours, because, at the time that the celebration was planned, my people were enjoying peace and prosperity; moreover, there is precedent for such displays of pageantry and rejoicing. I therefore consented to His Majesty's filial request, and decided to receive birthday con-gratulations at the Summer Palace. Who would ever have anticipated that the Japanese [literally, 'dwarf men'] would have dared to force us into hostilities, and since the beginning of the summer have invaded our tributary State [Korea] and destroyed our fleet? We had no alternative but to draw the

sword and to commence a punitive campaign; at this moment our armies are pressing to the front. The people of both nations [China and Korea] are now involved in all the horrors of war, and I am continually haunted by the thought of their distress; therefore, I have issued a grant of three million taels from my privy purse for the maintenance and relief of our troops at the front.

Although the date of my birthday is drawing close, how could I have the heart, at such a time, to delight my senses with revelries, or to receive from my subjects congratulations which could only be sincere if we had won a glorious victory? I therefore decree that the ceremonies to be observed on my birthday shall be performed at the Palace in Peking, and all preparations at the Summer Palace shall be abandoned forthwith.

This Decree was issued by the Emperor on the Empress Dowager's behalf, with the comment that Her Majesty had acted in accordance with the admirable virtue that always distinguished her, and that, in spite of his own wishes, he was bound reverently to obey her orders in the matter.

14 Aggression and Attack

Wu Ko-tu's last Memorial was typical of the outlook of a Confucian scholar and gentleman in the second half of the nineteenth century. It might have been equally typical in the fifteenth, ninth, or any preceding century. 'Outlook' is not the appropriate term for the thoughts and feelings it revealed : 'in-look' or 'back-look' would be more suitable.

Perhaps as the result of this habit of 'back-looking', the Chinese had acquired a leisurely manner of living and thinking unparalleled in any other civilized community. Whereas ever since the end of the eighteenth century, American Independence, and the Industrial Revolution, Europeans and Americans were thinking in terms of decades, the Chinese still measured human activities in terms of centuries. A couple of hundred years or so was no matter. In the Western world, the word progress had an almost fetishistic magic. As the Western nations grew more powerful, thanks to the unparalleled speed of development of pure and applied science and technology, so their ambitions expanded and their prosperity also. With the coming of the steamship their navies and merchant marines could master the oceans of the East with no fear of local interference; all they needed to guard against were the similar ambitions of rivals of their own race.

But in nineteenth-century China the word progress was not even a dirty one : it was non-existent, meaningless. And it was then that the Western Powers no longer troubled to knock at the doors of the Middle Kingdom, but burst them open.

The basic cause for the fumbling attempts by the Chinese Government to come to terms at last with the modern world and the foreign Powers was increased aggression, and impudent and unchecked encroachments on Chinese soil. In recent years these have been stigmatized by both British and American writers without exaggeration.

Peter Fleming called the aggressors 'The Vultures' and the Celestial Kingdom their 'Tom Tiddler's Ground'.

'Forty years of diplomacy, agitation, resistance and war,' wrote Chester Tan, 'resulted in China's complete yielding to the demands of the Western Powers in the field of trade and residence settlements for foreigners. European ambitions, however, were not confined to commercial concessions. . . . The early 'eighties unmistakably demonstrated the political ambitions of the Powers towards the Chinese Empire. One after another China's dependencies were hacked away.'

For, as Victor Purcell pointed out, 'when it was suddenly made plain that the country was defenceless against modern military organization and weapons, this encroachment turned into a scramble for concessions which seemed to foreshadow its actual territorial partition'.

Yet there was no unanimity among Chinese statesmen and politicians as to the best way of dealing with these dreaded foreign encroachments. The old school, of which Wu Ko-tu was a distinguished representative, wanted to have no truck whatever with the foreigners or their inventions, realizing that to open the door to them would bring about the doom of the way of life their nation had for thousands of years pursued without interference.

But a new school of thought, whilst sharing the intense desire of the other for the expulsion of all foreigners from China, took a more realistic view. There was no escaping certain obvious conclusions. The Europeans and Americans possessed weapons which had enabled them already to invade Chinese territory so successfully only because China did not possess them. The only way it would be possible to meet them on their own ground and to contain them would be for the Chinese themselves to acquire the necessary know-how of Western science and technology.

The Empress Dowager was completely on the side of the antiforeign group that preferred to have no truck whatever with such dangerous innovations. But the party favouring them was led by several of her favourite and most trusted administrators, the so-called new officials, who hoped that it might be possible to give their ancient country a New Look, within, of course, the old system. This group had at its head the famous general and viceroy Tseng Kuo-fan, victor of the Taiping rebellion, and his able assistant, the soldier, scholar and statesman, Li Hung Chang. They were in almost constant contact with Sir Robert Hart, whose advice Li Hung Chang was glad of when it was necessary to negotiate with the foreign devils of various nationalities.

Li Hung Chang became the greatest Chinese statesman of the nineteenth century. He was tall, distinguished-looking even to Western eyes, a Chinese gentleman without a drop of Manchu blood; yet he loyally devoted his indispensable services to the Ching dynasty, and in particular, to the Empress Dowager Tzu Hsi. This devotion was both patriotic and personal. Li himself was a strong and powerful character, with a first-rate intellect; in Her Majesty he recognized a sovereign who, although a woman, he considered worthy of his services.

On several occasions this distinguished administrator—general, viceroy, travelling ambassador to Europe, Russia, and the United States, and saviour of the Throne after the Boxer Rebellion—fearlessly stood up to the Empress Dowager. Time and again she flew into a fury with him and sent him away after depriving him of his honours. But invariably he was recalled and reinstated. Basically both of them admired and trusted one another. The Empress knew—and so did Li Hung Chang—that he was indispensable to her. So he was invariably taken back into favour, and finally, like Tseng Kuo-fan, simply worked to death.

Among the many daring innovations Li Hung Chang persuaded the Manchu régime gradually to sanction were the 'learning of foreign methods as well as utilizing the manufactures and services of foreigners. . . . He bought foreign machinery with which to set up the Kiangan Machine Building Works in Shanghai in 1865, and the Tientsin Machinery Works in 1867. It was he also who made a real attempt to create a Chinese navy from 1875 onwards with ships bought from Britain and Germany, and invited foreign officers to China to train his sea and land forces. It was Li Hung Chang, too, who finally initiated the building of railways and telegraph lines in China; and these are only a few of his innovations. . . . He incidentally managed to build up an enormous private fortune in the process of laying the foundation of China's industry.'

This fortune came mostly from money-lending in return for certain pledges: pawnbroking, in fact, which was a traditional Chinese means of self-enrichment, and considered perfectly proper. ●

At the beginning of the 1870s a new and nearer aggressor also began pressing for a slice of the melon: Japan, the vigorous young Asiatic nation that in the short space of forty-four years had succeeded in carrying out a complete and revolutionary reorganization of its internal affairs, bringing its economy and industry into line with those of the great non-Asiatic powers.

In 1874 Japan began aggressive operations against China, first by taking over the Liuchiu Islands, and a few years later aiming to absorb Korea, a kingdom that paid tribute to the Emperor of China and looked to him for support and protection when threatened or attacked. From 1885 Li Hung Chang managed to stave off the Japanese menace for nearly a decade by the conclusion of the Tientsin Convention, but Japan returned to the attack in 1894, with a navy built on the British pattern and an army similarly modelled on the two most powerful in the Western hemisphere, those of France and Germany. China, considering herself rightly under obligation to protect Korea, and, wrongly, capable of taking on and defeating the Japanese, thereupon declared war on Japan.

At the outbreak of this disastrous war for China, Li Hung Chang was the principal Chinese negotiator with the foreign Powers and Viceroy of the Province of Chihli, the key-post in relation to Peking. For some years previously Li had made intensive efforts to strengthen the Chinese armed forces; had built up an army of his own and the first modern Chinese navy, which was under the command of Admiral Ting Ju-chang. This navy was theoretically superior to that of the Japanese, but, when it went into action, turned out to be almost totally deficient in armour, partly owing to the fact that the money that should have been spent on guns had been squandered on restoring the Summer Palace.

When one of the eunuchs, if not Li Lien-ying himself, was asked about this misappropriation of the naval funds, he is reported as having commented that, 'Even if the money had been spent on the Navy, the Japanese would have beaten us all the same. As it is, at least we have the Summer Palace.' This stupidly cynical remark was well worthy of the Chief Eunuch. But his Imperial Mistress would not, of course, concede her own guilt in her country's disaster, and attempted to place the blame for it on her Viceroy.

In his *Memoirs* Li Hung Chang vigorously defended himself from the unfair charges brought against him by his Empress. After China's ignominious defeat, it was he whom she nevertheless appointed to conduct the difficult peace negotiations with the Japanese representative, Prince Ito, which led to the signing in 1895 of the Treaty of Shimonoseki. Li was also, meanwhile, negotiating with the Tsar's government, which was seeking concessions from China like the rest, and, well aware of the danger to Russian plans for Siberia of a Japanese stronghold on the mainland, was supporting Li Hung Chang, even to the extent of colossal bribery, which did not, however, blind that canny negotiator to Russian intentions.

'Russia is today,' he wrote, 'our greatest friend and our most-to-be-feared enemy. She is our friend because Great Britain and

France pose as friends also. She wishes to be a better friend than they. She is our greatest enemy because what Russians call the trend of destiny makes her so. She dominates all northern Asia, and hopes some day to have preponderating influence in China.' An analysis and a prophecy that still have a strangely topical ring.

The Russian Minister Muraviev played a very clever and unscrupulous game, backed by the Tsar, who in turn was in league with his cousin Kaiser Wilhelm II, in their rivalry with Britain, France, and Japan for the partition of Chinese territory.

On receipt of these friendly assurances from Russia, Li Hung Chang began to regain favour with Her Majesty.

'The Empress is a strange woman, contradictory and headstrong as the devil at times; but if she feels she has done a great wrong unjustly, she is ever ready to right it if her personal dignity is not too plainly at stake. Yesterday her mood was that of desiring me to say things in my own behalf. She had learned within an hour of their arrival of the good tidings from St. Petersburg. . . . Briefly we discussed the Russian letters, and Their Majesties are heartily grateful that Japan will not be permitted, either now or in the future, to seize upon any part of Manchuria or the Mainland.'

An amusingly characteristic episode in the peculiar relationship between Li Hung Chang and the Empress Dowager occurred after his attendance as Chinese Ambassador at the Coronation of the Tsar of Russia in 1896. Yehonala was then an old woman —turned sixty—but still retained her vanity. She had also by that time developed a keen interest in women of other countries. Li Hung Chang had been deeply impressed by the young Tsarina's beauty, and rather undiplomatically betrayed this when summoned in audience by his Empress :

I have received notification that I am to forfeit one year's pay for a breach of ceremony at the Palace. This is a small matter, the fine, but I would be pleased to know in what respect I offended Tzu Hsi.

But later on the same day :

> Messengers from the Throne have just arrived bringing a copy of the edict conferring upon me the Order of the Golden Dragon. The original edict was written, says the copy, by Tzu Hsi herself. I am inclined to think my breach of Court etiquette was not serious to her private mind, although her official mind fined me 37,000 taels for it.

Li Hung Chang was a brilliant statesman, but he was a man. More likely it was the Empress's private mind that had resented his too obvious admiration for the Tsarina.

15 Rebellion of an Emperor

Although Old Buddha was ostensibly, even ostentatiously, in retirement at the Summer Palace, at least once or twice weekly the Imperial Sacred Chariot could be seen proceeding there. On arrival the Emperor was made fully to realize who, in spite of appearances, was still the real ruler, admiringly nicknamed the Old Buddha and 'the only man in China'. Yet his contemptuous reception was more likely a proof of the great and increasing power of his old enemy, Li Lien-ying.

Almost the only characteristic the physically feeble and apparently pliable Kuang Hsu Emperor had in common with his obstinate cousin and predecessor, the self-assertive and impetuous Tung Chih, was a capricious temper, which from time to time, in spite of Kuang Hsu's fear of his majestic Aunt, would flare up. On one or two such occasions he had complained bitterly of the Chief Eunuch's insolence, and even demanded that he be beaten for it. Although on these occasions Li was invariably supported and exonerated by his Imperial Mistress, so long as they remained in the Forbidden City he found no means of avenging these slights. Li was capable of the greatest villainy and the most rapacious greed; but he never disdained opportunities for petty revenge—especially on the Emperor—nor, in spite of his increasing wealth, of relatively modest self-enrichment.

When the Emperor arrived at the outer gates of the Summer Palace in his Sacred Chariot, surrounded by his mounted escort, he was admitted. But at the inner gate His Majesty, like any lesser petitioner, was obliged to dismount from his palanquin, to await there humbly, on his knees, the summons to the presence of the Dowager Empress by the Chief Eunuch, who was supreme dictator there. And in this humble position Li would deliberately keep him waiting, half an hour, an hour, whilst the Emperor's attendants distributed the customary largesse to the lesser eunuchs—most of which later found its way into the Chief Eunuch's purse—before deigning to admit him to his audience with Old Buddha.

Although Li Hung Chang was obliged to bear the heaviest part of the blame for China's defeat by the Japanese, it was an open secret that the Empress and Li Lien-ying in particular were to a large extent responsible for it by their misappropriation of the naval funds. In 1895 one of the Censors, An Wei-chun, sent the Emperor a Memorial in which he pulled no punches at all:

> There are not lacking people who declare that this humiliating policy of peace has been prompted by the Empress Dowager's Chief Eunuch, Li Lien-ying. . . . What sort of a person is this Li Lien-ying who dares to interfere in Government matters? If there be any truth whatsoever in the rumour, it is assuredly incumbent upon your Majesty to inflict severe punishment on this creature, if only because of that House-law of your Dynasty which forbids eunuchs to concern themselves in State affairs.

As the Kuang Hsu Emperor knelt on the dusty paving-stones of the Summer Palace, he may well have whole-heartedly agreed with the Memorialist's forthright strictures on his enemy. But when at last he rose from his knees and was admitted to Her Majesty's presence, it was only to become the object of her blazing anger at the Censor's attack on herself and her favourite, and to receive from her the reply to the Memorial which she had dictated, and now ordered him to publish forthwith against her too-frank critic:

The Censor An Wei-chun has today submitted a Memorial based entirely upon rumours and containing the following sentence: "How can you possibly justify your position before your ancestors and to your subjects if you permit the Empress Dowager still to dictate to you, or to interfere in the business of the State?"

Language of this kind reveals depths of audacity unspeakable, the unbridled licence of a madman's tongue. Were we to fail in inflicting stern punishment in a case of this kind, the result might well be to produce estrangement between Her Majesty the Empress and ourselves. The Censor is, therefore, dismissed from office and sentenced to banishment at the post-roads on the western frontier, where he shall expiate his guilt and serve as a wholesome warning to others. His Memorial is handed back to him, with the contempt it deserves.

The Decree as usual contained an ironical twist, a hint that relations between the Empress Dowager and the Emperor were already bad enough, and a veiled threat on her part that they might deteriorate even further if the Emperor showed the least inclination to encourage any more criticism of Her Majesty—and Li Lien-ying. The severe condemnation of An Wei-chun served also to exonerate Li Hung Chang, a bitter enemy of the Censor's, who was by this Decree given the great satisfaction of the departure of the latter from Court and Government circles.

Nevertheless, a good deal of the mud thrown in the so-called gossip on which An Wei-chun had based his accusations still stuck and was by no means washed away by his punishment.

Although Yehonala had banished her faithless lover from her sight, she had had plenty of time to regret this necessity, and on the occasion of her sixtieth birthday, in 1894, she recalled Jung Lu, re-established him in full favour, and placed him in command of the Peking garrison. She had, as well, adopted Prince Kung's daughter, conferring on her the title Imperial Princess. And, of course, she kept up the closest intimacy with the Empress, her niece, whose relations with her husband, Kuang Hsu, continued to worsen, becoming more and more inimical. They were not improved by the fact that the Emperor was well aware that his First Wife was passing on every scrap of information she could glean about his private and public affairs to Old Buddha. Her Majesty had other loyal supporters in the Forbidden City.

The situation was in fact a potentially explosive one. After China's defeat by Japan there was a strong feeling in the country and especially in the south—always hostile to the Manchu dynasty and especially to the Empress Dowager—that a great deal more was needed to bring China into line with the modern world than the tentative efforts made until then by Li Hung Chang and one or two others in favour of a certain degree of industrialization. But what to do, and how to set about it?

The Manchu party, of whom the reactionary Kang Yi was a leader, saw in every Chinese effort at modernization a threat to tradition and, above all, to its own power. Certain Chinese politicians, unable to cope with the pressure of events, and, in particular, with the veiled or open aggression of the foreign devils, sided with them. There was always a streak of timidity, defeatism and masochism in the Chinese character, exemplified by the feverish search for precedents when an unexpected situation arose, a feeling that it was less dangerous to remain in the old-fashioned frying-pan which for centuries had served so well, than to jump into the uprising flames of the fire of reform. This harking-back to the past and refusal to come to grips with the future was an almost insuperable barrier to gradual and peaceful transition from the old order to the new, and to progress.

In all their efforts and intrigues to thwart the demand for reorganization, this reactionary faction looked to the Empress Dowager as their mainstay and prop. In her character there was not a trace of defeatism, but nevertheless, perhaps owing to the shock her pride and self-confidence had received by the disastrous attempt to grapple with the modernized Japan, for a short time she did appear to be in favour of some slight measures of reform.

In 1898, however, the Imperial Mother suddenly found herself powerless to prevent the hitherto outwardly docile and submissive young Son of Heaven from taking the bit between his teeth and galloping through a series of such revolutionary edicts as left the country almost breathless. There was then a continuous procession of petitioners to the Summer Palace, begging their Old Buddha to rescue them and the country from the young firebrands who were threatening the old China and the Manchu dynasty with disintegration and collapse. They implored in vain. Never before or afterwards did the Empress play a waiting game with such deep guile and patience as during that year.

The death of Prince Kung at this juncture was a national calamity. The Emperor's mother—Her Majesty's sister—had died two years previously, but even during her lifetime she had never been able to protect Kuang Hsu from the domination of his Imperial Aunt. Prince Kung was certainly an ally of the Empress and not of the Emperor and his faction, but as China's First Elder Statesman he still had a great deal of influence over Kuang Hsu, and might have counteracted or restrained the young Emperor's more impetuous advisers. During Prince Kung's last illness, both the Empress Dowager and the Emperor visited him several times—the highest mark of Imperial favour. In the Decree that Her Majesty issued on Prince Kung's death she recalled their earlier collaboration so long ago, and there was not a trace of insincerity in her mourning for him.

The fact of their subsequent differences and Prince Kung's temporary fall from her favour was tactfully and briefly dismissed.

The Kuang Hsu Emperor was still inexperienced in government when, to the consternation of the Manchu party and their Chinese sympathizers, he so suddenly asserted himself. Had the Empress remained in the Forbidden City, her mere daily physical proximity might have proved too much for him. But, in spite of his outward deference, her removal to the Summer Palace, not all that far away but far enough to allow him some respite from her bullying, seemed to have brought him to a consciousness of the supreme power that was his, if he chose to exercise it. And now he did so choose.

In 1898 the Kuang Hsu Emperor was twenty-seven years old, and without a friend of his own sex in the world. He was—and was destined to remain throughout his life—the loneliest monarch in history. As he grew older and his physical disabilities became more obvious, he was shamed and mortified by them. He had no personal magnetism, was an introvert, seemingly dull, apathetic and unattractive. From his early childhood onward he had been forced into an uncongenial world, and was repressed, tormented and bullied. When occasionally he did try to assert himself, his inner tension expressed itself in snappiness and irritability, which his courtiers feared, but which did not impress them. Malicious gossip dismissed him as a moron, and this libel was accepted as fact even by certain European writers—who of course had never set eyes on him—one of whom described him as 'so mentally un-developed as to be hardly more than half-witted'. But only those totally ignorant of elementary physiology would assume so rashly that because a man's gonads did not function properly, because his testicles had not descended during puberty, and because traditional factors beyond his control placed him in so hostile an environment, he must be entirely lacking in intellect or even ordinary intelligence.

According to one story, during the Emperor's boyhood the eunuchs, searching for playthings with which to amuse him, found in a small store kept by a Swiss in Peking, mechanical toys which immediately fascinated the child, as his great fore-runners had been attracted by the clocks brought to China by the Jesuits in the seventeenth century. And some years later he was also thrilled by the telephone, which he promptly installed in his private apartments, and a narrow-gauge railway track which was built along the banks of the Palace lakes and on which he used to invite the Court ladies to ride up and down with him in tiny carriages drawn by miniature steam engines.

There is no doubt that Kuang Hsu was well educated accord-ing to the highest traditions. And as he grew older his interest in foreign thought and invention increased—possibly as the result of his tutor's influence, who may first have brought to his notice the available Chinese translations of foreign books : notably a Chinese version of the Bible, which the young Emperor was said to have 'devoured with avidity'. If this was the case, he was certainly no moron, and if his mentor had over-estimated his pupil's intelligence, which although limited was both ardent and alert, the Reform movement of the year 1898 would never have occurred.

After China's defeat by Japan, Weng Tung-ho, the Emperor's former tutor, was as keenly aware as any of the enlightened scholar-statesmen of the period that if the Empire were to be rehabilitated a new policy must be worked out and instituted without further loss of time. He was one of the leaders of a group of advanced Peking intellectuals, but the only one who by virtue of his post possessed the life-long privilege of having free and constant access to His Imperial Majesty, now at last ruler and governor of his Empire. And this included the right to speak to the Emperor freely and openly, unhampered by all the restrictions and formalities which, like a barrier of prickly pear, hedged about the relations of practically all other officers and ministers of State with their master.

Since Weng had performed the ambiguous service to the Empress Dowager of bringing to her notice the infidelity of her servant Jung Lu, and in reward been promoted by Her Majesty to the Grand Council, it was inevitable that on returning to Court Jung Lu should have no particular liking for him. His success had made him other powerful enemies in the Empress Dowager's entourage and he was already lapsing from her favour. He was therefore steering a clever but tricky course between daring and disaster.

The events that followed the death of Prince Kung at the end of May occurred with breathtaking rapidity, and this time-factor was of considerable importance to their issue. Roughly a week later, Weng, realizing the delicacy of his position, applied for and was granted a week's sick leave. And his motivation was unmistakable : for three days after he left the Court the Emperor issued the first of his spate of Reform Decrees, which in its careful phrasing but uncompromising point of view indicated quite clearly that the Secretary to the Grand Council had either composed it himself with the Emperor's approval, or suggested the lines on which it was drafted.

This Decree was especially concerned with educational matters, as well as the reform of the Army. The latter reference was an astute one, since no one was more aware of the unsatisfactory state of military organization than the efficient soldier Jung Lu. In spite of his personal grievance against Weng Tung-ho, this reference met with his approval.

The kernel of this Decree, the revolutionary new proposals, then followed :

> The bases of education will continue to rest on the canons of the Sages, but at the same time there must be careful investigation of every branch of European learning . . . so that there may be an end to empty fallacies. . . . Parrot-like plagiarisms of shallow theories are to be avoided and catchwords eschewed. . . . The Peking University is to be made a model for the Empire, and all officials of the rank of Board Secretaries, officers of the bodyguard, future magistrates, sons of high officials and Manchus of hereditary rank, are to be entitled to enter upon a college course in order that their talents may be trained to meet the needs of these critical times. No procrastination or favouritism will be tolerated, nor any disregard of these, the Throne's admonitions.

Those reactionaries reading between the lines of this disturbing Decree realized what its revolutionary tendencies might mean to themselves : the immediate rather than future abolition of the venerated traditional educational and administrative systems and the substitution for them of European methods and techniques.

No, in the Middle Kingdom, the Celestial Empire, things had never happened nor would ever happen with such indecent haste. In China less than anywhere else in the world was it possible to make a clean sweep with old brooms—even if they were provided with smart new modern handles.

According to previous custom the Emperor dutifully proceeded to the Summer Palace to present his proposed Decree to the

Empress Dowager for her approval. Acutely aware as always of the political trend, Her Majesty realized that some expression of a desire for reform must be promulgated from the Throne. Jung Lu was also in favour of military reform, and was now appointed Viceroy of Chihli with orders to proceed to Tientsin and begin the much-needed reorganization of the northern army.

The Empress gave her assent to the publication of Kuang Hsu's first Decree, but, of course, on her own terms. In regard to all dynastic affairs, her relatives, and the Manchu clans, procrastination and favouritism were still to be tolerated, and none of the hereditary and customary privileges were to be infringed or disturbed. And with good reason Weng Tung-ho had feared Old Buddha's retribution, for the second condition for her assent was the Grand Secretary's dismissal from the Council. When, at 4 a.m. on the morning of his return from his diplomatic 'sick-leave', Weng arrived at the Summer Palace for the Council audience, an official handed him a Vermilion Rescript—a personal directive only to be issued by the Emperor, but this time of course dictated by the Empress—informing him of his instant dismissal—luckily for him, as it turned out :

A Vermilion Rescript. We have recently had occasion more than once to observe that the Grand Secretary Weng Tung-ho has failed in the proper performance of his duties, and that he is the object of very general criticism. He has frequently been impeached, and when questioned by Ourselves at audience, he has allowed his manner to betray his feelings, even daring to express approval or displeasure in Our presence. His conduct has gradually revealed a wild ambition and a tendency to usurp Our authority : it is no longer possible to retain him on the Grand Council.

No doubt the reactionaries and the Manchus thought themselves well rid of this dangerous radical, whose influence with the Emperor had so nearly undermined their security. Little did they realize, however, that before retiring to his native province of Kiangsu—to live there happily ever after until 1904—he had left a real firebrand behind : Kang Yu-wei.

16   Plot and Punishment

Kang Yu-wei was a Cantonese scholar and calligrapher who became famous amongst his colleagues on two accounts. He was a fervent and learned Confucianist, yet also one of the most radical thinkers of his time. His fame had spread as far north as Peking. Kang was no revolutionary, but a firm upholder of the Imperial system and the Ching dynasty. At the same time he was one of the chief opponents of the Empress Dowager, and like most southerners believed all the scandalous stories in circulation regarding her private life.

Had it not been for Weng Tung-ho, the Emperor might never have heard of Kang Yu-wei, nor, certainly, met him. For it was Weng who first introduced the name of this brilliant Cantonese scholar in conversation with his Imperial master, explaining Kang's views to him and arousing the lonely young Emperor's interest in this remarkable subject.

Before they could meet, however, certain traditional obstacles had to be overcome. According to immemorial custom, the Son of Heaven might not receive in audience any subject who was not an accredited official. So in order to conform with protocol the Emperor conferred on the Cantonese scholar a very minor post, which enabled him to be admitted in attendance.

Kang was handsome, enthusiastic and devoted to the Throne. From their very first meeting the Son of Heaven came under his spell, and very soon Kang was accorded the rare privilege of submitting his plans for reform as Memorials, directly to the Emperor. Their mutual attachment rapidly became as close as the enormous distance in rank between them permitted. To the lonely young occupant of the Dragon Throne, deprived of the wise counsels of his late uncle, Prince Kung, and more recently of his Grand Secretary's guidance, Kang appeared almost as a father-surrogate, a devoted, selfless servant with a modern outlook, competent to produce all the brilliant plans so urgently required to reform the country.

And there is no doubt about the impression made on Kang Yu-wei by his master, whom he found far from lacking in intelligence, patriotism or earnestness and only too willing and anxious to place himself at the head of the Reform movement.

Kang inevitably and quickly aroused bitter enmity at Court, and the opposition at once set out to prove that, far from being a respectful and wholehearted patriot, he was no better than an ambitious upstart, whose sole aim in acquiring this presumptuous influence over the Emperor was to make the Son of Heaven the pliable tool of his own advancement.

Whatever Kang's motives may have been, he made two fundamental mistakes in furthering his schemes. He made no secret of his views on the Empress Dowager and her interference in affairs of State. Whilst until then Kuang Hsu had not felt the full blast of Old Buddha's fury, he had already suffered enough from her to permit Kang to air views on her Sacred Person which in themselves constituted the crime of *lèse-majesté*. The Emperor's even greater mistake was to underrate the power of his enemy, hidden away in her palace in the Yi-Ho-Yuan, and to endeavour to rush through a series of decrees which, had they been carried out, would have reduced the administrative system, hallowed and ossified in the course of centuries, to chaos.

Relations between the Emperor and Old Buddha had not yet outwardly deteriorated. Kuang Hsu announced his intention of accompanying the Empress Dowager on a State visit to Jung Lu, after his nomination as Viceroy of Chihli. They were to review the crack regiments there, the troops trained by foreign military experts. The suggestion for this visit came, apparently, from Jung Lu. The Empress Dowager gave it her delighted approval. All the years of her life—with the exception of the flight to Jehol—Yehonala had been unable to leave the Great Within except for the short trip to the Summer Palace. Yet to travel was her secret passion, one that in her punctilious observance of etiquette she was obliged to deny herself. But she was not able to gratify it this time either. Before the lengthy and elaborate preparations for such an official jaunt could be completed there occurred the dramatic climax to the Reform movement and Kuang Hsu's Hundred Days of government.

A palace plot was hatched against Old Buddha, with a view to depriving her of the power to delay or quash the reforms. Was Kang, as his enemies and those historians who sided with the Empress Dowager declared, the initiator of it? Or was this almost insanely rash act decided upon by the Emperor on his own responsibility?

Kang is not mentioned at all in Johnston's version of this sinister and desperate scheme. According to him it was the Emperor who, although knowing the seriousness of the risks he was taking, nevertheless took them 'with his eyes open'. If this was indeed the case then it must have been the most perfect example of the proverb that there are none so blind as those who will not see. The Emperor's motive for the plan he proposed to carry out was that although until then the Empress Dowager had not vetoed the Reform Edicts he had already issued, she might at any moment do so and cancel them. His method of forestalling or preventing this action on her part was to seek 'someone whose power and influence in official circles were such as to make him feared and respected, who had command of an efficient body of troops, who was a strong and resourceful man of action, who held enlightened views on the subject of reform, and who was incapable of betraying a great trust'.

The individual on whom Kuang Hsu's choice unfortunately fell for this highly delicate operation was Yuan Shi-kai, a

protégé of Li Hung Chang. It was Yuan who, when Imperial
Resident in Korea, had mistakenly advised the dispatch of
Chinese troops to that country, which precipitated the Sino-
Japanese war of 1894; yet in spite of his political error he had
not lost favour in Imperial circles. And undoubtedly he was a
quite unusually able player of the games of intrigue and wily
manoeuvring prevalent there.

Jung Lu was Viceroy of Chihli; Yuan, at the age of nearly
forty, was holding the post of Judicial Commissioner in that
important province. The Emperor sent for Yuan Shi-kai, to
entrust him with—as Johnston put it more than mildly—'the
delicate duty of preventing the Empress Dowager from re-entering
public life on the side of the opponents of reform'.

There is, however, another authoritative and more sinister
version of the plot against Old Buddha, according to which it
was the work of Kang Yu-wei, the Censor Yang Shen-hsiu, and
three secretaries of the Grand Council called Tan Ssu-tung, Lin
hsu and Liu Kuang-ti.

Her Majesty had apparently already severely rebuked the
Emperor for 'even noticing Kang Yu-wei's suggestion'—which
had been reported to her—that his master should act more on his
own authority. 'Jung Lu, he knew, would always loyally support
his Imperial mistress; and there was not one prominent Manchu
in the Empire and, as far as Peking was concerned, hardly a
Chinese who would dare to oppose the Old Buddha. . . . But'—
and this was the crux of the matter—'if he [the Emperor] could
obtain control of Jung Lu's northern foreign-drilled army, the
reactionary party might yet be overthrown.' The conspirators
therefore suggested to the Emperor that he should have Jung Lu
put to death at Tientsin, before the Empress could be warned of
the plot, and bring a force of these troops to Peking, with a view
to surrounding and imprisoning the Empress Dowager in the
Summer Palace.

And 'at the same time the most prominent reactionaries in
Peking . . . were to be seized at their residences and hurried off
to the prison of the Board of Punishments'.

In attempting to weigh these widely differing accounts against one another it would appear that even if Kang Yu-wei and his friends were not responsible for the plot, he must, in view of his close relations with the Emperor during this crucial period, at least have been aware of Kuang Hsu's dangerous plan. Nor can it be doubted that, had it succeeded, this would in every way have been to Kang's advantage.

The choice of Yuan Shi-kai as the Emperor's instrument was dictated partly by his key position in Chihli, but also by the fact that Yuan, either on his own initiative or at the suggestion of someone in higher authority, had ostentatiously expressed his approval of the reforms. The Emperor called him into private audience and with reasonable caution on this first occasion did not reveal the full extent of his plans, but sounded out Yuan's loyalty with a view to placing him, as a preliminary move, in command of the troops that in due course would be required to surround the Summer Palace.

As the result of this satisfactory interview, Kuang Hsu issued a Decree promoting his trusted servant to the rank of Expectant Vice-President of a Board and placing him in special charge of Army reform.

The audience apparently took place at the Summer Palace, where Kuang Hsu was then in residence and where Yuan Shi-kai had been received by the Emperor in the Hall of Benevolent Old Age. As soon as it ended, the Empress Dowager summoned Yuan Shi-kai to her own apartments and closely questioned him as to what the Emperor had said. As Kuang Hsu had been careful not to show his hand too plainly at that stage, 'By all means let the army be reformed,' said the Old Buddha, 'the Decree is sensible enough; but His Majesty is in too great a hurry, and I suspect him of cherishing some deep design. You will await a further audience with him, and then receive my instructions.'

If the Empress Dowager did send so quickly for Yuan Shi-kai, and gave him such definite instructions, she was clearly aware that the Emperor and his faction were plotting against her. According to other accounts generally accepted, however, at that moment she was in blissful innocence of the plot, amusing herself as usual with amateur theatricals and water-picnics.

Kuang Hsu returned to the Forbidden City, where he soon summoned Yuan Shi-kai to further audiences. The Emperor's precautions at that point were apparently effective, for no information of his intentions appears to have leaked out, either through the spying eunuchs or the ministers devoted to the Empress. Nor, apparently, did Yuan Shi-kai at that stage return to Old Buddha and the Summer Palace with the sensational story he might then have told her.

In the usual posture of humble deference before his Imperial Master, Yuan Shi-kai bowed his head, and this presumably concealed his expression as the Son of Heaven revealed his fantastic plan to him. But his outward impassivity may not have corresponded to the mental turmoil with which he listened to his orders. For the Emperor was commanding Yuan Shi-kai to proceed immediately to Tientsin, where he was to remove Jung Lu from his command—forcibly, by assassination if necessary—take it over and return forthwith to Peking at the head of the troops which were to surround the Summer Palace.

Many years later Der Ling claimed that Kuang Hsu himself gave her his version of the instructions he had issued to Yuan Shi-kai. Three times he stressed that he wished no harm to come to Old Buddha; he only wanted to prevent her leaving the Summer Palace before he could make his Decrees operative—for if she did so she would wreck all his plans. And according to the Emperor, Yuan Shi-kai agreed with every detail of the plan advanced by Kuang Hsu and Kang Yu-wei, even adding some detailed suggestions of his own.

Finally the Emperor handed Yuan a small golden arrow as symbol of his personal authority to carry out his mission on arrival at Tientsin. On his secret journey there Yuan had time to think over the position very carefully indeed. A traitor he may have been, but he was certainly no fool. A man of his station and experience, who had risen to offices of importance and responsibility before his fortieth birthday, could not have helped being amazed, not only at the Emperor's daring, but at the sheer folly of this hastily conceived plot. He had only to compare the

strength of the Empress Dowager's character with the sudden
self-assertion of her hitherto weak and pliant nephew—obviously
under the direct influence of Kang Yu-wei—to realize that this
phase in Kuang Hsu's reign must be no more than a flash in the
pan. He could not have felt much confidence in the plot's ultimate success, even if he himself were in charge of the troops
needed to carry out this *coup d'état*. And should it fail, the consequences to himself were obvious even to the most unimaginative
of men.

Moreover, unknown to the Emperor, Yuan Shi-kai was, and
for a long period had been, on such close and intimate terms with
Her Majesty's reinstated favourite, Jung Lu, that they had some
time previously sworn an oath of blood brotherhood. So that if,
on his journey to Tientsin, Yuan, weighing up his tricky problem
in some such terms as those, concluded correctly that he was
faced either with betraying the Emperor, whose chances of success were at least precarious, or Old Buddha, ostensibly resting
from her Imperial labours in retirement, but still as potentially
dangerous as a coiled cobra, and in addition with breaking his
vow to Jung Lu and becoming his assassin, the conclusion he
came to was reasonable, practical, and not necessarily dis-
honourable.

On arrival, Yuan went straight to Jung Lu, but, instead of
placing him under Imperial arrest or worse, revealed to him immediately the Emperor's scheme in full detail.

Once again, as so many years ago at Jehol, Jung Lu rushed to
the side of his beloved mistress. Yuan Shi-kai had given him the
Emperor's secret Decree, appointing Yuan as successor to the
'late' Viceroy of Chihli. Provided with this documentary evidence, Jung Lu immediately left Tientsin by special train, arriving in Peking soon after 5 p.m. on the same evening.

On arrival Jung Lu wasted not a minute. He did not even
follow the prescribed custom of seeking an audience, but simply
rushed into Her Majesty's presence and, dramatically throwing
himself at her feet with the obligatory kowtows, exclaimed,
'Sanctuary, Your Majesty!'

'What sanctuary do your require,' Old Buddha replied, 'in the

Forbidden precincts, where no harm can come to you, and where you have no right to be?'—an unmistakable reminder of Jung Lu's former infidelity and his consequent banishment.

But this time Jung Lu knew that his breach of etiquette would readily be forgiven. He promptly gave Her Majesty the full story brought to him by Yuan Shi-kai. Old Buddha listened to him in silence, and, as always happened when her rage slowly gathered momentum, her features froze into mask-like immobility, only her eyes expressing her fury and resolution.

The moment to strike had come.

Among the flood of decrees issued by Kuang Hsu during his fateful Hundred Days of authority had been one sweeping peremptorily from office nearly all the members of the Government Boards and several Censors whose opposition he regarded as insurmountable. These disgruntled officials had proceeded in a body to the Summer Palace, in order to implore Old Buddha to save the country and themselves from this iconoclastic Son of Heaven. But at that moment Her Majesty was still playing a waiting game. She fully intended in due course to use the weight of her own authority to block the Reforms, but considered that to do so effectively she must move only once, but decisively, at the right moment. Now it had arrived.

Secret summonses from the Empress Dowager were sent immediately after Jung Lu's arrival to all members of the Grand Council, and to the two ministers and heads of the Boards whom Kuang Hsu had recently dismissed. Having joyfully read them, they collectively hastened to the Presence, where, knowing that there would be no refusal this time, they again formally implored Her Majesty to save their government and the realm. Meanwhile, Jung Lu's troops were brought to Peking, not to surround the Summer Palace but to replace the Emperor's guards on duty in the Forbidden City. The Empress was due to leave the Summer Palace at dawn in any case, to perform one of her routine duties: the offering of the prescribed sacrifices and prayers to the God of Silkworms. But before carrying out this ceremony, she departed from the Forbidden City to punish the rebellious Emperor.

It was customary, when the Empress Dowager left the Summer Palace for Peking, to light a flare visible there, so that her impending approach was known to the eunuchs in the Forbidden City whose duty it was to make the preparations for her reception on arrival.

On this tragic occasion, which was to mark the end of the Emperor's Hundred Days of rule, Kuang Hsu was fast asleep in bed, and not even in his wildest dreams did he suspect his betrayal by Yuan Shi-kai, of which he was now to suffer the consequences. A loyal eunuch, informed by the signal of the Empress Dowager's departure, hastened to awaken him. What then happened the Emperor himself told Der Ling five years later :

'I knew instantly that I was lost ! . . . I did not know what to do. So I dressed myself, sent word to Kang Yu-wei that he must leave the Forbidden City and Peking at once, and make no attempt to return as he valued his life—and prepared to go out to my acounting with the Old Buddha !'

This last note, scribbled in haste by the Emperor, was a pathetic one :

I have a very great sorrow in my heart, which cannot be described in brush and ink. You must at once proceed abroad and devise means to save me.

According to another version, however, Kang Yu-wei left Peking before Yuan Shi-kai betrayed the Emperor to Jung Lu and Old Buddha. Some time previously, learning that the Cantonese reformer had been making slanderous attacks on her personal conduct, the Empress Dowager had summoned her nephew to the Summer Palace, and ordered him forthwith to dismiss this presumptuous critic. Kuang Hsu was obliged to promise to do so, but took the occasion to circumvent these orders by writing to him personally, in his own hand, although guardedly in an official Decree, which his confidential eunuch, Sung Yu-lien, brought to Kang Yu-wei in Peking. This was as follows :

On a previous occasion we commanded the Secretary of the Board of Works, Kang Yu-wei, to take charge of the Government Gazette Bureau at Shanghai. We learn with astonishment that he has not yet left Peking. . . . His duties are evidently of no light responsibility and funds having been specially raised for this enterprise, we now command him to take himself with all dispatch to Shanghai; he shall on no account procrastinate any longer.

Kang lost no time in obeying these Imperial instructions, through which the red light shone clearly. He left Peking by the next train on the following morning, and on arrival in Shanghai appealed to the British consul there for protection. This was granted, and in due course he found refuge in Hong Kong. Old Buddha did not hear of his escape until too late. Although she telegraphed to Jung Lu to have Kang arrested when he passed through Tientin, the Viceroy, still ignorant of the Emperor's plot to have him assassinated, did not do so. Subsequently every effort was made by the Empress Dowager's agents to recapture Kang. A large price was put on his head, and even in Hong Kong he was in danger, despite the protection of the British Government. He soon left for Singapore and ultimately, wrote Johnston, for Europe and America, 'always with a price on his head, always in danger of his life from watchful spies and agents of the imperial government. As long as the old empress-dowager lived he was a homeless wanderer'—but he finally did return to China.

When the Empress's procession entered the gates of the Forbidden City, the Son of Heaven, following the usual precedent, went to meet it and flung himself on his knees before her.

During the Hundred Days of Reform the Emperor had acted manfully and daringly, although rashly and unwisely. But always until she had retired to the Summer Palace, in the physical and overpowering presence of Her Majesty her nephew behaved like a rabbit mesmerized by a snake. Now, for the first time in his life, knowing how real was his reason to fear her fury and power, Kuang Hsu was a guilty rabbit. His fear was so great that his whole body trembled as if he were suffering from a high malarial fever, and his powers of speech left him. They were both aware of the gravity of the dynastic crime he had committed. Even had Kuang Hsu indeed not wished a hair of Old Buddha's head to be touched, his offence was still a terrible one, meriting the severest punishment. Merely to have suggested confining the Holy Mother and ancestress against her wishes was an outrage on all Confucian tradition and a shocking infringement of dynastic law. If, as the Empress undoubtedly believed he did, Kuang Hsu had plotted her arrest and subsequent murder, this was the worst crime imaginable : matricide. And when the news of that night's tragedy leaked out there were very few prominent officials or even private citizens in the whole of China—excepting members of the Reform Party—who did not side with the Empress Dowager in the measures she took to punish her guilty nephew.

Seeing the quaking Kuang Hsu prostrate before her, Old Buddha curtly ordered him to rise, but said no more. They then went indoors, from the darkness preceding the dawn to the almost equally dark great audience hall in which the eunuchs had hastily lit the coloured lanterns and candles flickering in the draught.

This was Kuang Hsu's account of what then happened, as Der Ling claimed he had told it to her.

The suite had not yet followed Her Majesty into the great audience hall. And there, in that voice of velvet, she quietly asked her nephew :

'Do you know the law of the Imperial Household which deals with punishments for one who raises his hands against his mother?'

Indeed he did know it, and could only nod his bowed head to signify so.

The majesty of Old Buddha's wrath was then slowly and with deadly quietness unleashed against Kuang Hsu :

'I have treated you as a son,' she reminded him. 'You have taken the place with me of the son I lost, and this is how you repay me! I save your life and you seek to take mine. You are ungrateful! You are unfit to rule from the Throne of the Manchus! You have fallen into the trap set for you by the Cantonese, whose one desire is to drive out the Manchus and usurp the Throne! What you have done may be instrumental in causing the downfall of the great Ching Dynasty. . . . Do you know the punishment,' she repeated, 'for raising your hand against the person who stands as mother to you in the Imperial Household?'

Briefly and clearly, in those few short sentences, Old Buddha put the case against the Emperor to him. And added:

'You have four hundred millions of people to look to you for advice and guidance, and you have betrayed them!'

This was rightly or wrongly Her Majesty's view, but had certainly not been Kuang Hsu's design. Never was a road to hell paved with better intentions than that of this well-meaning but incompetent young monarch. He did not of course attempt to defend himself.

'Punish me according to the law! I deserve it! I am not fit to rule!'

Old Buddha then called in Yuan Shi-kai and Jung Lu. In Kuang Hsu's own words:

'I stared steadfastly at Yuan Shi-kai, and my betrayer could not face me. He kept his eyes on the floor. He realized the depth of his infamy, yet now, if he would save his life, he could not rectify the wrong he had done me. So he stood there, pale as ashes, looking everywhere but at the sovereign he had betrayed, and every expression on his face showed that he realized the horror of his betrayal. Yet there was nothing I could say. I *had* ordered him to throw soldiers around the Summer Palace to prevent Old Buddha's leaving until I could put my decrees into effect; and this act merited punishment in itself. But I had never even suggested that Yuan Shi-kai or anyone else, raise a hand against Her Majesty.'

The Empress then pronounced the first part of Kuang Hsu's sentence depriving him of his throne:

'Make a decree then, here and now . . . abdicating the Throne of the Manchus! Write that decree yourself, returning me to power. . . . '

Eunuchs brought writing utensils—brushes, ink and paper; then the Emperor, still violently trembling, seated himself at a small table and in the following Decree announced his abdication :

The nation is now passing through a crisis, and wise guidance is needed in all branches of the public service. We ourselves have laboured diligently, night and day, to perform OUR innumerable duties, but in spite of all OUR anxious energy and care WE are in constant fear lest delay should be the undoing of the country. We now respectfully recall the fact that Her Imperial Majesty the Empress Dowager has on two occasions since the beginning of the reign of H.M. Tung Chih performed the functions of Regent, and that in her administrations of the Government she displayed complete and admirable qualities of perfection which enabled her successfully to cope with every difficulty that arose. Recollecting the serious burden of the responsibility WE owe to OUR ancestors and to the nation, WE have repeatedly besought Her Majesty to condescend once more to administer the Government. Now she has graciously honoured US by granting OUR prayer, a blessing indeed for all OUR subjects. From this day forth Her Majesty will transact the business of Government in the side hall of the Palace, and on the day after tomorrow WE ourselves at the head of OUR Princes and Ministers shall perform obeisance before Her in the Hall of Diligent Government. The Yamens concerned shall respectfully make the arrangements necessary for the ceremonial. The words of the Emperor.

Among those who waited in dead silence in the cold dark audience chamber for Kuang Hsu to finish composing this tragically euphemistic document was Li Lien-ying, in attendance, as usual, on his Imperial Mistress. Old Buddha, sternly ignoring her wretched nephew, now gave her orders to Li :

'Imprison the Emperor on Ying Tai ! Give him only the barest necessities in the way of food ! See that he is never unguarded ! Assign a eunuch you can trust to be at his side perpetually.'

The Empress Dowager then turned her back on the poor wretch who crouched in front of her and, followed by her suite, left the Forbidden City.

The Emperor was placed under close arrest and taken by four eunuchs on Li Lien-ying's staff to Ying Tai, the Ocean Terrace, a little promontory jutting into the Winter Palace Lake, where in semi-darkness and total misery he was to expiate his guilt during the following two years. The setting was idyllic, surrounded by rippling waters and glossy foliage. But his dwelling, barred and bolted to prevent any attempt at escape, consisted of four small rooms, cold, draughty, and furnished hardly better than cells; his bed was a rough one, and his food the kind thrown to coolies, which even the lesser eunuchs would have disdained. His four guards treated him with contempt, modelling their conduct towards him, their deliberate insolence, on their master's. All his former personal servants were either killed or banished.

Kuang Hsu was quite powerless to save himself, and even more so to prevent the tragedy which overtook his Pearl Concubine, who now found herself the unprotected victim of Old Buddha's spite, as once A-lu-te had been. The only person the Emperor was permitted to see was his Empress, the Matriarch's niece and spy.

The Empress Dowager went to visit the deposed Emperor in his prison on the Ocean Terrace. Ostensibly this was to inform him that for the time being she intended to spare his life. Presumably, however, with her usual thoroughness she wished to satisfy herself that he had no means of escape. The publication of the Abdication Decree was followed by a brief announcement stating that, 'The Emperor being ill, the Empress Dowager has resumed the Regency.' This gave rise to considerable anxiety, since it seemed to suggest that Kuang Hsu would very soon mount the Dragon and go to join his ancestors.

There seems little doubt that Her Majesty would have preferred this final and simple solution to the situation, which could easily have been arranged. But her sudden dethronement of the Son of Heaven had displeased and alarmed other officials besides Li Hung Chang, including the powerful Viceroy of Nanking, Liu Kun-yi, who sent in memorials protesting against it. The Empress Dowager was even more intensely annoyed when the heads of certain foreign legations, notably the British, unequivocally in-

formed the Tsungli Yamen of their governments' disapproval of
the Emperor's abrupt removal from office and conveyed indirect
but unmistakable threats of more positive action should his life
become endangered.

Nor had Old Buddha forgotten the deep national dissatisfac-
tion, culminating in the suicide of Wu Ko-tu, when she had
failed to provide the Tung Chih Emperor with a spiritual heir.
She had still not fulfilled her promise to do so. Realistic as ever,
she thought it wiser not to encourage further unrest at that
moment. To repress revolutionaries and reformists with dangerous tendencies was one thing, but to alienate her most powerful
and trusted advisers was another. Jung Lu, as he always did,
advised caution. For dynastic and diplomatic reasons, therefore,
the Emperor must live. Meanwhile a tragic farce was staged to
give some justification to the statement that he was ill, and should
she later decide on his death, to account for it.

The most eminent physicians from all over the Empire were
summoned by Imperial Decree to attend His Majesty. This was
the custom when an Emperor fell ill, and such summonses were
not welcomed, for, should he die, his unsuccessful medical
advisers might perish also, or at best be disgraced and banished.
The procedure was not specially invented for the Kuang Hsu
Emperor's benefit, but was the normal course followed, even
when Her Majesty herself was obliged to call them in. One of
the doctors summoned to attend on this occasion was a very old
and distinguished practitioner from Soochow, Chen Lien-fang.
An account of his visit appeared in *The Times* on 31 March
1899.

The Emperor was brought by his eunuch guards to a hall in
one of the palaces in the Forbidden City. No doubt the appalling
shock and strain he had suffered, in addition to subsequent close
confinement and malnutrition, were enough to account for his
obvious weakness, pallor and fever.

According to routine, Dr Chen, after being ushered into the
presence on his knees, having performed the ritual three kowtows,
in that humble posture wriggled across the wide floor until he
found himself in front of the august patient. On a dais above

him, the Emperor and Empress Dowager sat facing one another across a low table.

The old physician's comment on this examination was not without sardonic humour: 'It is difficult to look at a patient's tongue when his exalted rank compels you to keep your eyes rigidly fixed on the floor.' His final prognosis was masterly: 'Asked if he considered the Emperor's condition critical, he replied oracularly that if he lived to see the Chinese New Year, his strength would thereafter gradually return with the spring and the complete restoration of his health might be expected.'

Among other medical men called in was the French doctor, M. Dethève—an astute move by Old Buddha to calm any impertinent questionings by her foreign critics—whose diagnostic methods aroused as much hilarity amongst his Chinese colleagues as did their own in Legation circles. Yet Chinese medical practice was by no means merely a mumbo-jumbo of spells and potions. It had behind it sound homoeopathic experience, and the Chinese pharmacopoeia contained certain remedies, such as the use of some forms of ephedrine, centuries before their adoption by European pharmacology. The Chinese also invented acupuncture.

But although Kuang Hsu's life was spared, his martyrdom had only begun. For Old Buddha kept him permanently under her own or Li Lien-ying's vigilance, partly in order to prevent any possibility of his rescue or escape, and partly in order to exhibit him on State occasions, gorgeously arrayed as in the past, when he performed his ritual State duties. When the Court moved to the Summer Palace, the Emperor was still a prisoner, in a small place poetically called Yu-Lan Tang—the Hall of the Waters of Rippling Jade—of which he barely caught a glimpse. His bedroom, 'small and ill-ventilated', lay next to a dim reception-room or throne-hall, with two small wings on either side. But according to Johnston, who visited the place later, 'throughout the whole length of the inside of . . . the two side buildings there was a solid unbroken brick wall . . . ' and these two interior walls 'shut him off from every view on both east and west, whilst his own living-quarters and the locked gate in front of his courtyard shut him off equally effectively from north and south'.

In one or the other of these prisons Kuang Hsu spent his time keeping a diary and otherwise eating his heart out in bitterness —yet never, apparently, resenting his harsh treatment by Old Buddha. He was completely sincere in his repentance for his offences against her and the dynastic code. His hatred was solely directed to Yuan Shi-kai, who became an obsession with Kuang Hsu, so much so that on his death-bed ten years later he bade his brothers to 'remember his long agony and promise to be revenged upon the author of his undoing'.

17 Sinister Reaction

'She is once again in name, as she has ever been in fact, the Ruler,' Li Hung Chang wrote in his diary.

Having so spectacularly returned to full power, the Empress lost no time in exercising the undisputed autocratic authority she was to wield until her death.

Once more she owed her freedom and possibly her life to Jung Lu. Almost immediately she appointed him to the Grand Council, as well as Controller of the Board of War and Supreme Commander of the northern army. After she had taken the necessary steps to ensure that the Emperor would never again have an opportunity to raise an opposition against her, she proceeded to deal equally thoroughly with all those who had supported his plans and plots and to destroy the Reform party and their movement root and branch.

Kang Yu-wei, to her lasting fury and mortification, escaped her vengeance. The second of the Reform leaders, who was also a distinguished scholar, Liang Chi-chao, was equally fortunate and found refuge in Japan. But six of the ringleaders of the movement were arrested, and an Imperial commission was immediately set up to investigate their guilt and to pronounce the inevitable death sentences.

In proceeding against these reformers the Empress Dowager was closely advised by Jung Lu, and he had no reluctance in now turning the tables on the conspirators. He personally conducted the examination by the Board of Punishments of the six prisoners. During these proceedings they showed to the very end qualities of dignity and courage in marked contrast to the grovelling pusillanimity of the Emperor. Their executions were a foregone conclusion.

In the search that took place of the house of one of them, Yang Jui, papers were allegedly discovered proving conclusively how deeply implicated in the plot against Old Buddha the Emperor himself had been. Certain letters from him were said to have been found there expressing bitter criticisms of the Holy Mother. A Memorial by Yang was also found accusing Her Majesty of gross immorality and illicit relations with several persons in high positions, one of whom was Jung Lu : this document was annotated in red ink by the Emperor's own hand. It quoted songs and ballads current in Canton, scurrilous comments on Her Majesty's alleged vicious practices. Small wonder then, said the Empress Dowager's advocates of drastic reprisals, that having seen for herself, in the Emperor's handwriting, that these treasonable utterances met with his favour and support, Old Buddha was determined to put an end once and for all to such sinful rebelliousness.

In order that the ferment aroused in Peking and throughout the Empire by the sudden reversal of power should be dampened down as quickly as possible, haste was made to execute the ringleaders. In addition to Kang Yu-wei's brother, the group included four secretaries of the Tsungli Yamen, and one of the Censors. An enormous crowd gathered to witness their decapitation. Before the executioners dispatched them these martyrs for reform still cursed the Empress Dowager. They died bravely, predicting that for each one of themselves to give his life in their cause a thousand others would carry on the struggle.

The Emperor was once again publicly humiliated and forced to sign the Edict drawn up by the Empress and Jung Lu, containing a confession of his own guilt. This Edict further urged the proper authorities to arrest and put Kang Yu-wei to death, and announced the sentences on his collaborators.

Jung Lu strongly advised Her Majesty to confine the sentences and punishments to the ringleaders of the Reform movement. And in appearance she did take this advice, for the Emperor's Edict contained a statement that Kang's followers had for the most part been led away by his immoral doctrines. It admitted that there were very many of them—'their number is legion and the Throne has taken note of their names'—but it had been decided by the all-abounding Imperial clemency to drop further prosecutions.

The Empress Dowager would not, however, have been true to herself had she not pursued with retribution all the Emperor's supporters whom she could reach, both in Peking and the provinces. All officials who had in one way or another actively shown sympathy with Kuang Hsu's reforms were dealt with in due course. Amongst them were Manchus as well as Chinese. A sharp rap was administered even to the Imperial Clansmen. Prince Tsai Chu, who had rashly supported the Emperor during the Hundred Days, was sentenced to perpetual confinement in the Empty Chamber, the punishment quarters of the Clan Court. His disgrace was another interesting instance of Old Buddha's cunning in marrying off her nieces to men of the Imperial clan and using them as her spies, for Tsai Chu's disloyalty was reported to her by his wife.

That the Empress was vindictive is unquestionable. But that her severe treatment of the Emperor and her ruthlessness was merely due to personal spite is not altogether correct. His chief crime was endangering the power of the great Ching dynasty.

Whether or not the documents found in Yang Jui's house were forgeries, whether or not the Emperor had seen and endorsed them, it was indisputable that such libels on the Empress Dowager were current in Kwangtung and other southern provinces. Canton remained the centre of the anti-Manchu opposition, of which Her Majesty was keenly aware, and on which she was continually kept informed. Whether or not she was actually guilty of the vices imputed to her by the Cantonese is a matter on which there was not, nor ever will be, direct or conclusive evidence. Undoubtedly her sense of responsibility to her dynasty was the basis of all her public proceedings and policies.

Her Majesty's official title was not, in fact, Empress Dowager of China, but Empress Dowager of the Ta Ching, or Manchu realm. Moreover, when the previous dynastic line, the Ming, fell from power, the spiritual cause of this was held by all literate Chinese to be that it had lost the mandate of heaven on account of bad government. This mandate was then conferred on the northern conquerors. The Empress had good historical precedents for claiming that in allying himself with the Cantonese-inspired Reform party the Emperor had betrayed this mandate. And her view that he had committed this unpardonable error was widely endorsed by millions of the Emperor's Chinese subjects, including most of the leading scholars and statesmen like Li Hung Chang, Viceroys and Governors.

Li realized very clearly that disastrous consequences to the internal and external affairs of his country would ensue as the result of the Emperor's intellectual subservience to Kang Yu-wei and his colleagues. He knew that their rash endeavours to modernize China almost overnight must fail, and would enormously enhance the power at Court of the reactionaries, of whom he also strongly disapproved. As early as June 1898, he was 'determined to see Tzu Hsi herself and present the situation to her in the plainest manner', gloomily foreseeing the calamities ahead. 'For more than two hours after midnight,' he wrote on 11 July, 'I was at the Empress Dowager's own palace, and for more than one-half of that time I was in secret audience with that woman, who had often said that twenty minutes was sufficient time for her in which to give orders and answers to the Council, the Cabinet, and the Foreign Office combined.'

But he was too late. The reactionaries had already won over the Empress: 'and their influence over Tzu Hsi is indeed deplorable. . . . If she would but listen to the wise counsels of Prince Ching and Jung Lu her manner . . . would soften. . . . I believe with the flight of time her ambition grows, and she hopes to live on for ever.'

Yet his sympathy and loyalty remained with the Empress.

On returning to power, Old Buddha proceeded to publish a large number of Decrees, which revealed with what zest and vitality she was tackling the most diverse and complex problems of administration. Nor did she forget the sufferings of the unfortunate peasants and farmers : especially those resulting from the terrible destruction and devastation in Shantung Province caused by the overflowing of the Yellow River, that great and turbulent river that was known as China's Sorrow.

This disaster, incidentally, offered Her Majesty a splendid opportunity to find employment away from Court for her too outspoken servant, Li Hung Chang, whom she appointed as Special Commissioner to visit the devastated regions and to advise her on the action required.

The reorganization of the Army was always one of the Empress Dowager's chief preoccupations. In another Decree, however, she stressed that she had never resorted to conscription or the levying of *corvées*. Jung Lu was given a free hand to press on with Army reorganization. But after the Emperor's disgrace he begged the Empress Dowager to give up her plan to visit the troops at Tientsin, as he feared that her life might be endangered if she persisted in it. Very reluctantly she cancelled it.

In another Decree Her Majesty pointed out that,

> We have always excluded Chinese women from service as subordinates in the Palace.

But all the eunuchs in Imperial service were Chinese—since it was unthinkable that a Manchu should become a *castrato*. The Palace administration—the Imperial Household Department—was, however, exclusively staffed by Manchus, whose loyalty, according to Johnston, was entirely reserved for 'their own rice-bowls'. The greater the waste, extravagance and pomp at Court, the fatter were their pickings and perquisites, to which, like the eunuchs, they clung tenaciously.

The Edict dealing with education was definitely reactionary. Because Kang Yu-wei and his fellow Reformers were outstanding Confucian scholars, they understood better than most Chinese and nearly all Manchus how urgently the Chinese educational system needed to be brought up to date at the turn of the nineteenth century. The Confucian system had become fossilized and had degenerated into theoretical hair-splitting.

Tests every bit as pedantic were to be found in plenty of Western university examinations. But there they were offset by the amazing upsurge of scientific method and discovery during the nineteenth century, and their application to technical and practical problems. As the Reformers clearly understood, China was by that late period desperately handicapped by clinging to her exclusively literary educational system. Yet when the Emperor had boldly attempted to tackle it, making it compulsory to include in the curriculum some more practical and contemporary subjects, those scholars still clinging like limpets to their old intellectual habitats were outraged. All the greater was their joy when, to the lasting detriment of China's intellectual and material progress, the Empress Dowager reversed the situation. The Decree in which she did so may not have been written by herself, yet it clearly mirrored her point of view, her real fear and detestation of all experiment in education. Oddly enough she was completely right in the assumption that this could only, in the end, lead to revolution.

The Decree dealing with the maladministration of justice—a constant and legitimate cause for complaint—the problems of crime and the reforming of criminals contains a genuinely motherly passage. Sighed Tsu Hsi,

If only they could be turned from their evil ways to service in our Army or to agriculture, they might become good citizens; how preferable such a result to seeing them cast into prison and finally dismembered. . . . Here in the remote seclusion of our Palace we think only of our people's welfare, and we long for the time when virtue may prevail and punishment become a thing of the past. We therefore now implore you, our children, to remember how real is our sympathy in all your troubles. . . .

Millions of humble Chinese folk who had never set eyes on her nevertheless did believe that she was their Holy Mother and had their welfare at heart. But whether or not they hoped that these well-meant Decrees would stop the Yellow River from overflowing, purge the administration of corrupt magistrates, fill empty stomachs and clothe ragged bodies, in practice of course they did nothing of the kind : any more than the Emperor's over-hasty attempts at reform.

When Li Hung Chang expressed his great anxiety regarding the reactionaries who had won the Empress Dowager's favour, he cited three names. These were the general Tung Fuh-siang, the administrator and member of the Imperial Council Kang Yi, and the Imperial Prince Tuan. Even Jung Lu was unable to counter their sinister influence. There were others as well, including Hsu Ying-Kuei, who had been dismissed by the Emperor but whom the Empress Dowager immediately reinstated.

Her Majesty admired strength of character, and always had a weakness for able military commanders, whether, like Jung Lu, they were of her own clan, or great scholar-generals like Tseng Kuo-fan, the suppressor of the Taiping rebellion, or, like Tung Fuh-siang, whom she now summoned to Peking, merely coarse strong-arm warlords. He was one of those colourful military adventurers who recurrently appeared on the scene at times of crisis in Chinese dynastic troubles. He was a former rebel, a Moslem, of whom there were large numbers in the remoter western provinces, who in the past had organized insurrections on a vast scale and given considerable trouble to the central government. Tung had taken service under the Manchus, risen to the rank of general, and commanded a private army of his own, a body of irregular but good soldiers he had recruited in Kansu.

Kang Yi had long been one of the Empress Dowager's favourites, largely because he was an exceptionally skilful manipulator of finance and produced the revenue of which the Imperial purse was in constant need. He was jokingly referred to by the British as the 'Lord High Extortioner', this mock-title being a topical adaptation of the famous 'Lord High Executioner' in Gilbert and Sullivan's *Mikado,* set in Japan, and first produced at the Savoy Theatre in London on 14 March 1885.

But perhaps the Empress Dowager's most sinister favourite was Prince Tuan, a grandson of the Tao Kuang Emperor, a nephew of Hsien Feng and Prince Kung, and a first cousin of the Tung Chih Emperor and the unfortunate Kuang Hsu, between whom and himself there was bitter hatred and rivalry.

Overriding all the opposition of the Imperial Princes, and violating the dynastic code, the Empress Dowager had daringly placed her nephew on the Throne. She endeavoured to pacify the outcry that followed this impudent stroke with the promise that one day she would provide a suitable heir from the Blood Royal to perform the Rites for the pacification of Tung Chih's soul and the ancestral shades. But it was only after Kuang Hsu's betrayal that she decided to do so. She had intended his death. But when that proved politically impracticable, she knew that at any rate he would never become a parent, or even be in a position to nominate his successor. The moment appeared to have arrived for her to do so.

In 1898, when she resumed power, the Empress's intuition and cunning, which until then had been so amazingly sure, deserted her. This may have been due partly to advancing age and partly to the genuine shock or trauma, from which she never fully recovered, caused by the Emperor's betrayal and her very narrow escape from imprisonment or even murder. The death of Prince Kung deprived her of the one really able statesman of Imperial blood. When she had received Li Hung Chang, at his own request, she at first seemed anxious for his advice, and even asked him frankly where he would be found in the event of a great trouble. At this interview she seemed so graciously inclined, that Li asked Her Majesty very daringly—since protocol strictly forbade any subject to question her—whether there was some premonition in her mind, and would she not take him into her confidence regarding her plans? Her attitude then instantly changed.

'She had been so cordial and amiable in comparison with her

ordinary wont that I did not believe that my further query would offend her : in an instant she was alive with wrath and angry words, and I immediately withdrew. I have seen women something like her before,' he commented with dry humour, 'but they were in my house, and it was not necessary for me to get on my knees to them.'

The reason for Her Majesty's sudden temperamental outburst might have been Li's infringement of etiquette, for which she was always a stickler. But more likely it was due to her fear that she had given herself away to him, shown him a glimpse of the anxious and worried female behind the figurehead of Imperial impassivity that was her usual pose when receiving her ministers in audience. *She* sat in silence, like an idol, on her Throne, whilst *they* submissively reported to her; *she* alone asked the questions and gave the orders, which *they* had to carry out.

And the factor in the male character which Her Majesty, like most successful and powerful women, tended to underestimate, was masculine guile. The Chief Eunuch was an adept at flattery and adulation; but he was not the only one at the Manchu Court. Even the coarse Prince Tuan had learned to practise the less subtle techniques of ingratiation.

It was this Prince's son whom in 1899 Her Majesty unfortunately appointed as heir apparent to the Emperor, and ritual heir to the late Tung Chih. He was of the right generation to carry out the obligatory Rites, but otherwise turned out worse than useless, a born trouble-maker and layabout. As soon as he was introduced into the Forbidden City, where no males were allowed to reside excepting the Emperor, who was impotent, the heir apparent speedily proved in the most shocking manner that all youths and men of the Imperial clan were by no means undersexed. His carnal appetite was as refined as that of a young bull in a field of heifers and no serving-maid was safe from his lust. The Empress suffered severe loss of face by her choice of this rampant young lecher as successor to the Throne.

She took stern measures to discipline him, but punishments and beatings had little effect. His tutors were powerless to inculcate him either with knowledge, culture or decorum. Her Majesty concealed her discomfiture as best she might until an opportunity should arise to demote this coarse youth whom she had so unwisely chosen as the future Son of Heaven.

His father's position, however, was immensely strengthened by the lad's promotion. Prince Tuan artfully took advantage of it to play on the Empress's greatest phobia of all : her hatred of the foreign devils.

18   'All One Family'

The Empress's bitterest complaint against the missionaries was due to a belief held in ignorance, but with whole-hearted fanaticism, by herself and the majority of her people, that they experimented upon Chinese children with foreign medicines. It was even firmly believed that the missionary doctors took out the eyes of such little children from which to make medicines.

It was this belief that had caused the dreadful Tientsin massacre of the Catholic nuns in 1870, and in 1899 it was one of the most powerful underlying motives of the Boxer Rising, which was already gathering momentum in the provinces. No use trying to explain to the Chinese that the nuns, seeing all round them children with the horrible endemic eye disease, trachoma, leading inevitably to blindness, took in these unfortunate little victims to help and care for them. The underlying Christian theory of compassion for the unfortunate was beyond the imagining of any rational Confucianist. No good Confucian would so uselessly waste time and trouble on those penalized by fortune to succour them and keep them alive in spite of their handicaps. This simply did not make sense to the Chinese mind. Since no rational good motive for such behaviour might be adduced, the Chinese—

peasants, merchants, magistrates, princes and Her Majesty also—had perforce to satisfy their own sense of logic by substituting an evil one for it.

Generalities apart, Her Majesty was also personally embittered by the attitude taken by the diplomatic corps, and especially by the British Minister, to her treatment of Kuang Hsu. She was furious when Sir Claude Macdonald informed the Tsungli Yamen that in the event of any serious worsening of the Emperor's health, Queen Victoria's government would not like it at all. Almost certainly Kuang Hsu owed the rest of his unhappy life to that humanitarian intervention, but this made it even more distasteful to the tyrant in whose power that life lay.

The Empress's reaction to this situation, however, was one almost of genius, and specifically feminine genius at that. The best way to convince the foreign envoys that the Emperor was still alive and as well as could be expected, was to put the unhappy man on display. Since this could not be done unless Her Majesty herself were present and in command of the event, she decided to invite the wives of the diplomats to a party. Early in December, when the Empress Dowager was informed that the Legation ladies would like to pay her their compliments on the attainment of her sixty-fourth birthday, she graciously agreed to receive them on the 15th of that month.

The seven ministerial wives were borne in a procession of sedan-chairs to the Forbidden City, at the gates of which they were met by some of the Imperial Princes and officials from the Tsungli Yamen. They there changed from their own chairs into Imperial sedans carried by the Court eunuchs in splendid uniforms as far as the Marble Bridge, where they entrained in the miniature railway coaches in which in happier days Kuang Hsu had amused himself by riding with the Court ladies. The visitors then disembarked at the Audience Hall, where they were formally received by Prince Ching, surrounded by a bevy of princesses and ladies-in-waiting in dazzling Manchu costumes, wearing their high black silk head-dresses studded with jewelled gold pins, a shimmering and flashing kaleidoscope of gorgeous colour.

The foreign ladies were also wearing their Sunday best in the very latest European fashion: picture hats with flowing ostrich feathers, ribbons and flowers; ankle-length dresses of lace and velvet and satin, with leg-of-mutton sleeves; their waists tightly laced in and their busts protruding under the pressure of the whaleboned corsets beneath their several petticoats. There was much feigned admiration and unspoken criticism of their clothes on the part of the Manchu ladies, who smiled and giggled so delightfully that the foreigners never for one moment imagined how ludicrous they and their prominent bosoms looked to those dark and sparkling eyes.

Costume was one of Her Majesty's greatest interests. When receiving such foreign visitors she gave her ladies-in-waiting minute instructions as to the dresses and ornaments they were to wear in order to create the loveliest colour schemes, and not a detail of their appearance escaped her eagle-eyed inspection beforehand. Nor could Lady Macdonald and her companions guess with what keen interest their features, complexions (which she thought hideously coarse), dresses and deportment were inspected by those penetrating eyes, when, after being served with tea in exquisite porcelain cups, they were ushered into Her Majesty's presence.

The Empress Dowager, the Motherly and Auspicious, was seated on the Dragon Throne backed by a superlative jewel-encrusted screen. She wore the heavy brocaded ceremonial robes of tradition, the Manchu head-dress in which were pinned and sparkled some of the loveliest pearls, jade and diamond jewels from her collection; long ear-rings to match them, and on the fingers of her hands, reposing in her lap, were the golden jewel-studded nail-protectors. Her famous necklace of three hundred enormous perfectly matched pearls fell to below her waist, around which was a jewel-studded belt; on her feet were the satin bootees on their high platform-heels from which dangled pearl tassels. Compared to her European and American guests this woman was tiny; yet in her poise and bearing were the heavy dignity and benevolent charm of one who knew herself to be the world's most powerful female ruler.

Her welcoming smile was absolutely guileless as she observed the reaction of her guests to seeing, on a smaller throne below her own, the Kuang Hsu Emperor, pale, silent, motionless, but nevertheless very much alive still, as he now also smiled in hospitable welcome at the foreign ladies, and, moreover, after their presentation, shook each one of them by the hand in their own fashion.

Lady Macdonald read an address of congratulation to Her Majesty, on behalf of herself and her companions, Prince Ching acknowledging their good wishes in Chinese for the Empress. Then, with the utmost graciousness, Old Buddha also shook the hands of her guests, and as she did so took from the attendant eunuch a heavy gold ring set with a large pearl, which she slipped on each lady's finger. This audience then ended, the ladies bowing deeply to Her Majesty as they left the Audience Chamber.

The party, however, continued for a while. The ladies were led into another hall, where Prince Ching, his wife and five other princesses entertained them to luncheon. They thereupon adjourned to a third hall for tea, and in due course returned to the banqueting hall. Here they once again met Her Majesty, seated in a chair of Imperial yellow satin. And now she spoke to her guests in that irresistible voice of hers, which never failed to beguile those whom it was intended to win over.

The tremendous impression she made on her visitors was summed up by the American Minister's wife, Mrs Conger:

> She was bright and happy and her face glowed with goodwill. There was no trace of cruelty to be seen. In simple expressions she welcomed us, and her actions were full of freedom and warmth. Her Majesty arose and wished us well. She extended both hands to each lady, then, touching herself, said with much enthusiastic earnestness, "One family—all one family."

The visitors were then entertained by a performance in the Imperial Theatre, after which the Empress received them again, to say goodbye to them. She hoped that they had enjoyed themselves, and according to custom deplored the fact that the entertainment she had been able to offer them was no doubt inferior to that of their own countries. The ceremony ended as tea was again served, and Her Majesty, according to Mrs Conger, 'stepped forward and tipped each cup of tea to her own lips and took a sip, then lifted the cup, on the other side, to our lips, and said again, "One family—all one family." ' More presents were then given them, and the visitors left the Presence to enter their sedan chairs, 'full of admiration for her Majesty and hopes for China'. An account by one of the visitors, published in the *Hong Kong Daily Press,* stated that the Empress Dowager's manner was 'affectionate amiability personified'.

Sir Claude Macdonald informed Lord Salisbury that, 'Her Majesty made a most favourable impression, both by the personal interest she took in all her guests and by her courteous amiability.'

The events that occurred six months later were, however, more than a family quarrel between Old Buddha and her foreign 'sisters'. Those few words of hers were then remembered as an instance of typical Oriental duplicity. Before entering into this matter it might be helpful to bear in mind the smile of Mona Lisa. The Empress had never set eyes on this masterpiece, but her own expression on that day must have closely resembled it. What was her smile to mean, how were her words and gestures to be correctly interpreted?

When she received them so beamingly the Empress Dowager did not love the foreign women more, nor hate their countries and their policies towards China less. She did not forget that the British were occupying large slices of Chinese coastline territory, from Hong Kong to Wei-hai-Wei; that the French had plunged their arms up to the elbow into her Western possessions; that the Russians were heading right across northern China, driving their railway to maritime outlets on her eastern coast; nor that the Japanese had only been thwarted in their attempt to grab the vassal State of Korea because the Allies, thinking that the Treaty of Shimonoseki gave these Oriental upstarts too large a slice of the melon, forced them to relinquish their hold on it.

The Kaiser, the Tsar, Queen Victoria, and their governments were all her enemies. China's trials were becoming more and more unendurable to her.

Her invitations were given from motives of policy. According to the traditional Chinese laws of hospitality, the party was of great sumptuousness. It followed the usual custom of sending away one's guests loaded with presents—and incidentally also a deep sense of obligation—but no more. Such conventional entertaining was never meant to imply any further commitments on the Empress Dowager's part, nor to raise hopes for China's capitulation to the policies of the foreign powers. Those famous words 'All one family' were only another gesture of politeness and nothing more. Their implication was merely that Her Majesty was welcoming the diplomatic ladies into her superlatively magnificent home as warmly *as if* they were members of her own family.

Taken as it was meant to be taken, at its face value, the party had been given to prove to the outside world the fact that the Emperor was alive and well, despite all rumours of his ill-treatment and imprisonment. That was its first and principal objective. The second was to create to the highest degree an impression of the Empress Dowager's benevolence and goodwill. Both these objectives were successfully accomplished. But it meant and was planned to mean nothing more. To assume that it did so was a serious error of judgment on the part of Her Majesty's feminine guests and their husbands. This was partly deliberately and partly involuntarily induced by the smiles and flattery dictated by the traditional Chinese code regarding the entertainment of guests.

The policy of the Reformers, like that of the liberal-minded elder statesmen such as Li Hung Chang, was based on two main premises: firstly, that owing to their superior know-how the foreign devils were so firmly entrenched in China that it would be impossible to dislodge them; and secondly, that China's only hope of achieving some parity with them in course of time was to copy Western techniques as speedily as possible, meanwhile appeasing the aggressors. It was a policy of weakness, based on a pessimistic political outlook.

Such a policy was unlikely to commend itself to the Empress Dowager. Temperamentally she was an invincible optimist, a shrewd gambler and a fervent patriot, who, throughout her reigns until the end of the nineteenth century, had prevailed over her opponents by fair means if possible, but by foul when necessary.

The reactionary methods she adopted when she resumed power in 1898 were based on her temperamental unwillingness ever to admit defeat, her sense of China's vast superiority over all other nations, and indomitable physical and mental courage. Her unhesitating intention was to govern her country, and to meet those who would tear away portions of it, from a position of strength, not weakness.

The first evidence of this was her appointment of Jung Lu as Supreme Commander, instructed to provide the largest and best organized military effectives with which to stem further aggression, and in the political field to make no further concessions but to oppose all aggression calmly, yet with the utmost firmness. In the circumstances the latter was a risky policy, but when put to the test in February and March 1899 it succeeded surprisingly.

In February of that year the Italian Government, not to be outdone by the British, French, Germans and Russians, demanded that China should cede to it Sanmen Bay in Chekiang Province as a naval base. This demand the Chinese Government politely but definitely refused, and when the Italian minister issued an ultimatum, pressing his demand, an Imperial Decree instructed the Nanking Viceroy, Liu Kun-yi, to use any force necessary to repel an Italian landing. And the Governor of Chekiang was at the same time ordered to attack 'without hesitation but with all might' any Italian penetration of Chinese territory. The Chinese attitude was so unequivocally firm that the Italian Minister had no option but to renounce his claim, whereupon, with considerable loss of face, he was recalled by his Government. So, for the first time since China's ignominious defeat by Japan five years earlier, the Middle Kingdom scored a military and political success.

'Audacity, more audacity, and always audacity' seemed now

to be the Chinese policy. It was put to a severer test only a month later. Germany, at that time Europe's most quickly rising military nation, was a far more powerful adversary than Italy. Kaiser Wilhelm II had no intention of being outgrabbed in seizing Chinese territory by his European rivals, Russia, Great Britain and France. His opportunity came in 1897 when two more missionaries were murdered by incensed Chinese, and these victims were Germans.

> . . . The Kaiser struck at once, seizing the port of Kiaochow in Shantung and forcing the Chinese Government to legalize this depredation by granting the Germans a ninety-nine years' lease of Kiaochow Bay and the city of Tsingtao as indemnity for the murdered missionaries, as well as extensive railway and mining concessions in Shantung.

Two years later a further incident occurred. In March 1899 some infuriated local villagers killed three more Germans. Reprisals were swift : German troops razed two villages to the ground, occupied the city of Jihchao near by, and held it. This time the Chinese again reacted very firmly. The Chinese Minister in Berlin was told to protest strongly to the German Government. But in addition, Yu Hsien, the Governor of Shantung, received unequivocal orders to dispatch a strong force to the area, 'not to act with undue haste, but at the same time not to be intimidated'; and on 11 April he received further instructions, 'not to accede unendingly to the aggressive demands of the Germans' although he should not himself attack them. The Germans withdrew and the incident was closed, but for a second time it was made clear to the astonished Western world that there was a new firmness in China's determination to resist further aggression.

This policy was expressed in an Imperial Decree issued to all the Viceroys and Governors of Provinces throughout the Empire on 21 November, worthy of a proud nation no longer prepared to accept unending humiliation :

> Never should the word "peace" fall from the mouths of our high officials, nor should they harbour it for a moment in their

breasts. Let us not think of making peace, nor rely solely upon diplomatic manoeuvres. . . .

and the Decree concluded with the highly charged sentence,

. . . Let each strive to preserve from destruction and spoliation at the ruthless hands of the invader his ancestral home and graves. Let these our words be made known to each and all within our domain.

In this Decree the Empress Dowager proudly spoke to her Viceroys, Governors and people. Whilst the mandarins may not have taken it more literally than they did other edicts and decrees streaming out of the Forbidden City, this time the Empress's words closely corresponded with the bitter emotions of the common people. For already there existed a formidable movement of a totally unofficial and revolutionary kind which had begun to take the offensive against the foreign devils and especially their missionaries. The members of this movement were called I Ho Chuan or Patriotic Peace Fists, or, more shortly, the Boxers. And it was owing to the extraordinary alliance that occurred in 1900 between Her Imperial Majesty Tzu Hsi and the Boxers as the result of their common aims, that she became in a sense the Motherly and Auspicious Ancestress of the Chinese Revolution which only forty-eight years later culminated in the People's Republic.

19   The Boxers

The term 'the masses' is a loose and amorphous one much favoured in Communist propaganda. It only acquires some more accurate definition if one breaks it down, as it were, into its components: several hundred or thousand or million *human beings*.

Nowhere in Europe, even in the worst slums, does one feel so acutely conscious of population density as in Asia.

The Chinese, both men and women, whether city dwellers and industrial workers or farmers and peasants, were and are humble, patient, generally docile, and industrious as industry was never conceived of in the Western world: in many respects the most lovable people on earth. To anyone approaching them as a friend, an admirer of their ancient and superb culture, of their simple but solid virtues, and not an exploiter of these, all groups and classes extended instant courtesy often bordering on affection.

The historical process, with its switches and changes in social organization, sometimes slow, sometimes dramatically swift, has little effect on racial character or characteristics, which have a continuity of their own and a much slower rate of change.

It is more than a little difficult for the educated Western mind to appreciate the limitations set on human thought and all higher mental activities by illiteracy. Yet in China, until the middle of the twentieth century—as in many other parts of the world—with the exception of a very thin uppercrust of intensively educated men, and even fewer women, nearly all the teeming and toiling population was illiterate. In consequence, before attempting to follow the Chinese revolutionary movements during the past centuries, culminating in the Boxer Rising of 1900, it is necessary to glance at the means of communication, information and instruction available both to their leaders and to the rank and file.

News and information could only be spread amongst the people, the city proletariat and the peasants—a vast majority—orally, by one to another. And it was if as those to whom the written word was inaccessible suffered from a condition similar in a way to defective speech or hearing. Only approximations to or distortions of fact were available to them. The three great religions of China—Buddhism, Taoism, and in a wider sense Confucianism, which controlled human relationships and behaviour—in their pure forms were systems of philosophy also. But their teachings reached the common people in distorted and irrational versions. They were almost inextricably mixed up with myth, legend, magic and superstition, sometimes of the crudest and most absurd kinds. These garbled tales, practices and rites were propagated by priests and lay leaders as illiterate as their followers. And total ignorance of the causes of tragic natural phenomena such as devastation by perennial flood and drought, or loss of life on a colossal scale due to sweeping endemic or epidemic diseases partly caused by these and partly by poverty, overcrowding, hunger, and non-existent hygiene, bred an atmosphere of constant anxiety or worse, leading to outbreaks of panic and mass hysteria.

In primitive communities—and Chinese rural communities were indeed primitive—belief and conduct based on distorted traditions were also influenced by other important factors. These traditions were kept alive by the many seasonal rituals and by the cult or worship of ancestors, heroes and gods. Story-tellers handed down tales of these, embroidered according to the teller's gifts of visualization and imagination. Human ghosts swarmed around the outskirts of the burial-grounds adjacent to every hamlet, village and town. In forest and jungle there were many wild and dangerous animals, and their ghosts could be even more dreadful. Finally, most fearsome of all, there were just ghosts.

Perhaps the simplest manner of reconstructing this atmosphere is by recalling a similar state of affairs in Europe during the Dark Ages. And in China also there were not only story-tellers, but magicians, conjurers, tightrope-walkers, wrestlers, boxers, and finally the bands of strolling players who acted out all these beliefs and fears in improvised or traditional plays in which the supernatural characters became incarnate, visible and touchable. To their innocent audiences these performances seemed frequently bordering on the miraculous : the gods, demons and other frightening apparitions became real. And in such conditions a crude form of spiritualism played a very important part. It was difficult to draw the line between inspiration and impersonation. The performers' amazing prowess was often due to a trance-like state they engendered in themselves by auto-suggestion, the audience responding in a kind of mass hypnotism. They were filled with a sense of wonder and euphoria and were uplifted by the experience, so that everything seemed possible to them.

But even the Chinese peasants, grubbing a hard living from a reluctant soil and, when they did so, harassed by grasping overlords and landlords, did not always find magic and magicians capable of supporting their struggles for survival. Docile, endlessly hardworking, respectful of their rulers, worshipping them, their gods and their ancestors, the majority might well be. But throughout the ages there was always a minority in the Celestial Kingdom that rebelled against their harsh fate and sought, aggressively, a way of escape. These hardier and more virile minorities were not content passively to starve to death below the necessary subsistence level. They banded together, sometimes in large numbers, to achieve a better standard of life. Their aims were aggressive, and in general took two forms : either banditry on the open road or the forming in towns and cities of underground pressure-groups that became secret societies, with their own peculiar rites and rituals, signs and signals, but with a common objective; the re-exploitation of their exploiters.

Such secret societies had existed in China since time immemorial. One of the most enduring of them was the White Lotus Society. Others were the Eight Diagram Sect, and the Red Fist Society. The White Lotus Society was suppressed by the authorities in 1808, but this only meant that it went a little deeper underground. It never lost its hold on the people, and by 1899 it was exceedingly powerful, notably in the provinces of Shantung and Chihli, where it was partly, but not wholly, responsible for the emergence of the Boxers. These were bound together, as invariably occurs in secret societies, by oaths of allegiance and loyalty, the betrayal of which was punishable by instant execution and the decimation of all relatives.

As their name implied, the Boxers were lusty, athletic fellows, with great skill in fisticuffs and wrestling. But they were also well armed with every kind of weapon, from swords and knives and rusty muskets to those of a more modern kind which they were able to acquire, by fair means or foul, from the regular forces. There were various groups and grades among them, distinguished by the colours of their turbans and sashes, mostly blood-red or green. Women were also admitted to the special female corps they organized, which acted as a kind of commissariat department. Originally their aims were frankly revolutionary, and as conditions in the northern provinces worsened they attracted more and more recruits, mostly from the starving and desperate peasantry.

But by far the most powerful attraction the Boxers exercised on the people amongst whom they operated was due to the high proficiency they had developed in arts more occult than the merely physical. These occult practices were similar to those in many other primitive and illiterate communities. They sprang from ancient sources : an imperative subconscious need for divine intervention and assistance, the basis of all religious beliefs and ritual. The divinities to whom the Boxers looked were the gods such as, in their non-understanding of the higher and purer forms of their religions, they imagined them to be. Their incantations were appeals to such divinities.

Their performances and rites were designed to induce those powerful gods to descend into them, take possession of their bodies, and once this phenomenon had occurred the mediums of the Boxer sect and their awed onlookers were utterly convinced that the possessed ones had become invulnerable and immortal, immune to bullets or any other weapons with which they might be attacked.

The Boxer movement reappeared in strength in Chihli and Shantung in the eighteen-nineties and soon spread through the north-eastern provinces like a prairie-fire. It was fanned by flood, famine, land-hunger, depredations and the sufferings of the people due to maladministration and corruption, the ruthlessness of their foreign invaders—especially the Germans—and the hatred felt for Christian converts and missionaries.

At first it seems to have been a popular and semi-revolutionary movement, with leaders who slightly resembled the glamorous Robin Hood of Sherwood Forest in Merrie Olde England : it even had its Friar Tuck, a Buddhist priest.

The best known—the Robin Hood—of these early leaders was Chu Hung-teng, who in 1899, at Pingyuan in Shantung, rallied round him a large group of rebels, enthusiastically following his banner, on which was proclaimed the slogan *Fan Ching Mien Yang,* or 'Overthrow the Ching—Destroy the Foreigner'. Chu and his guerrillas at that time seem only to have attacked Chinese Christians, and foreigners. Government troops were sent to suppress them, and in a series of fierce battles they were defeated. Chu Hung-teng was captured and later executed.

Although some sources state that even before that event Chu Hung-teng had changed his slogan to the one that afterwards became the definitive Boxer war-cry, it seems more likely that this was a later development. The new slogan, 'Uphold the Ching and Exterminate the Foreigners' was a complete change of policy, with no revolutionary undertones at all; rebellion against the

Manchus and against the dynasty disappeared completely from the Boxer aims. And the new slogan fitted in too well with the views and policies of successive Viceroys and Governors of Shantung and Chihli—with the solitary exception of Yuan Shi-kai—to have been merely coincidental.

Three years before the capture of Chu Hung-teng, in July 1896, Li Ping-heng, the Governor of Shantung, sent a Memorial to the Throne in which he described a local organization known as the Big Sword Society, and its aims:

> . . . Last year, as the coast was not peaceful, the people, believing that this sect was invulnerable against guns and cannon, flocked to it, with the result that its members appeared everywhere. Now, while the stupid [the common people as usually described by the educated] consider it a means of protecting their lives and families, the dishonest seize the opportunity to indulge in their violence. . . .

This distinction between the 'good' and the 'bad' Boxers was to influence all official policy towards them during the next four years. And as happened when Chu Hung-teng and his followers were defeated, the line officially taken was to punish the ring-leaders only, whilst disbanding their followers with no more than cautioning. Suppression of the leaders was to go hand in hand with pacification of the rest: an ambiguous policy, open to such interpretation as those who attempted to administer it liked to give it.

By May 1898, when fresh riots had broken out in Shantung, Chang Ju-mei, who had succeeded Li Ping-heng as Governor, was commanded by Imperial decree to investigate the situation and restore order. He, like his predecessor, minimized the gravity of the matter, stating that the movement was known as the Boxers, but that there were no riots. In fact the Boxers were openly proclaiming in their handbills their determination to kill all Christians.

In March 1899 matters took a more definite turn in favour of the Boxers of Shantung. Chang Ju-mei was succeeded as Governor of that turbulent province by Yu Hsien, who did not at all conceal his own vehement anti-foreign bias. Only a month later the Boxers were more or less openly in possession of many villages, and with considerable justification boasted that they enjoyed the protection of the Governor. Yu Hsien, astutely realizing that his and their aims towards the hated foreigners were identical, encouraged all their anti-foreign and anti-Christian activities. In order, however, to make use of them in this respect, it was necessary to his purpose that they should not emerge as rebels and opponents of the Manchu dynasty, but as its supporters. The disappearance of their original slogan—anti-Ching—and the substitution for it of the pro-Ching characters on their banners, appears to have been his personal contribution to the Boxer Uprising.

Six months later the Boxers and their supporters had another demonstration of the absurdity of their claims to immunity, when several hundred of them attacked the local converts. There ensued a fierce battle between them, and the troops sent from Tsinanfu to restore order. When it ended, twenty-seven Boxers lay dead, the rest having fled. This, however, had no effect on their faith at all, nor, apparently, on Yu Hsien's support of them. When he heard of the event, he proceeded viciously against all the local officials who had opposed them : the local district magistrate was peremptorily dismissed, and the head constable, who had taken his orders too literally, was imprisoned. The commander of the Government force—who happened to be Yuan Shi-kai's brother—was also dismissed. Inevitably, the Boxer movement spread with renewed vigour, and the criminal elements sheltering within it took advantage of this new immunity to murder, burn and plunder on a vastly greater scale.

But reports of these events had reached Peking. Mr Conger, the American Minister, protested against the anti-Christian activities of the Boxers to the Tsungli Yamen, and on 7 December 1899 wrote to the American Secretary of State that, 'It is generally understood that the governor, Yu Hsien, is strongly anti-foreign, and believed that he is by no means doing what he could and should do.'

. . . As you will see [his dispatch continued] from my note to the Tsungli Yamen, I have, without demanding it, suggested the necessity and propriety of his removal, and I am glad to report that yesterday General Yuan Shi-kai, of the Imperial Guards, was appointed Acting-Governor. He is an able, brave and courageous man, has mingled much with foreigners, and it is believed that, if the right kind of orders are given him from the Throne, the rioting will be stopped and order restored.

'If the right kind of orders are given him from the Throne,' Mr Conger wrote, almost wistfully, and with good reason. But meanwhile Yu Hsien was recalled to Peking, ostensibly to report personally on the situation, and Yuan Shi-kai replaced him as Acting-Governor of Shantung.

Ever since he had chosen to serve the Empress instead of Kuang Hsu Emperor, Yuan Shi-kai had enjoyed high favour. When he made this decision, after careful consideration—for this able and intelligent man, who kept faith with no cause but his own, was an extremely clever politician—it was not because he himself was a reactionary. He was a disciple and protégé of Li Hung Chang, and, like his master, believed that China had to reform if she was ever to advance in the modern world. He had no faith, however—and rightly—in the ability of the Kuang Hsu Emperor and his mentor, Kang Yu-wei, to carry out their whirlwind Reform programme of the Hundred Days. In this view events had justified him. To highly educated and politically skilled mandarins like Li Hung Chang and Yuan Shi-kai, the Boxers and their whole ideology were anathema. And indeed no intellectuals such as they were could for one moment have subscribed to the absurd beliefs, rituals, magic and methods of those uneducated and 'stupid' rebels. When, therefore, Yuan Shi-kai took over in Shantung, it was with the determination once and finally to suppress and eradicate the Boxer Movement there. And he would have completely succeeded in this aim had he, as Mr Conger vainly hoped, been given 'the right kind of orders from the Throne'.

Yu Hsien was recalled to Peking on 7 December to make his

report. On 26 December Yuan Shi-kai received the first of a series of Imperial Decrees ordering him to tone down his measures very considerably.

Yuan replied to them in a very tactful Memorial on 13 January, which showed a balanced and sensible attitude to a problem that to him, on the spot, seemed not a particularly formidable one. He emphasized the fact that the Boxer groups contained many bandits and criminals, who must be ruthlessly exterminated.

But it was obviously too late to attempt to quell the violent emotions of the anti-Christian Chinese by such eminently reasonable and statesmanlike arguments.

Yuan Shi-kai made no bones about disposing of the Boxer rabble by force. Had his policy been supported in Peking, or applied in neighbouring Chihli, the Boxers would have been either suppressed, wiped out, or dispersed in a very short time. This, however, was not to be.

The Empress Dowager's policies at that time were undoubtedly tinged with wishful thinking: a passionate desire to deal with the foreign Powers from a position of strength. With Jung Lu as her principal instrument, she was striving to the utmost to provide China with large, well-disciplined armies. And, in addition, she took up with enthusiasm the plan of raising a nation-wide People's Militia in support of the regular troops. This idea was not the Empress's, but had originally been conceived by the man whom she had branded as an arch-traitor, the reformer Kang Yu-wei. Nevertheless, Her Majesty took over the scheme and propounded it as if it were her own.

None of her three most prominent advisers—Jung Lu, Yuan Shi-kai and Li Hung Chang—were in theory opposed to the raising of a People's Militia. But with good reason they did not regard the Boxers as suitable material for providing it.

Yuan Shi-kai had expressed his views as frankly as he dared in his Memorial to the Throne of 13 January. But by that time his predecessor as Governor of Shantung, Yu Hsien, the Boxers' protector, had already won Her Majesty over to this plan. Yu's two most powerful allies at Court were the reactionary 'Lord High Extortioner', Kang-yi, and the even more implacable Prince Tuan.

Li Hung Chang despaired as he foresaw the perils ahead, which he had no power to avert.

The truth of the matter was, however, that her Majesty's mind was still not quite made up, although the hour of fatal decision was rapidly coming nearer.

Throughout the Spring of 1900 Prince Tuan continued to urge the cause of the Boxers on the Empress.

As head of the national forces, Jung Lu's position was a difficult one. In a long private letter to an old friend, the Viceroy of Fukien province, who was a Cantonese—throughout the Rising the South remained implacably against the Boxers—Jung Lu gave him a detailed account of them, their attacks on the Christians in Chilhi and Shantung, their absurd beliefs and magical practices, and their false claims to immunity. And he concluded that 'if we imagine for a moment that . . . we shall thus be able to rid ourselves of the accursed presence of the foreigners, we are very much mistaken, and the attempt is foredoomed.'

Yet this was the grandiose vision the reactionaries had succeeded in implanting in the Empress's mind. Jung Lu, despite his loyalty and devotion to his former love, was not swept away, as she was, by wishful thinking and furious indignation. Aware of the great personal risk he was taking, he nevertheless concluded his letter to the Viceroy of Fukien :

My advice, therefore, to Your Excellency, is not to hesitate in disobeying the Edict which commands you to raise these train-bands. . . . You should, of course, act with great discretion, but the main thing is to prevent the Throne's Decree from becoming an excuse for the banding together of disorderly characters.

A Court recorder gave an account of the meeting called on 16 June to deliberate on the situation. This was, of course, presided over by Her Majesty, who summoned in Council 'all the Manchu princes, dukes, nobles and high officials of the Boards and Ministries'. A representative of the Foreign Office, Yuan Chang, was sufficiently daring on this critical occasion to point out the unreliability of the Boxers. He was interrupted by the Empress Dowager :

> If we cannot rely upon the supernatural formulas, can we not rely upon the heart of the people? If we lost it, how can we maintain our country?

These were noble and crucial words, of immense importance when assessing Old Buddha's personal attitude to the Boxers and their collaboration in her plan to rid China for ever of foreign domination.

Another version of the Empress Dowager's acceptance of the Boxers as her last weapon against the foreigners contrasts sharply with the objective account of this important Council meeting given by the recorder. Although written by her devoted lady-in-waiting, it agrees far more closely with the condemnations of Her Majesty's policy by her enemies than with the adulations of her admirers. This is the story told by Der Ling of Old Buddha's acceptance of Tuan's protégés, in spite of Jung Lu's desperate attempts to foil it. This highly dramatized version leaves out altogether the previous bloody attacks by the Boxers on the Christian Chinese and missionaries in Chihli and Shantung.

Prince Tuan had for some time been a secret member of the White Lotus Society. Several of the Imperial princes, including his younger brother, Duke Lan, high officials and army officers also belonged to it.

Der Ling asserted that Tuan had a penchant for low life and had become a member of those Boxer groups who were strolling players, conjurers, swordsmen and wrestlers, and had taken part in their performances. In order to win over Old Buddha to the popular belief in their invulnerability, the Prince persuaded her to allow him to bring three of their best performers to Court, and to give her a demonstration of their arts. Two of them, armed

with spears, attacked the third, who in unarmed combat,
repelled all their attacks.

The malodorous fellows were then dismissed. Apparently Jung
Lu also witnessed this performance, and 'wrung his hands in
anguish inside his long sleeves' as he noticed how deeply Her
Majesty appeared impressed by it.

Sir Robert Hart commented with regard to this demonstration
that, 'the Chinaman is really an extravagant believer in the supernatural, and so he readily credits the Boxer with all the power
he claims.' Yet this was quite untrue in the case of Jung Lu, as
well as Yuan Shi-kai, all the southern Viceroys, and even the
Emperor, who, although a weakling and by then quite unable to
stop the drift to disaster, was no fool.

Yet Hart also pointed out, in 1900, that, 'In 1898 the eclipse
of the Sun on the Chinese New Year's Day foreboded calamity—
especially to the Emperor'—which was indeed a prophecy fulfilled
—'and in September that year the Empress Dowager usurped the
Government; then, as chance would have it, this year, 1900, is
one in which the intercalary month for the Chinese year is the
eighth, and an eighth intercalary month always means mis-
fortune. When such a month last occurred the Emperor Tung
Chih died, and accordingly the popular mind was on the look-
out for catastrophe in 1900, and perhaps the people were
morbidly willing to assist folklore to fulfil its own prophecy.'

Whether or not Old Buddha did for a short time believe in the
Boxers' alleged invulnerability, unquestionably she had as strong
a faith as her people in the planets and the forecasting of events
by the Court star-readers.

'Those of us,' Hart admitted, 'who regarded the movement as
likely to become serious and mischievous, put off the time of
action to September; our calculations were wrong.'

As head of the Chinese Imperial Customs, Hart was eagerly
consulted during this anxious period by the foreign diplomats.
His admission of an error in his calculations aroused their indignation. They even went so far as to suggest that his obvious bias
was due to the undoubted financial advantages he had gained
by his thirty-year occupation of this lucrative post. That he was

biased in favour of the Chinese was indisputable. For this very reason Hart's account of the events leading up to the siege of the Legations is unique. In striking contrast to the vituperative Kaiser, who coined the world-famous term 'The Yellow Peril' for those despised Asiatics, and even the mild and courteous American envoy, Mr Conger, Hart was one of the rare foreigners who genuinely attempted at that critical period to analyse Chinese motives and the deplorable mistakes into which they led Her Majesty the Empress Dowager from the point of view of this much-wronged nation.

Hart concisely summed up the situation when, wise after the event, he wrote,

> We cannot say we had no warning. . . . If there was one cry to which our ears had grown accustomed it was this Chinese cry of "Wolf!" . . . The last half of the nineteenth century saw the Taiping Rebellion, the *Arrow* war, the Tientsin massacre [of missionaries and nuns] the Franco-Chinese misunderstanding, the war with Japan, and the surrender of Cochin-China, Burma, Kiaochow, Port Arthur, Weihaiwei, etc. to the foreigner.

These last surrenders were the result of the Battle for the Concessions, waged against one another by the Great Powers for Chinese territory—on Chinese soil and in complete disregard of the interests of those helpless people to whom that territory belonged.

The time had come to call a halt to such cynical aggression.

On 13 June 1900, the wolves of China, at last unleashed by the Motherly and Auspicious Empress Dowager, descended on their enemies and launched their vicious attack on the Legations of Peking, determined to wipe them out.

20   Siege of the Legations

The first attacks by the Boxers were made on Chinese Christian converts. But on 31 December 1899 they murdered their first British victim in Shantung: Mr S. A. Brooks, a missionary. At that time the policy of the moderates in Peking still prevailed. Treaty obligations towards the foreigners had to be honoured. A Decree was issued ordering the punishment of the local neglectful officials, and the arrest, followed by execution, of the Boxer murderers. This Decree was promulgated on 4 January 1900. But only a week later Yu Hsien had apparently won over Her Majesty. For on the 11th she published another Decree. This emphasized the distinction between 'good' and 'bad' members of the secret societies very definitely. Local authorities and magistrates were instructed to draw the line between them quite sharply.

In spite of Sir Robert Hart's contention that the Legations had expected no real trouble from the Boxers until September 1900, all the foreign envoys in Peking did quite clearly hear the baying of the Chinese wolves in the ominous last sentence of that Decree.

On 27 January the British, American, French, German and Italian Ministers unanimously protested in identical terms to the

Tsungli Yamen against this Decree. They no longer made tactful suggestions in Mr Conger's previous style, but firmly demanded that another decree be immediately published ordering that the two principal offending Secret Societies, both connected with the Boxers, the Fists of Righteous Harmony and the Big Sword Society, should once and for all be suppressed. Their protests and demands, however, were ignored : ignored again and again. The envoys sent further similar notes on 2 and 10 March, with equal lack of success. So much so that a further Decree, published on 17 April, repeated with only very trivial modifications the instructions given to the local authorities on 11 January.

The Boxers' attacks on the missionaries continued alarmingly. But in May, in Chihli, a new development in their offensive occurred which was positively ominous. This was their aggression against the railway. The murders of Christian converts and missionaries were clearly criminal and in contravention of all the Chinese treaties with the Powers. But the attempted destruction of the railways was immediately recognized as a threat to the very lifelines of the residents in the Legations of Peking. The Chinese peasants still had a superstitious fear and hatred of the Iron Dragon that moved on wheels on metal lines laid down for it by foreign engineers : lines that cut indiscriminately through and across arable and sacred land. The arable land, so precious in that intractable earth, only belonged to the farmers, who, poor devils, were utterly helpless to protect their soil from such depredations by the foreign engineers, who could not care less if those living and working on it were thus deprived of their already meagre means of subsistence. The sacred land consisted of the straggly untidy burial grounds outside every village and township, where the revered ancestors of the local population were laid to rest. To disturb their graves was desecration. It would raise a multitude of protesting ghosts, and these wraiths would inevitably bring every kind of calamity on their impious descendants in revenge. The Germans in particular showed a positively brutal disregard for Chinese filial piety in destroying these hallowed graves.

On 28 May the news arrived in Peking that the Boxers had

torn up the rails and cut the telegraph wires at Fengtai, the junction of the Peking-Tientsin railway line. The diplomats thereupon decided to act firmly for their own protection. They informed the Tsungli Yamen forthwith that they were going to call in European guards for their Legations. These were a mixed force of soldiers, sailors and marines of the various foreign nationalities normally on coast patrol to protect the concessions. The Chinese government was requested to provide the necessary transportation for this force. The Tsungli Yamen attempted to procrastinate, stating that Chinese troops had already been sent to the railway trouble spots to restore order.

Most of these troops, however, turned out to be either themselves members of the secret societies or overt allies of the Boxers.

On 30 May all the heads of the diplomatic corps paid a joint visit to the Tsungli Yamen, where they roundly informed the officials that with or without their permission, and without further ado, they were sending to Tientsin for the guards. If the Chinese would not co-operate in bringing them to Peking, the ministers would ask for an even larger contingent than they had originally intended.

To the great relief of the foreign civilians, between 1 and 3 June a mixed detachment of their armed compatriots at last arrived in Peking. This force consisted of seventy-five Russians, Britons and Frenchmen; fifty Americans; forty Italians, and twenty-five Japanese, who immediately took up their duties at their respective legations.

But by then the impetus of the Boxer movement on the capital could no longer be checked. Incident after incident occurred. In one of these a party of French and Belgian engineers were rescued by a detachment of twenty-five Russian Cossacks, who had ridden out to save them. The 'invulnerable' Boxers fought with frenzied fanaticism. They lost many killed and wounded but simply redoubled their attacks on the railways. In spite of the arrival of Chinese troops uncontaminated as yet by their fury, who killed several hundred of them, the Boxers as a whole remained invincible, and surged onwards towards Peking. They had powerful backing, for by then all attempts by the anti-Boxer

Viceroys and Governors to check these insurgents, whom they still described as rebels, were thwarted by Imperial Decrees.

The Commander of the Chinese troops who had fought with and defeated the group of Boxers on 4 June, at the Huangtsun station of the Peking-Tientsin railway was General Nieh Shi-cheng. His feelings must have been grim when on the following day he received a telegram from his Commander-in-Chief, Jung Lu. 'The uniforms of your troops,' it ran, 'make them look like foreigners, and the ignorant villagers may mistake them for foreign troops. The Boxers are the children of China. You should earnestly explain to them and make every effort to disperse them.'

Although this telegram was dispatched by Jung Lu, the wording of it was unmistakably that of Tzu Hsi, the Motherly and Auspicious. The Boxers were the children of China—and therefore hers.

This situation was highlighted by the arrival at Chochou on 7 June of Kang Yi, the 'Lord High Extortioner', as Imperial Commissioner. On this occasion it was a question not of raising finance, but of direct interference with the Army : presumably in spite of Jung Lu's nominal authority over it. Kang Yi cancelled all the anti-Boxer measures taken by General Nieh, and went all the way with the insurgents, summoning their leaders in conference, listening to their demands, and in spite of the protests of all the leading local military and civilian officials, even including the Viceroy Yu Lu, acceding to them. His mandate was a direct one from the Throne and could not be contravened. The Imperial troops were withdrawn to Tientsin. The Boxers scored perhaps the only victory that confirmed their claim to invulnerability and protection from on high, since it was a walk-over for them in which they did not shed a drop of blood.

The crisis was now approaching its climax. Before Kang Yi's return to Peking, on 10 June Prince Tuan was appointed President of the Tsungli Yamen in succession to the amiable and moderate Elder Statesman, Prince Ching : an appointment that justifiably threw the foreign ministers into alarm and despondency.

A counter-initiative had already been begun by the British

Minister, Sir Claude Macdonald, who was keeping in close touch telegraphically with Admiral Sir Edward Seymour, the British naval commander at Taku Bay. Sir Claude was still vacillating. For on 9 June he sent him three messages. The first asked that a relief force be dispatched immediately to Peking; the second countermanded this request as the situation seemed momentarily less alarming. But two hours later Sir Claude sent a third and final message, renewing his appeal for help, as by then the situation was hourly becoming more serious.

According to Peter Fleming, what apparently brought home this fact to the British Minister was the burning of the grandstand on the private British racecourse only three miles from Peking by a band of Boxers making for the capital. Although for weeks past missionary refugees had been thronging into the city with horrifying stories of their perils, this attack on the sacrosanct centre of British sportsmanship was 'the straw that broke the camel's back'.

The Seymour relief force, consisting of rather more than two thousand men of various nationalities, was expected to arrive by train in Peking on 12 June. Among the foreign diplomats who rode out to the station to welcome these eagerly expected compatriots was the Chancellor of the Japanese legation, Mr Sugiyama. The troops did not arrive, however, and on his way home the defenceless diplomat was dragged from his vehicle by Chinese soldiery encamped near the Temple of Heaven, and cruelly clubbed to death.

13 June was the fateful day.

The Throne issued a strong Decree, ordering Viceroy Yu Lu and Generals Nieh and Lo to 'resist any further foreign reinforcements and to stop the Allied force from coming to Peking'.

It was hardly necessary for the commanders to carry out these orders.

At Lang Fang, about forty miles from Peking, Admiral Seymour found the railway line broken. His efforts to repair it were completely thwarted.

'As fast as one bit was mended,' wrote Hart, 'another was torn up by the crowds of Boxers that swarmed around, so that, what with failure of food and drink and fuel, and an increasing number of enemies in front and rear and on both sides, the Admiral and party were soon in such a plight as no mixed force ever before. . . . '

The failure of this rescue expedition, compelled to retreat, was an appalling loss of face for the foreigners, and an equally great triumph for the Boxers. It appeared to vindicate all the claims, on their behalf, of Kang Yi and Prince Tuan, that they would annihilate or drive out of China every remaining foreign devil.

An infuriated, fanatical mob, filled with blood-lust, armed and brandishing weapons of all kinds—from stolen rifles to their dreadful fire-raising torches—now descended on defenceless Peking. Amongst the dedicated Boxers, members of the cults and secret societies, were thousands of desperate starving peasants and coolies, criminals and looters, wild-eyed and avid for blood and plunder. They carried the blazing torches through the narrow windswept streets and lanes with their dense, huddled, terrified population, the poorer members of which joined in their frenzied advance.

Hart, the least sensational reporter of their deadly work, wrote that, 'After setting fire to the missionary chapel in the Ha-ta-men Street . . . the incendiaries continued their work, and destroyed every foreign house they could touch, and every Chinese establishment selling foreign goods or connected with foreigners; of course adjoining buildings caught fire, too, and in some districts their conflagrations made a desert of the richest and most populous quarters. In this way, the Austrian, Italian, Dutch and French Legations, the Customs Inspectorate, Postal and College buildings, the extensive missionary premises . . . the Russo-Chinese and Chinese Imperial banks, Imberg's Stores and Chinese houses without number were destroyed. Even we ourselves, in the various Legations, were obliged to burn everything near us in self-defence, and from first to last a fire inside a Legation was what all dreaded most.'

Naturally enough, the foreign commentators—contemporary eye-witnesses, such as Robert Hart, and also later writers, like Peter Fleming—emphasized the horror of the situation from the foreign point of view; they were also justified in praising the admirable self-control and courage shown by their besieged compatriots. But the worst sufferers in this holocaust were the utterly helpless Chinese Christian inhabitants of the city. Their tragedy was overwhelming and remained unavenged.

They fled to the churches for sanctuary, pursued by the Boxers and their devilish torches. Hundreds of victims were burned to death as their refuges caught fire. A large Roman Catholic cathedral blazed to the destruction in which the aged priest-in-charge and his flock were roasted to death. There was, however, an occasional epic rescue. Catholic missionaries, as well as the Sisters of Charity and the twenty Chinese nuns whom they were sheltering, were brought to safety from the South Cathedral by a posse of French volunteers, almost minutes before the building was fired. This happened on 14 June. The famous correspondent, Dr G. E. Morrison, organized on the following day an international troop of Marines, to search for survivors and bring them to safety, shooting at sight any marauding Boxers they encountered. 'Awful sights,' wrote Morrison, met their horrified gaze : 'women and children hacked to pieces, men trussed like fowls, with noses and ears cut off and eyes gouged out.'

The Boxers were beserk, drunk with blood-lust and a sense of illimitable power. And occasionally their conviction of immortality, which in spite of their losses remained unshakeable, seemed oddly confirmed. Hart told of the astonishment of a Legation guard, who 'had fired seven shots at one of the [Boxer] chiefs on the northern bridge, less than two hundred yards off; the chief stood there contemptuously, pompously waving his swords as if thereby causing the bullets to pass him to right or left at will; he then calmly and proudly stalked away unhit. . . . '

Prince Tuan, apparently by instruction of Her Majesty, 'offered a bounty of five hundred taels,' wrote Der Ling, 'for every dead foreigner.'

And by night the Prince and his supporters would ride out to enjoy the spectacle and encourage the Boxers in their fearful excesses.

Meanwhile, 'in the seclusion of her palace', the Empress Dowager was in constant consultation with her ministers. And there Prince Tuan played a disgraceful trick upon her. At the beginning of June Her Majesty was not yet officially encouraging the Boxers, but by the scheme he devised Prince Tuan felt confident that he would finally win her over completely.

Until then this Prince was by no means always in Old Buddha's favour. According to one Court gossip he was 'horribly afraid of Her Majesty, and when she speaks to him he is on tenter-hooks, as if thorns pricked him, and the sweat runs down his face.'

On one occasion, his son, the loutish heir apparent, 'dressed himself up as a Boxer and was going through their drill in the Summer Palace grounds. . . . The Old Buddha saw him and promptly gave orders that he be confined to his rooms . . . unseemly behaviour she called it.'

Jung Lu was still trying to save Her Majesty from committing herself disastrously, and Prince Tuan and Kang Yi 'despaired of ever being able to induce her to support the Boxers wholeheartedly' so long as she continued to listen to Jung Lu's advice.

The foreign ministers never had direct access to the Court but only to the Tsungli Yamen, dominated, since his recent appointment there, by Prince Tuan.

At the Imperial Council meeting held in the afternoon of 16 June, the Prince presented the Empress Dowager with an alleged ultimatum from the Powers, which in fact was a forgery. It contained four principal demands :

1. A special place of residence was to be assigned to the Emperor, who all this while was a helpless prisoner, although he attended the Council meetings, where for form's sake the Empress Dowager even pretended to ask his advice, but where he was utterly unable to prevent catastrophe.

2. All revenues were to be collected by the foreign ministers.
3. All military affairs were to be committed to their hands.
4. The Emperor was to be restored to power.

No reasonable person might have been expected for one

moment to take these absurd conditions seriously. But, as Tuan expected, the threat to reinstate the Emperor so infuriated Her Majesty that she was in no reasonable frame of mind, and never for a moment suspected this document's authenticity. She regarded it as a challenge to war, which she promptly accepted.

'Now they have started the aggression,' she declared, 'the extinction of our nation is imminent. If we just fold our arms and yield to them, I would have no face to see our ancestors af er death. If we must perish, why not fight to the death?'

Thereupon she ordered three of her ministers—Hsu Yung-i, Li Shan, and Lien Yuan—to inform the foreign ministers 'that if they really wanted to start hostilities they could haul down their flags and leave China'.

When the reluctant three called on the British Minister, Sir Claude Macdonald, on 18 June, neither side had declared war. The matter of the alleged ultimatum was apparently not mentioned; in fact Li Shan drew the attention of his colleagues to the reasonableness of Sir Claude's attitude. Since the failure of the Seymour expedition to reach Peking, the Boxers had arrived and were sacking the city unchecked. The foreigners were more desperately than ever awaiting the relief force. And Sir Claude patiently explained to the envoys that 'far from British troops coming up with any hostile intentions towards the Chinese Government, their presence would be of material assistance in preserving order, and so preventing incidents which would have serious consequences, both for the Government and for the dynasty itself.'

The dynasty, however, of which the Empress Dowager was the supreme embodiment, took the opposite view. And her anti-foreign bias received encouragement from the news arriving from Tientsin on 19 June, in a dispatch from the Viceroy of Chihli, Yu Lu. The allied admirals had presented an ultimatum to him, demanding the surrender of the Taku forts. On his refusal they opened fire, but were repelled after severe fighting. On receiving this report of successful resistance to foreign aggression at last, Her Majesty decided immediately to break off relations with the powers, whose ministers were to be told to leave Peking within the next twenty-four hours.

At a meeting of the Grand Council the Empress Dowager, 'speaking with great vehemence, declared that . . . until yesterday, until in fact she had read the dispatch addressed to the Tsungli Yamen by the Diplomatic Body, it had been her intention to suppress the Boxers; but in the face of their insolent proposal that she should hand over the reins of government to the Emperor, who had already proved himself quite unfitted to rule . . . no peaceful solution was possible.'

Prince Tuan's plot had succeeded.

In the very long speech she then made, the Manchu Empress pointed out to the Chinese representatives present the great benefits conferred on China by her dynasty. She optimistically told them that at that moment China could rely on millions of her brave and patriotic volunteers. And she finally declared that 'she had always been of the opinion that the allied armies had been permitted to escape too easily' in the year 1860. 'Only a united effort was then necessary to have given China the victory. Today, at last, the opportunity for revenge had come.'

This was the nub of Old Buddha's wishful thinking, which dominated all her foreign policy.

Ever since her youth, when she had vainly pleaded with Hsien Feng to resist the British, when they entered Peking after his flight to Jehol and sacked her beloved Summer Palace, Yehonala had borne this hatred for them steadfastly and unswervingly. Now, exactly forty years later, her longed-for moment of revenge appeared to have arrived.

Having made her own views quite clear, the Empress then turned to the Emperor, pretending to ask his opinion as the next highest dynastic representative present. The unfortunate Kuang Hsu's 'deadly pallor' revealed his distress of mind. 'His Majesty, after a long pause and with evident hesitation, urged her to follow Jung Lu's advice, to refrain from attacking the Legations, and to have the Foreign Ministers escorted in safety to the coast. But, he added, it must be for her to decide. He could not dare to assume any responsibility in the matter.'

Others, however, had more courage. Never could the Empress Dowager have appeared more terrifying to her Councillors than at that fateful meeting. Yet one of them, Yuan Chang, knowing that by what he was about to say he was risking his life, still informed Her Majesty that he 'did not believe in the authenticity of the dispatch demanding her abdication, which Prince Tuan professed to have received from the Diplomatic Body. In his opinion [as a minister of the Tsungli Yamen] it was impossible that the Ministers should have dared to suggest any such interference with China's internal affairs.'

'At this Prince Tuan arose and angrily asked the Empress whether she proposed to listen to the words of a Chinese traitor. Her Majesty rebuked him for his loud and violent manner of speaking, but ordered Yuan Chang to leave the audience hall. No one else dared to say anything.'

Her Majesty's will to resistance was fortified on 21 June, when a second optimistic report was received from the Viceroy of Chihli, giving the news that two foreign warships had been hit by shells from the Taku forts, and that the allied troops at Tientsin had been repulsed with the aid of the Boxers.

Among the many female Boxers was one woman, a former prostitute in Tientsin, who in that city became briefly famous by the name of 'The Yellow Lotus Holy Mother' and a local Boxer leader. Possibly she possessed unusual divinatory powers. She may at one time have held court to her lovers; during the rising she apparently presided over a kind of Boxer court of justice. Those suspected of being anti-Boxer were dragged before her for judgment : she held the power of life and death. Li Hung Chang's eldest son was one of those who were thus imperilled. But even in Boxer circles, apparently, 'squeeze' was still powerful. On payment of the sum required, the 'Yellow Lotus' graciously spared his life. Li Hung Chang later, and perhaps ungratefully in the circumstances, ordered her execution.

But Yu Lu, the Viceroy at that time, an ardent supporter of the Boxers, received the prophetess with high honour, even kowtowing to her in official dress. He begged her to deliver China from the foreign aggressors, to which the 'Yellow Lotus' replied with great confidence that she had made arrangements for 'an angelic host to destroy them with fire from heaven'.

Meanwhile the Tsungli Yamen did offer to evacuate the diplomats and their families from Peking, and conduct them safely to the coast. The foreign ministers, having been in constant conference during these harassing and uncertain days—'eleven anxious weary men'—replied, asking for an appointment at 9 a.m. on the following morning. As no answer was received by 9.30, the majority of the ministers still preferred to wait where they were, since it would be undignified to go to the Yamen and sit there waiting for the Princes.

The German Minister, however, whom Sir Claude Macdonald described as 'a very passionate and excitable man', lost patience. Banging his fist on the table in a rage, he declared that he was determined to go to the Yamen and sit there until the Princes did come, even if he had to sit there all night.

The Russian Minister thereupon, more prudently, advised that they all went together, in a body, and with an armed escort to safeguard them from attack, either by marauding Boxers or out-of-hand Chinese troops. But in spite of the murder of the Japanese Councillor, Mr Sugiyama, the German Baron von Ketteler nevertheless set off by himself, in his bright green-and-red diplomatic sedan-chair, in which he was a sitting target. And having nearly reached his destination, he was shot dead at point-blank range by a Chinese soldier called En Hai, who was later on arrested and executed by the Germans for this murder.

At the time, however, this grave incident was ignored by the Tsungli Yamen in the reply to the diplomats' request, which was received a few hours later. It merely repeated the offer of evacuation for them and their families.

By this time they were justifiably alarmed. It was not a moment too soon. After the burning-down of all the other legations, those foreign civilians whose homes had been destroyed and whose lives were in serious danger—missionaries and all the members of the diplomatic corps—were taken into the British Legation on 20 June, together with a crowd of around two thousand Chinese Christian refugees. The Legation grounds contained about a dozen buildings, all of which were now packed almost to suffocation. But from the first moment the refugees—men, women and children of all nationalities—behaved with admirable courage, self-control and mutual helpfulness. Sir Robert Hart, who was one of them, particularly praised the women : 'Every lady made her share of sandbags—and it was wonderful where needles and thread came from!' All the men were organized for the defence, but as their ammunition was limited, used it as sparingly as possible. An all-round-the-clock watch was set up. Fire was still regarded as the greatest immediate danger.

The siege of the Legation began at 4 p.m. on the afternoon of 21 June, when Chinese troops fired the first shots into the grounds from the city wall overlooking them. These attackers were commanded by Old Buddha's rough-neck Mohammedan general, Tung Fu-hsiang. They were armed with repeating rifles, Krupp guns, and cannons, which they mounted on the wall. Hundreds and hundreds of rounds were fired by them, more or less at random, which did surprisingly little damage. The noise was a trial to which the defenders gradually became accustomed. It was increased when the troops also let off fire-crackers, an ingenious and old Chinese device for frightening an enemy. The defence was alerted at critical moments by the ringing of the famous alarm-bell known as the Jubilee, when the defenders ran to their action stations.

The Boxers, meanwhile, kept up their efforts to burn down the Legation. One of the most terrifying moments in the siege occurred on 24 July. The library of the famous Han-lin Academy, the ancient treasure-house of Chinese learning, was set alight by Boxers who hoped that the flames would spread to the adjacent Legation buildings. This horror was averted by a chain of tireless and heroic volunteers : men, women and even children old enough to carry and pass up buckets of water. So they staved off the dreadful menace of incendiarism. But the Boxers did succeed in destroying the priceless store of their own national literature : the fruits of centuries of culture, and irreplaceable.

Another heroic defence was organized by the isolated Roman

Catholic bishop and missionaries in the Peitang cathedral, against whom the Christian-hating Boxers concentrated perhaps their most vicious and ruthless attack, in which regular troops also occasionally joined. The French bishop, Favier, his priests and nuns, had only a tiny guard of forty-three French and Italian sailors to defend them. The cathedral compound contained various buildings in which the refugees—with the exception of fewer than one hundred Europeans, they were all Chinese converts, including eight hundred and fifty young girls—were sheltered. The wells of Peking were choked with the bodies of such girls, who had been raped by Boxers and drowned themselves in shame. The protection of the Bishop's converts was their only safeguard against similar martyrdom.

The heroic band of Christians in the cathedral and its precincts were sustained more by faith than by victuals. Being totally cut off from the outside world and all supplies, their daily ration was a pound of millet, rice, or beans at the beginning of July. A month later the last remnants of the rice and the last tough mule (they had slaughtered the others already for nourishing their defenders) were reserved for the men. The Chinese, adepts from long and bitter experience at living on next to nothing, made soups from lily and dahlia roots and even leaves from the trees.

The refugees in the British Legation had brought with them what they hoped would be ample provisions for a week or two, hoping that the Relief Expedition would arrive long before the stocks were all eaten. They also took in with them a string of sturdy little mountain ponies, used in happier times for riding and racing. But as the supplies dwindled, and the siege still dragged on, the food had to be strictly rationed : in the case of adults, consisting mainly of rice and, for protein, alas, the ponies, had to be sacrificed to this utilitarian purpose. Milk from the one precious remaining cow was of course reserved for the babies, whose inevitable ailments added to their mothers' worries. Water, also, was precious, owing to the need to reserve it at the beginning of the siege—in the dry season—for the most urgent protection against incendiarism. At first, however, there was a good stock of champagne, for all supplies had been taken in from the three large European commercial stores adjacent to the Legation.

Even most of the women smoked : with the exception of the Russians, this was 'not done' as a rule by European ladies at that time. Now, however, they found it calmed their nerves and above all slightly counteracted the inevitable stench of so many unwashed bodies crowded together in such confined conditions. And in the hot season the reek of the thousands of rotting corpses in the city occasionally became almost unendurable.

There were, however, one or two curious contributions to the food supply—from the besiegers themselves and from an even more surprising source.

'There were noteworthy differences,' Sir Claude Macdonald reported, 'between the troops on different sides of us; those to the north and east—all Kansu men under Tung Fu-hsiang—remaining sullen and suspicious. From other directions, and especially on the east, where Jung Lu's troops were posted, it was possible to obtain supplies (small but welcome) of eggs and vegetables, the sellers being smuggled through the Chinese soldiers' lines in spite of the prohibition of their officers, and it was from this side that messengers came with all later letters.'

On 20 July a larger and even more welcome contribution was made from a higher quarter. The Tsungli Yamen sent four cartloads of vegetables and four of water-melons. This gift, supplemented by a load of rice and a thousand pounds of flour, was repeated a week later. It was indicated to the recipients that these provisions were sent on the orders of Her Majesty, the Empress Dowager!

It was obvious after a time to the beleaguered diplomats that they had a friend on the other side.

'There must have been some protection,' wrote Sir Robert Hart, 'but it was not the Chinese Government that gave it.'

The siege had an intermittent pattern.

'We were under fire from the 20th to the 25th June; from the 28th June to the 18th July; from the 28th July to the 2nd of August'—roughly at weekly intervals. During the first two weeks of August, 'night and day rifle bullets, cannon balls and Krupp shells had been poured into the various Legations from the gate in front of the Palace itself, from the very wall of the Imperial City.'

'Yet,' he commented on this peculiar situation, 'that somebody intervened for our protection seems probable. Attacks were not made in such numbers as the Government had at its disposal— they were never pushed home, but always ceased just when we feared they would succeed—and had the force round us really attacked with thoroughness and determination we could not have held out a week, perhaps even a day . . . somebody, probably a wise man who knew what the destruction of the Legations would cost Empire and dynasty, intervened between the order for our destruction and the execution of it, and so fortunately kept the soldiery playing with us as cats do with mice.'

As the Legation was in such close proximity to the Forbidden City, those within it could hear quite plainly the 'continued and heavy firing, telling the Palace how fiercely we were attacked and how stubbornly we defended ourselves, whilst its curiously half-hearted character not only gave us the chance to live through it, but also gave any relief forces time to come and extricate us, and thus avert the national calamity which the Palace in its pride and conceit ignored, but which someone in his wisdom foresaw and in his discretion sought to put aside.'

The subject of this indirect reference to the Palace was not Prince Tuan, whom Sir Robert Hart need not have hesitated to name. It was, of course, the Empress Dowager, the final arbiter in this acute crisis for the dynasty and country as well as for the foreigners. As they gradually became aware that they had a protector on the other side, it was not, however, immediately clear to them that he could only be Jung Lu—as was later proved to have been the case. For as Commander-in-Chief of the Imperial force he was regarded at the time by most foreigners as almost the villain-in-chief of the attack upon them.

In trying to interpret the course of events during the siege from behind their sandbags and barricades, the diplomats were further confused by the erratic course of Chinese policy. The cat-and-mouse game—which even in normal times was one of its clumsy and confused methods—was brought to its highest pitch during the siege of the Legations in those summer months of 1900. It can perhaps, best be illustrated by a time-table of some of the events of that bizarre period :

17 *June:*   The Taku forts opened fire on the allied squadrons.

18 *June:*   The allies occupied the Taku forts and began their attack on Tientsin.

19 *June:*   The Tsungli Yamen requested the foreign ministers to evacuate the Legation Quarter of Peking.

20 *June:*   Murder of the German Minister, Baron von Ketteler.

    4 p.m. Beginning of the siege of the Legations.

21 *June:*   An Imperial Decree was issued to Viceroys and Governors throughout the Empire, ordering them to organize the Boxers into train-bands or militia to resist the foreign aggressors. In Peking, Prince Chuang and Kang Yi were placed in command of them, and Prince Tuan organized 1400 bands of them.

20 & 25 *June:*   The Throne received Memorials from the southern Viceroys, urging that the Boxers be suppressed and that peaceful relations with the foreign Powers be restored.

29 *June:*   A Decree was issued to all Chinese ministers accredited to the foreign governments. This stated that 'China had no intention of making war on all countries' and that the Imperial Government would 'strictly order the commanders to protect the Legations to the best of their ability, and to punish the rebels so far as circumstances permit.'

3 *July* :   The Chinese Emperor (still the titular head of the Government, although a helpless on-

looker at events of which he wholly disapproved yet had no power to halt or change)
appealed to the rulers of Russia, England and
Japan, requesting their good offices for the
settlement of the crisis.

Yet on that very same day another Decree
was issued in the Emperor's name, informing
the Viceroys and Governors that there was
absolutely no possibility that China would
immediately negotiate for peace, and exhort-
ing them in categorical terms that they must
'sweep the word "peace" from their hearts'.

13 *July:*   The allied force captured Tientsin.

14 *July:*   The Throne received a joint Memorial from
the thirteen southern Viceroys and Governors.
This important document contained the
following requests :

1) the protection of all foreign merchants
   and missionaries according to the terms
   of the treaties.

2) Asking that an Imperial letter be sent to
   the German Government, expressing
   regret for the death of Baron von
   Ketteler.   Similarly, Imperial letters
   should also be sent to the United States
   and France, as those countries had been
   omitted in the list of previous letters to
   Russia, Britain and Japan.

3) A list of all those foreigners to be com-
   pensated for losses due to Boxer disturbances should be compiled by the Viceroy
   of Chihli and the Prefect of Shuntienfu.

4) An express Decree should be sent to the
   Viceroy of Chihli and military officials,
   ordering that any riots by rebellious
   'bandits' or troops should be forcibly
   suppressed.

At that time also warnings were served by the Powers on the Imperial Government that it would be held responsible for any injury suffered by the foreigners in the Legations.

On that same day the Tsungli Yamen again offered to evacuate the foreigners from Peking.

16 *July:* This offer was again repeated, but was refused jointly by the foreign ministers, whereupon the Chinese Government ordered a truce in the hostilities for further negotiation.

17 *July:* An Edict was issued embodying all the recommendations made by the southern Viceroys in their memorial of 14 July.

20 *July:* The Tsungli Yamen sent the presents of victuals to the defenders.

26 *July:* A second delivery of these was dispatched. But on that date the temporary truce came to an end.

These contradictory trends were all part of the same underlying pattern.

In 1900, with the possible exception of the Christian converts, who were nearly all 'stupid people', the whole Chinese nation as well as the Manchus longed for the expulsion of the foreigners from their soil. The Boxers personified this national desire. The only difference between the reactionaries and the moderates was one of the methods they favoured to achieve this end. The former would not stop at murder, nor at employing a rebellious rabble to attain it. The latter did not believe in any short cut to solving the problem, for they foresaw, rightly, that in the end it would lead to dreadful retaliation.

There was one person, however, who during those crazy months of turmoil and upheaval was simultaneously committed to *both* sides. That person was of course the Empress Dowager, playing the game so typical of her principle throughout her tenure of power : 'Heads I win; tails I also win.' But it was never so clearly demonstrated until then. This was the reason why the obviously contradictory policies of June and July were pursued until the sudden breaking-off of the truce on 26 July.

The Manchu Empress was committed to upholding the honour of her dynasty and the heritage of which she was the guardian : Imperial China. She was only too willing to ally herself with the Boxers in order forcibly to annihilate the hated foreigners attempting to carve up that heritage. Yet she cannily realized the necessity for some form of political insurance in the event of her failure to do so. Such insurance lay in the policy advocated by the moderates. That was why Old Buddha was blowing now hot, now cold, on alternate days : sometimes even within the same twenty-four hours.

The southern Viceroys—moderates to a man—were greatly exercised by the problem of preventing the conflict from spreading to their own territories whilst betraying no disloyalty to the Court at Peking. At so great a distance they could only submit memorials to the Throne. They nevertheless took measures which they considered necessary to restrain their hotheads.

It was the ingenious Director of Railways and Telegraphs who devised the face-saving formula which enabled them to dodge the duty of supporting the war effort enjoined on them by Imperial Decree. When hostilities had already begun at Taku, but before any actual declaration of war, he suggested to Li Hung Chang that 'such hostilities had started without orders from the Throne, and therefore peace should not be considered broken'.

Viceroy Li Hung Chang then took it upon himself to telegraph from Canton to the Chinese Ministers abroad that 'fighting at Taku was not ordered by the Throne' and to take steps for a truce and a negotiated peace. After the fall of Tientsin and the reception in Peking of the joint memorial of 14 July, the Viceroys seemed to be gaining ground. But a dramatic switch in the situation thwarted their efforts. The pro-war party in Peking was powerfully reinforced by the arrival there on 26 July of Li Ping-heng, the former Governor of Shantung.

Even at that late date Her Majesty the Empress Dowager was

not totally committed to Prince Tuan's side. After he had in-
veigled her into declaring war, the Prince became increasingly
bold and reckless. He even dared to lead a large party of Boxers
into the Forbidden City at six o'clock one morning. Their
declared aim was to search out and kill any converts who might
be hiding there.

Their intentions may, however, have been more sinister. Hsu
Tung, one of their most ardent supporters at Court, hated the
Emperor, knowing that for all his helplessness to prevent it,
Kuang Hsu was steadfastly opposed to the aggression against the
foreigners. This official may have invented and certainly repeated
one of the Boxer slogans in typically picturesque and threatening
metaphor: 'Before we can hope to drive these foreigners into
the sea,' he said, 'we must exterminate one Dragon, two tigers,
and thirteen sheep.' The Dragon was of course the Emperor; the tigers were Her Majesty's steadfastly anti-Boxer
advisers, Jung Lu and Li Hung Chang, and the sheep those other
high officials, Viceroys, Governors and statesmen, who supported
them.

The Emperor was still asleep in the Palace of Peaceful
Longevity. The Empress Dowager was drinking her morning tea.
Prince Tuan noisily demanded that the Emperor come out,
declaring that he was protecting the foreigners. But on hearing
the commotion, it was Old Buddha who suddenly appeared at
the top of the steps. She glanced down in cold fury at the Boxers
milling around in the sacred courtyard below her. Instantly
taking command of the situation, she asked Prince Tuan whether
he thought that he was Emperor. How dared he behave in
this insolent manner? She alone was the supreme power in the
land. Having made his son heir apparent, she might at a moment
wipe him out. She ordered the Prince and his Imperial abettors
to leave on the instant and to return only at her command. First,
however, they would prostrate themselves and humbly ask His
Majesty's pardon for their appalling behaviour. As a punishment,
they would be deprived of one year's emoluments. As for the
Boxer chiefs accompanying them, who had created this uproar
in the sacred Presence, they were condemned to instant behead-

ing by the Imperial Guard on duty at the gates, the sentence being carried out on the spot.

Sir Robert Hart's theory that a friend was withholding the full force of the attack was confirmed when Jung Lu's second-in-command, Tung Fu-hsiang, bitterly complained that his superior was depriving his Kansu troops of the artillery they needed to destroy the Legations utterly.

In his usual truculent form, and 'in a towering rage', Tung 'made straight for the Forbidden City, although the hour for audiences was long since past'. Defying all protocol, he burst in on his Imperial Mistress, whom he found quietly painting a design of bamboos on silk. Old Buddha was furious. Tung, too, was given the rough side of her tongue.

'Be silent!' she angrily commanded him. 'You were nothing but a brigand to begin with, and if I allowed you to enter my army it was only to give you an opportunity of atoning for your former misdeeds. Even now you are behaving like a brigand, forgetting the majesty of the Imperial Presence. . . . Your tail is becoming too heavy to wag. Leave the Palace forthwith. . . . '

Li Ping-heng, however, was a very different person from the brutal Prince Tuan and the uncouth Kansu general. He was that rare phenomenon amongst Chinese generals and officials, a completely honest public servant. 'After twenty-five years,' he wrote, 'attaining as high as governorship, what I have accumulated is a debt of 20,000 taels, but not a single month's food.'

Li Ping-heng had distinguished himself in the Sino-French conflict of 1885. After the murder of the two German missionaries in 1898, the German succeeded in having him deposed from the governorship of Shantung. But in the following year he was appointed Imperial Inspector of the Yangtze naval forces. Li was a genuine die-hard, an implacable opponent of all modernism, and one of the earliest supporters of the Boxers. He was against every foreign method and invention: such new-fangled things as railways, post offices, modern schools, mining, paper currency—the lot. But unlike his southern colleagues, when receiving the command to assist the war effort, Li did not prevaricate. He at once enthusiastically offered his services, which were as eagerly accepted. Three times he was ordered to speed up his arrival in Peking. And the effect of his appearance there was immediately apparent. A couple of days later the truce was broken and hostilities against the Legations were resumed.

When he was received in audience by Her Majesty, General Li's theme was that, 'Only when one can fight does one negotiate for peace.' This aggressive attitude reinforced Old Buddha's combative feelings with the authority of a successful commander. She was so pleased with him that she conferred on him the honour of riding within the Forbidden City and using a sedan-chair borne by two attendants. General Li was appointed Deputy-Commander of the four northern armies, of which Jung Lu was still Commander-in-Chief. And he finally swung over the Empress Dowager, who even then was still vacillating between her counsellors, to the side of the reactionaries.

They thereupon took advantage of this fortunate turn of events to liquidate those politicians who had so courageously opposed them in the Imperial Council; who had denounced the Boxers, and, when sent by Her Majesty with threatening messages to the British Minister, had deliberately distorted them into assurances of protection. Five brave men and able statesmen thus lost their lives. In addition to other charges, Li Shan, the Manchu, was accused of having protected the heroic defenders of the Peitang cathedral.

The Peking moderates were powerless. Prince Ching, an Elder Statesman of the Tsungli Yamen who had been replaced by Tuan, on 27 July sadly informed the southern Viceroys that, 'the Boxers in and out of the capital daily increase. It is true that they should be suppressed, so as to deprive the foreigners of their pretext for revenge. But the responsibility is too great for my humble abilities, and as the power is exercised by the Court [Her Majesty] I really dare not make any request.'

Jung Lu telegraphed to the southern Viceroys that, 'I have argued with all my efforts, but without in the least saving the situation. . . . The Boxer societies swarm in the streets like locusts, several thousands of them. . . . Death I do not mind, but the guilt I shall bear for all ages! What a grief!'

On 6 August Li Ping-heng left Peking for the Chihli front, where by that time the situation was looking grim for the Chinese army. General Nieh was defeated at Tientsin, when he was attacked both by the allied force and swarms of Boxers avenging themselves for his attempts to suppress them. He died in battle there. When the attackers routed the Chinese troops at Yangtsun, the previously over-optimistic Viceroy committed suicide, thus making the traditional honourable amends for his errors. Li Ping-heng arrived too late to turn defeat into victory. On 11 August, after the Chinese were decisively beaten at Tungchou, he also took his own life, true to the end to his overlords, his country and his convictions.

On the previous day, 10 August, news was at last received by the British Legation that the Relief Force was well on the way to Peking. The final onslaught on the weary defenders was a vicious one : there were several more killed and wounded. But on August 8 the firing slackened and the Tsungli Yamen sent letters to the Minister, expressing condolences on the deaths of the King of Italy and the Duke of Edinburgh—for throughout the siege such touches of comic fantasy were never wholly absent.

On 12 and 13 August the attack was considerably intensified, and a shell actually landed in the British Minister's bedroom. To the clanging of the Jubilee Bell the defenders prepared for a last overwhelming assault, which they feared would be the final one. But on the very next day they heard a new sound and their hearts rejoiced at it, for this was the fire of the Relief Force, as it blazed its way to their rescue at last. At 3 o'clock that afternoon the first of their rescuers entered the British Legation. The siege was over.

In his account of the Boxer uprising, sixty years later, Victor Purcell claimed that although 'to those beleaguered it must have been a terrifying experience, and to those actually engaged in the fighting a dangerous one, the total casualties on the foreigners' side only amounted to 66 killed and 150 wounded', and that this dramatic episode, which made so profound an impression on the Western world in 1900, 'was a small incident in the vast history of China'. From the Chinese point of view, however, this was not the case. It was the first nationalist and patriotic response organized by the Manchu dynasty to foreign occupation and the attempt of foreigners to foist on the people of China a foreign religion unwanted by the majority of them, whether rightly or wrongly. It was a futile, abortive attempt, foredoomed to failure, yet invested with an Oriental and savage grandeur : a popular uprising by the illiterate, semi-starving and fanatical Boxers and their allies, as well as the last bid to throw off the burden imposed by the unequal treaties made by the desperately pressed Empress Dowager.

The Venerable Old Buddha, the Motherly and Auspicious, living in the sacred precincts of the Forbidden City in a luxurious setting unrivalled by any European Court since the days of Versailles and Schönbrunn, the focal point of intriguing princes and politicians, was temporarily drawn into alliance with the northern Chinese populace—'the children of China' as she called them—with tens of thousands of her ragged subjects : freedom-fighters with empty bellies, whose red turbans and sashes in due course became as significant for the modern Chinese world as the French tricolour of 1789 for France.

There were many dramatic, absurd, and even comical incidents during those fifty-five days at Peking. Perhaps the most extraordinary and indirectly influential episode—that sent a thrill of horror throughout Europe—was one that never occurred at all. This was the story of the so-called Peking Massacre, reported by the Shanghai correspondent of the *Daily Mail,* F. W. Sutterlee, an 'Old China Hand'—a businessman of doubtful integrity, turned journalist. He had picked up various sensational and quite untrue reports about the fate of the Legations in the Shanghai vernacular Press. His dispatch was received in Europe 'with rage, grief and horror' as the truth. Sutterlee stated that in the night of 6-7 July the Chinese bombarded the British Legation and broke down the defence system :

Desperate fighting went on all night. Time and again the waves of attackers were hurled back. But at length the Europeans began to run out of ammunition. Early in the morning

of the 7th they . . . were overwhelmed. Every one alive was put
to the sword in the most atrocious manner.

When this sensational horror-story was printed the effect was
shattering. A Memorial Service for the victims was organized at
St Paul's Cathedral in London, to take place on 23 July. It was
only cancelled in the nick of time when the American State
Department received a telegram from the admirable Mr Conger,
revealing to the world that although the situation was a grim
one, all was not yet lost. 'For one month', it ran, 'we have been
besieged in the British Legation. Quick relief only can prevent
massacre.' Had the Relief Force not arrived on 14 August,
Sutterlee might only have been accused of anticipating the truth.

At the time, however, the false news had an electrifying effect,
especially on the German Emperor, Wilhelm II. He had already
invented the famous picture of the Yellow Peril. Like Adolf
Hitler, the Emperor fancied himself no end as an artist. He made
a sketch which was copied by a professional, Professor Knackfuss
of Cassel, and this was then engraved for propaganda purposes.
This picture, as described by its Imperial creator, showed 'the
powers of Europe represented by their respective Genii called
together by the Arch-Angel Michael—sent from Heaven—to
unite in resisting the inroad of Buddhism, heathenism and barbar-
ism, for the Defence of the Cross.' The European nations were
symbolized by a group of female figures recalling the Wagnerian
Valkyries with a very reluctant Britannia doubtfully holding back.

The *North German Gazette* described this famous Yellow Peril
cartoon as showing 'the path trodden by the Asiatic hordes in
their onward career . . . marked by a sea of flame proceeding
from a burning city. Dense clouds of smoke twisting into the form
of hellish distorted faces ascend from the conflagration. . . . '

Wilhelm II had been inspired by this vision five years before
the Boxers arrived in Peking. In 1897 the murder of the two
German missionaries in Shantung gave the Kaiser a providential
opportunity to dispatch a naval squadron there. He informed
Chancellor von Bülow that, 'Thousands of German Christians
will breathe more easily when they know that the German

Emperor's ships are near, hundreds of German traders will revel in the knowledge that the German Empire has at last secured a firm foothold in Asia.' And finally, 'hundreds of thousands of Chinese will quiver when they feel the iron fist of Germany heavy on their necks.'

China might well have reciprocated the Yellow Peril cartoon with one of her own, showing herself menaced by the 'Red-faced' peril. But her attempt to shake it off was defeated by the failure of the Boxer Rising.

When the European Powers organized the relief expeditions to rescue and avenge their nationals in Peking, the Kaiser, as usual, took a very high line. The German contingent was placed under the command of General von Waldersee. As he inspected these crack troops, glittering with metal, spit and polish, before they left Bremershafen on 27 July, the Kaiser made a speech to them. The unfortunate simile he then chose was to be quoted derisively ever afterwards by Germany's enemies:

> Let all who fall into your hands be at your mercy. Just as the Huns a thousand years ago, under the leadership of Attila, gained a reputation by which they still live in historical tradition, so may the name of Germany become known in such a manner in China, that no Chinese will ever again dare to look askance at a German.

In 1900 an allied enemy force entered Peking for a second time in forty years. On this occasion retribution even more savage and terrible was exacted from the unfortunate Chinese people.

21　*Flight from Peking*

At four o'clock in the afternoon of 14 August, Duke Lan, a younger brother of Prince Tuan, burst into the Presence unannounced, shouting as he did so:

'Old Buddha, the foreign devils have come!'

He was followed by Kang Yi, who had seen a detachment of turbaned troops in the grounds of the Temple of Heaven.

'Perhaps,' Her Majesty suggested hopefully, 'they are our Mohammedan braves from Kansu, come to demolish the Legations?'

They were in fact Indians, Sikhs under British command. Kang Yi insisted that Her Majesty must leave immediately, or they would take her life.

As had happened forty years previously, the Empress Dowager was very reluctant to leave. When she finally decided to do so, she set about organizing her departure with her usual thorough efficiency. Whilst those around her were in a state of panic Old Buddha remained calm and unflurried. At 3 a.m. the next morning, having had only one hour's rest, she changed from her fine silken robes into the ordinary blue cotton clothes of a Chinese peasant woman. For the first time in her life she discarded the aristocratic Manchu coiffure and had her hair dressed in the Chinese manner.

'Who would ever have believed it would come to this?' she wondered.

Three ordinary travelling carts, similar to those used all over the country, were ordered to stand by. Their drivers no longer wore the Imperial uniform.

Her Majesty decided that for safety's sake her party must be as small and inconspicuous as possible. At 3.30 a.m. she summoned the Emperor's concubines to inform them that they would not be going with herself and the Son of Heaven.

Among these young women was Chen Fei, the Pearl Concubine, who had once been so beautiful, but who had incurred the wrath of the Empress Dowager during the Hundred Days and had been kept in wretched semi-imprisonment ever since. She was no longer lovely, but half-starved and almost in rags. Yet with singular courage and rashness the poor girl threw herself at Her Majesty's feet, begging that the Emperor should be allowed to remain in Peking.

In this moment of crisis it was more than ever essential to Old Buddha to keep her nephew close to her own person. The Pearl Concubine's daring suggestion immediately aroused the Imperial fury.

'Throw this wretched minion down the well!' she commanded the eunuchs on duty.

At last Kuang Hsu mustered sufficient courage to intercede for the unfortunate concubine whom he still loved. He, too, fell on his knees, begging that her life be spared. Her Majesty sharply reminded him that this was no moment for argument. She repeated her command :

'Let her die at once!' And added, 'as a warning to all undutiful children, and to those *Hsiao* birds who when fledged peck out their mother's eyes.'

The eunuchs Li Lien-ying and Sung then seized the weeping concubine and threw her down a large well which was close to the Palace of Tranquil Old Age. Ever afterwards, it was believed to be haunted by the spirit of the unfortunate Pearl Concubine.

The reference to the *Hsiao* bird in this sentence of death was clearly understood by all those present. It was a direct allusion to the Emperor's insubordination two years previously, and to the important part played in his plotting at that time by his favourite. The Empress Dowager, as Matriarch, was dynastically the 'mother' of the Emperor and also of his First and Secondary wives. According to this code the unfilial behaviour of the Pearl Concubine was punishable by summary execution. The Empress's words and the drowning by the eunuchs of this rebellious daughter might therefore be interpreted as a death sentence immediately carried out according to traditional rules.

Had Chen Fei kept silent at that moment of crisis and general alarm, she might possibly have been overlooked by Her Majesty and left behind, together with the forgotten concubines of the late Tung Chih Emperor, to lead an obscure life in some quiet corner of the Forbidden City.

An official later version, which was undoubtedly inspired by the Empress Dowager herself, asserted that the Pearl Concubine had nobly and voluntarily committed suicide in the heroic tradition, by throwing herself into the well. Yet recalling the fate of A-lu-te, the First Wife of the Tung Chih Emperor, it seems unlikely that any young woman who might one day have emulated Yehonala's own example, if given the opportunity, had a very good prospect of longevity. At the dramatic moment of the flight from Peking, the Empress was given the chance to rid herself for ever of the lovely but over-ambitious Pearl Concubine, and, with her usual ruthlessness, promptly seized it.

As usual, when under strong emotional pressure, Kuang Hsu was trembling with grief and wrath. But, implacably, Old Buddha, still in supreme command of herself and everyone else, issued her orders to him and the others.

'Get into your cart and put up the screen,' she commanded Kuang Hsu, 'so that you are not recognized.' Like Her Majesty, he had already changed from his Imperial robes, and wore a plain black cloth gown and trousers. She commanded Prince Pu Lun to ride on the shaft of the Emperor's cart and look after him. The heir apparent, Pu Chun, was to ride similarly on the shaft of Her Majesty's own cart. As for Li Lien-ying, she told him that although he was a poor rider, he must shift as best he could to keep up with them. And as she was entering the common cart that was to carry her away from the Forbidden City and her enemies, Old Buddha ordered the carters to drive their hardest, and if any foreign devil should stop them to say nothing. She herself would speak to them and explain that they were but poor country folk, fleeing to their homes. She then ordered them to go to the Summer Palace.

So they set out, leaving by the *Te-sheng-men,* the Gate of Victory, on the north-east side of Peking. Already there was beginning a mass exodus from the fallen city. The Imperial carts with their disguised passengers had to wait in the queue like any others in that traffic jam, until they in their turn passed through the gates. But no foreign devils molested the Imperial refugees. When in due course Their Majesties arrived safely at the Summer Palace, the soldiers on duty there could not at first believe that this wrinkled old peasant woman was indeed their feared Mistress. They were only convinced that this was so when in furious tones Old Buddha demanded whether they failed to recognize her?

After a brief rest there, next day the Empress Dowager and the Emperor, with his First Consort and the Imperial Princesses, left on their long and arduous trek to safety. It was given out in the usual manner that His Majesty had gone on a tour of inspection. For the first time, now, Old Buddha was to meet her people.

The local district magistrate in a little town called Huai-lai, seventy miles from Peking, was Wu Yung, another of those scholar-administrators who for centuries managed to keep the internal economy of the country working somehow, despite drought and inundation, famine, riot and revolt. Wu had been fearless in facing his local Boxers, who repeatedly threatened to kill him. But he felt genuine terror when at only a few hours' notice he was instructed to meet Their Majesties at a little posting-station, Yu-lin, eight miles from Huai-lai, and to provide suitably for them.

Fleeing Boxers and deserting soldiery had ravaged and pillaged the whole district. When his sovereigns arrived and he fell to his knees in fear at their meeting, all Wu could offer them was a cauldron of millet porridge which he had had to guard at his peril throughout the preceding night. But the Empress Dowager—who until then had never sat down to a meal of less than one hundred courses—was kind.

'If you have millet porridge,' she told the trembling magistrate, 'that is good. Bring it quickly. In times of distress that is enough.'

After a feverish search, Wu had discovered five eggs in the kitchen-table drawer of a deserted shop. These he gave to Li Lien-ying.

'Old Buddha enjoyed the eggs very much,' the Chief Eunuch informed the gratified magistrate. 'She ate three, the remaining two she gave to the Lord of Ten Thousand Years.'

In the headlong flight, the eunuchs responsible had forgotten to provide food for the Imperial cavalcade, assuming that this could be bought or impressed from villagers or peasants along the road. But the countryside was devastated.

Li Lien-ying had not, however, forgotten Her Majesty's little medicine chest of sandalwood, divided into compartments containing such proven prophylactics or remedies as dried ginger-roots for colds and chills, Ten-thousand Cure Pills, and the famous Tiger ointment: a preparation of mentholated cream used throughout the realm to rub on wounds or sores.

Her Majesty dosed the miserable Emperor, suffering understandably enough from bouts of nausea, with some of these remedies. The young Empress was unable to stop herself from crying, which seriously annoyed Old Buddha, who at the best of times was irritated by any show of feminine weakness, and more than ever at this crisis. She gave the First Wife tranquillizers —probably opium pills—commanding her to take them and cease weeping.

When summoned before the Imperial Presences, Wu had tears in his eyes as he beheld their pitiable state.

'The house,' he wrote later, 'was divided into two rooms.' It was hardly better than a shack. 'In the centre was a square table, with a chair on either side. The Empress Dowager, dressed in cotton clothes, with her hair done in a simple knot on the top of her head, was sitting in the right-hand chair. . . . '

Her Majesty then almost broke down also, as she told him how she and the Emperor fled, having nothing to eat or drink.

'We were both cold and hungry.'

The wells along the roads were choked, many with floating human heads.

'Last night,' she said, 'the Emperor and I had only a bench between us, and we sat shoulder to shoulder, watching the sky for morning. At daybreak the cold was intense and chilled us through. . . . It is two days since we had food.'

After her delicious meal of eggs Old Buddha recovered, and wished to smoke her water-pipe. Wu also managed to provide her with five spills with which to light it. 'Having eaten her fill she had a contented look and her clothing was more in order.'

When his august guests arrived at Huai-lai, Wu put his official residence at their disposal. There they were a little more comfortable.

'When we left the palace,' Her Majesty told him, 'we were in a great hurry and did not bring many clothes. I have only what I am wearing. I am cold. Can you get us a few garments?'

Wu humbly explained that his wife was dead and he only possessed a few clothes that had belonged to his mother, and these, he feared, were too coarse for Old Buddha, who until then had always been swathed in the most precious silks and furs.

'That,' she replied, 'does not matter. If they warm my body, that is enough.' But the Emperor and the Imperial Princesses were in even worse plight.

Wu presented the party with all his own and his family's garments and toilet articles. When Her Majesty received him to thank him for these gifts, she and the Emperor were both wearing the clothes he had sent, and he saw 'that dignity had to some extent returned to their appearance. The two princesses also had on my long coats. . . . They no longer looked like dejected jackals.'

Her Majesty, even when she was dressed like a common

Chinese peasant woman, cold, tired and hungry, remained in command of the situation. As soon as she felt herself relatively safe from pursuit, she discarded her disguise and began again to grow the long Imperial fingernails which even before her hasty flight she had not forgotten to cut, in order that they might not betray her status. In spite of the physical hardships she had endured, the indomitable Old Buddha remained in robust health, enjoying with a good appetite what food was available, and finding herself for the first time, in her middle sixties, freed from the stringent restraint of protocol and the Forbidden City, eager to see what she could of her country and her subjects.

Fearing the outcome of the peace negotiations which Li Hung Chang and Prince Ching had meanwhile begun in Peking, the Empress Dowager was highly nervous of the consequences to herself of her last desperate attempt to liquidate the Christians and foreigners by means of the Boxers. This had failed, and now, she knew, retribution would be demanded of her. In order to forestall any attempt by the allies to capture the Emperor and herself, Old Buddha decided to settle in the province of Shensi, several hundred miles from Peking, to await events. On 23 August instructions were sent to the Governor of that province to prepare a palace for Their Majesties. Meanwhile they crawled along at leisurely pace, spending some weeks at Taiyanfu, where the 'Benevolent Countenance' beamed with delight on being shown the gold and silver vessels that had been made in 1775 for the use of the great Chien Lung Emperor. On another occasion, when a huge crowd of the 'stupid people' were pressing around Her Majesty, she told the harrassed officials trying to clear them away, 'Let them crowd around us as much as they like. It amuses me to see these honest country folk.'

And at other times she held up her cortège in order to view famous temples and ancient monuments.

At Taiyanfu there was also another, more sinister, entertainment. Yu Hsien, the Governor, who had been the Boxers' chief protector in his province, in the courtyard of his residence demonstrated to Her Majesty how he had had all the foreign missionaries in his district beheaded. At the height of her persecution of the Christians the Empress had telegraphed her governors, commanding that 'All foreigners—men, women and children—be summarily executed. Let not one escape, so that my empire may be purged of this noisome source of corruption, and that peace may be restored to my loyal subjects.' Yu Hsien had thoroughly carried out these instructions, and now described to his Imperial visitor the executions of the 'First Hairy Ones', as the missionaries were called, whilst the heir apparent, brandishing the huge executioner's sword brought in for this demonstration, pranced gaily around the courtyard.

The Imperial Council was depleted, for in the panic flight from Peking most of the ministers had been left behind. However, on 18 August the aged Grand Councillor Wang Wen-shao caught up with the Sacred Chariots, bringing with him the State Seal to be affixed to the Decrees, and gradually some system was restored to the travelling administration.

The Court finally reached Sianfu, the capital of the province of Shensi, on 28 October. In order to maintain some standards of comfort in this provincial setting, although it was far inferior to the luxury of Peking, and to provide for the protecting troops, eunuchs, ministers and officials who had gradually rejoined Their Majesties, the Imperial chest urgently needed refilling. Messengers went out to all Viceroys and Governors with the command that funds and tribute be sent immediately to Sianfu. And as these gradually arrived and accumulated the eunuchs soon reverted to their past habits.

About this time a letter was written to a friend in Peking by a Soochow official who had borne tribute from his province to the Imperial chest at Sian, in which he remarked that, 'The chief eunuch does not seem to be abusing his authority as much as usual ... most of his time and attention being given to the collection and safe keeping of tribute. If the quantity and quality is not up to his expectations he declines to accept it, and thus infinite trouble is caused to the officials of the province concerned.'

The Empress Dowager, this gossip wrote, 'looks very young

and well. One would not put her age at more than forty, whereas she is really sixty-four.'

The Emperor, although he had put on weight, as usual looked depressed. The letter continued with a detailed account of the peccadilloes of the tiresome heir apparent, who was consorting with the local actors and other riff-raff, causing brawls in the town 'which were bringing him into disrepute with respectable people', in spite of the fact that Old Buddha had had him severely whipped. His last offence was to commence an intrigue with one of the ladies-in-waiting on Her Majesty. He was 'much in the company of Li Lien-ying' who, following precedent, was leading him into 'the wildest dissipation'.

This letter ended with a significant passage.

Far from showing the least signs of repentance, Old Buddha was still cherishing hopes of defeating the foreigners. She had been particularly delighted by a Memorial in which an 'aboriginal tribesman' was recommended to Her Majesty by one of her courtiers, who offered 'to lose his own head and those of all his family, should this heaven-sent warrior fail to defeat all the troops of the Allies in one final engagement'.

There was little chance that this pipe-dream would be realized. Meanwhile, however, with her unfailing intuition, Old Buddha had removed herself and the Emperor far out of reach of their vindictive enemies. She was determined that when she did return to Peking it would be in her own good time and Imperial style.

22   *The Allies Exact Vengeance*

The double-edged policy of Her Majesty during the siege of the Legations had been a shrewd one. The Boxers had proved themselves a broken reed. But already at the beginning of July the Empress had taken the necessary steps to prepare for peace negotiations with her enemies.

On 12 July, to his considerable annoyance, old Li Hung Chang had been appointed Viceroy of Chihli. He had no intention of travelling north while Prince Tuan, whom he despised and detested, was still in supreme favour. On 23 July Li received in Shanghai—where he was temporarily resident—a telegram from the Empress Dowager.

'Li Hung Chang,' it ran, 'is to obey without question our earlier Decree, and is to hasten north regardless of other considerations. He must know that the crisis is very serious and that he can, therefore, offer no further valid excuses.'

The Court fled from Peking on 14–15 August; by the 18th the old statesman, nearly eighty, had arrived in Tientsin on his way to the capital, to take charge of the peace negotiations.

In spite of the calamities the criminally stupid policy of the reactionaries had brought on the dynasty, even in Sian Old

Buddha remained loyal to those who still served her faithfully. Prince Tuan, by no means in disfavour as yet, was actually made head of the Imperial Council, and Her Majesty's grief was great and sincere on learning that that most virulent reactionary, her devoted servant Kang Yi, had died in the course of flight, on the way to rejoin her. In defeat the remainder of the pro-Boxer faction clung tenaciously to their Motherly, if no longer so Auspicious, benefactress. Old Wang Wen-shao, who had never openly supported the Boxers, but had not dared, either, to oppose those who did so, was the only liberal member of the Council, until to Her Majesty's immense relief and delight she was re-joined by Jung Lu, of whom she was now going to have greater need than ever, as a kind of liaison officer between herself and Li Hung Chang in far-away Peking.

After the fall of the capital, Jung Lu's position was for a short time a very dangerous one. It was not until much later than the summer of 1900 that he was finally fully vindicated as a secret sympathizer with the foreigners, who had deliberately with-held from his fiery deputy, Tung Fu-hsiang, the guns that could have wiped out the Legation defenders in a matter of hours. When the allied troops entered Peking, the Chinese attack collapsed immediately and completely. Jung Lu was unable to maintain any discipline among his men, who fled in all directions. He himself, knowing that his life was threatened, wisely left for Paoting and safety.

It was Li Hung Chang who with his usual astuteness, knowing Jung Lu's reliability as well as his enormous influence over Tzu Hsi, suggested to Her Majesty that her Commander-in-Chief be appointed to the Grand Council. For the terms the allies were imposing on China were harsh indeed.

This desire for vengeance and insistence on the maximum penalties for the principal war-criminals who had provoked the siege of the Legations was not unnatural. Many innocent foreign men, women and children had been cruelly tortured and suffered horrible deaths. Only the severest retribution, on Old Testament lines, their Christian compatriots maintained, would avert any future recurrence of such horrors.

Yet even in defeat, and safely ensconced at Sian with this very eventuality in mind, the Empress Dowager fought like a mother tigress to preserve her Imperial relatives from retribution.

Jung Lu knew as well as Li Hung Chang, Yuan Shi-kai, and the southern Viceroys, who at a distance were intervening actively and judiciously in the negotiations between Peking and Sian, that the condign punishment of Prince Tuan and his associates was inevitable.

Realizing at last that she must swiftly take some steps to comply with the demands of the victors, on 25 September Her Majesty issued an Edict depriving Tuan of all his offices : he was to be handed over to the Imperial Clansmen's Court for further punishment. The lesser princes and dukes who had supported him were also to be deprived of their titles. The Board of Censors was instructed to deal with the reactionary ministers.

But these mild measures met with such emphatic opposition from the irate Powers in Peking that at the end of October Li Hung Chang informed Her Majesty that he could make no further progress with the peace negotiations until much severer penalties were imposed on the pro-Boxer faction at Court.

Finally and very reluctantly, after procrastinating as long as possible, Old Buddha was obliged to give in. Announcing this in an Edict published in the Emperor's name, she provided herself at the same time with an alibi in terms that might have brought tears to the eyes of a crocodile :

> The dangers that have been incurred by Her Majesty the Empress Dowager and myself are simply indescribable, and our hearts are sore, aching with unappeased wrath at the memory of our sufferings. . . .
>
> Prince Tuan, already cashiered, was the leader and spokesman of the Imperial Clan, to whom was due the declaration of war against foreigners; he trusted implicitly in Boxer magic, and thus inexcusably brought about hostilities. Duke Lan, who assisted Prince Chuang in drawing up the proclamation which set a price on the head of every foreigner, deserves also that he be stripped of all his dignities and titles; but remembering

that both these Princes are our near kinsmen, we mitigate their sentence to exile to Turkistan, where they will be kept in perpetual confinement.

This Decree also ordered the execution of Yu Hsien, ex-Governor of Shensi; the posthumous degradation of Kang Yi; the compulsory suicide of Ying Nien, Vice-president of the Censorate, and of the Grand Counsellor Chao Shu-chiao. The Empress Dowager fought for a long time before she agreed to this last execution—of one of her special favourites—but in the end was obliged to decree it.

The Allies were also demanding the execution of the Kansu general, Tung Fu-hsiang, who had led the most vicious attacks on the Legations; but Jung Lu protected his subordinate. In any case the Moslem leader had a great following in his native Kansu: his troops, still numbering 15,000, were stationed in Sian and might have given serious trouble had their general's life been taken. So Tung had the good fortune merely to be deprived of his command, and ordered back home.

Old Buddha's chief preoccupation, however, was to protect herself from any attempt by the allies to deprive her of power. She clearly foresaw that in order to retain it, she must give herself a new image, and her future policies a new look. Therefore, by a stroke of superlative hypocrisy Her Majesty ordered that all her pro-Boxer Decrees and Edicts be expunged from the records of the Ching dynasty.

Her Majesty applied another thick coat of whitewash to her pro-Boxer activities in a Penitential Decree the Emperor was compelled to issue on the same day. In this Kuang Hsu took the blame for the Boxer catastrophe on himself, whilst referring to 'Our Mother', Tzu Hsi, in glamorous terms, recalling her gifts of wine, fruit and vegetables to the besieged Legations, and, in a well-turned dramatic passage, describing how,

When our Capital fell . . . Her Majesty the Empress Dowager and ourselves decided to commit suicide in the presence of the tutelary deities of our Dynasty. . . . But at the critical moment of dire lamentation and confusion, we were

seized by our Princes and Ministers, and forcibly led away
from that place where bullets fell like rain and where the
enemy's guns gathered thick as forest trees. . . . The imminent
danger of Her Sacred Majesty, the overwhelming ruin of our
ancestors' inheritance, our prosperous Capital turned to a
howling wilderness, its ravines filled with the dead bodies of
our greatest men; how can it possibly be said that the Throne
could protect the rebels who brought such disasters upon us?

And it was true that the unfortunate and impotent Emperor,
now forced to make atonement, was not responsible for them.

There still remained one embarrassment to be removed. After
Prince Tuan's disgrace it was obvious that his son could not continue to be heir apparent to the Emperor. He had, moreover,
proved himself utterly unworthy of the high honour Her Majesty
had bestowed on him. She now withdrew it. As she could not
loose face by thus admitting the error of judgment she had made
in conferring it, the recipient was compelled to petition for his
own demotion on the grounds of his father's guilt. Old Buddha
further marked her displeasure with the young lout by degrad-
ing him to the lowest rank an Imperial Duke might hold, with
no salary or emoluments.

The Allies insisted also—with the full approval of Li Hung
Chang and Prince Ching, and no doubt also the Emperor, had
he been allowed a say in the matter—on posthumous honours
being awarded to the dead ministers who, after their vain attempt
to stop the attack on the Legations, were condemned to death
and executed during the brief triumph of the reactionaries.

And posthumous honours were also later awarded by the im-
penitent Matriarch to the Pearl Concubine, who was praised for
her admirable courage, 'which led her virtuously to commit
suicide when unable to catch up the Court on its departure' from
Peking.

The peace negotiations were protracted and complicated,
bedevilled by the rivalries between the victorious allies.

China was not the only bone of contention at that time

between the European Great Powers, whilst Japan was the rival of them all in the struggle for hegemony in the Far East. Russia and Japan were in deadly competition for the mastery of Manchuria; but at that stage of the game both of them found it expedient to pose as China's friend. In view of Germany's and Great Britain's antagonism to Li Hung Chang, whom they regarded with some justification as a heavily bribed Russian agent, the Russian representative in Peking took the Chinese plenipotentiary under his protection. The Russians professed to have no interest in severely punishing the Chinese for the Boxer atrocities, since they had no missionaries in the country whose murders they were out to avenge. Li Hung Chang had no particular illusions about Russian motives, but he immediately appreciated Count Witte's point when that minister of the Tsar urged him to begin the peace negotiations before the arrival in September of Field-Marshal von Waldersee, the Kaiser's representative.

In spite of the murder of Sugiyama, the Japanese were also posing as friends of China, giving their protection to the aged and timorous Prince Ching, who, although appointed most reluctantly as the representative of the Imperial Family and Court, in fact left these highly difficult and complicated negotiations almost entirely to Li Hung Chang.

Germany, more implacable than ever since the murder of von Ketteler, regarded the Russians as more in alliance with the Chinese than with the other European Powers. With typical Prussian arrogance, Count von Waldersee went out of his way to offend the Chinese by installing himself on arrival in Peking in the *I-luan-Tien,* the private palace of the Empress Dowager, and flatly refusing to receive Li Hung Chang, whom the Germans and British quite wrongly treated as if he were the friend and and representative of Prince Tuan, the arch war-criminal. The German soldiery obeyed their sovereign's order to behave like the Huns so conscientiously that the Chinese people hated them more intensely than all the other occupation troops.

The United States showed far greater tolerance and moderation towards the defeated Chinese. On 3 July, whilst the Legations were still besieged, the American Secretary of State, John Hay, telegraphed to the other Powers that his Government was concerned to ensure 'permanent safety and peace to China' and unlike the rest of them at that time, to preserve 'Chinese territorial and administrative entity'. Nor had the American admiral joined in the attack on the Taku forts. The American Government now objected to the ultimatum served on Li Hung Chang by the other Powers, and especially to their demand that before any negotiations began at all the pro-Boxer ministers be handed over to the Allies for punishment.

After a good deal of such wrangling with one another, the Powers at last agreed on the expectedly harsh peace terms. These were set out in a joint Note presented to the Chinese negotiators on 24 December. It contained twelve articles:

Article 1 stipulated that an Imperial Prince was to head an expiatory mission to Berlin for the murder of Baron von Ketteler, and that a monument to that diplomat was to be erected on the spot where he was killed.

Article 2 provided for the severest punishment of the pro-Boxers, and in retaliation, in clause (b), the suspension of all official examinations for five years in all the towns where foreigners were massacred.

Article 3 demanded honourable reparation to the Japanese Government for the murder of Mr Sugiyama.

Article 4 that expiatory monuments should be erected in desecrated Christian cemeteries.

Article 5 dealt with the prohibition of the importation of arms and war material.

Article 6 dealt with the crucial matter of the indemnities to be paid to governments, societies, private individuals, as well as for Chinese . . . in consequence of their being in the service of foreigners.

Article 7 arrogated to each Power the right to maintain a permanent guard for its Legation, and to place the Legation quarter (in which no Chinese were to be allowed to live) in a strong state of defence.

Article 8 insisted on the razing of the Taku forts and others that might impede free communications between Peking and the coast.

Article 9 stipulated that by mutual agreement the Powers should have the right of military occupation of certain strategic points between Peking and the sea.

Article 10 insisted on the perpetual prohibition under pain of death of being a member of an anti-foreign Society.

Article 11 demanded that the Chinese Government negotiate amendments favourable to the Powers to existing Treaties of Commerce and Navigation.

Article 12 finally, dealt with protocol, demanding that the Chinese Government reform the office of Foreign Relations, and modify the Court ceremonial relative to the reception of foreign Representatives.

The crux of the matter was in *Article* 6 : the question of the indemnity. What was the maximum sum that could be extorted from the Chinese? The United States Minister made a valiant attempt to have this sum fixed at what the Chinese might in fact be considered able to pay, namely 40,000,000 pounds. But he was overruled by his colleagues, who fixed the indemnity at the colossal sum of 450,000,000 taels of silver (67,000,000 pounds).

'With accrued interest over the period of thirty-nine years, the sum exceeded 980 million taels. An addition of 20 million pounds a year was thus added by the protocol to the burdens of the impoverished Chinese people. . . . Europe's treatment of China in the whole period from 1895 onwards had been devoid of all consideration and all understanding,' wrote one British authority, who described these terms as humiliating and crippling, whilst an American stated that, 'hardly anywhere in the diplomatic correspondence does one find any appreciation of the feelings of the Oriental or any sympathy for the crude efforts made at reform.'

When news of the Boxer Rising was received in St Petersburg, the Russian War Minister, according to his colleague, Count Witte, the Finance Minister, declared : 'I am very glad. This will give us an excuse for seizing Manchuria. . . . '

All the Russians were concerned with was to drive their railway line through Manchuria to the seaboard, and gain control of the three northern provinces. When the Boxers tore up the rails and did other damage to the railroad, the Russians seized on the necessity to restore order as a pretext for occupying these provinces, and in their turn committing atrocities on their inhabitants. Their alibi in Peking, meanwhile, was to pose as the friends of the Chinese during the peace negotiations. As Peter Fleming wittily put it, 'if you earn the gratitude of a half-drowned man by successfully applying artificial respiration, there is a chance that he will overlook the fact that you have stolen his wallet in the process. . . . '

In Manchuria, the Chinese troops under the Tartar general Tseng Chi were totally defeated by the Russians, and, without memorializing the Throne, the general then concluded a treaty of surrender with the Russian general, Alexeieff. The Manchu Empress had a special allegiance to the land of her forebears, and was not unnaturally furious when news of this agreement first reached her at Sian via a report of it in the London *Times* of 3 January 1901. Yet China could not afford to antagonize the Russians, and the Chinese plenipotentiary in St Petersburg, the ambassador, Yang Ju, was instructed to negotiate a new treaty. Triangular and complicated negotiations between St Petersburg, Peking, and Sian—with the southern Viceroys also intervening in this case—continued throughout the winter and spring of 1901. In spite of Russian coaxing and bullying, Yang Ju managed successfully to resist signing a separate treaty with that country whilst negotiations for a general agreement with the Joint Powers were continuing in Peking. And, matching the Russian moves, the southern Viceroys cunningly managed to 'leak' information of the negotiations to the diplomatic representatives in their provinces.

The British, Germans, and the Japanese in particular, were implacably opposed to Russia's designs on Manchuria. In her weakness, China's only means of defence was to take this advantage of the discord among her enemies. In 1895 the Western Powers had frustrated Japan's attempts to seize Korea. This time, in April 1901, their mutual rivalries compelled the Russians to abandon their attempt to negotiate this separate agreement.

The Peace Protocol between the foreign Powers and the Chinese representatives, based on the Joint Note of the previous January, was finally signed in Peking on 7 September 1901. More than a year had passed since Her Majesty's flight from the Imperial City. Yet in spite of repeated demands from the Powers that the Court should return to Peking, the Empress Dowager still tarried in Sian. Her Majesty was fully determined only to return to Peking on her own terms. Once she was assured that she might do so safely, she hesitated no longer. She had fled from her capital in appalling conditions. She would re-enter it in such triumph as no previous monarch in history ever achieved.

23   Her Majesty's Triumph

Presumably there was no time to consult the Court astrologers before the flight from Peking, but before the return this was done very carefully indeed.

After much consultation, the date fixed for the Court's departure from Sian was the 24th of the 8th moon: 20 October 1901.

The party, headed by Her Imperial Majesty and the Son of Heaven—who was obliged always to travel a little in advance of the Motherly and Auspicious in order to welcome her with the obligatory kowtows at each halting place—included Kuang Hsu's sullen young Empress; the Princess Imperial, Old Buddha's adopted daughter; the wife of Jung Lu; and Court Ladies in attendance. There were not quite as many eunuchs as in the past, but under Li Lien-ying their numbers increased, as those who had deserted during the evil days now rejoined the Imperial service. There was, of course, a strong military bodyguard, both for the Sacred Chariots and for the almost equally sacred treasure, in vast quantities, that they were bringing back with them to their capital. In addition to many taels of gold and silver, this included priceless carpets, woodwork and porcelains for the refurbishing and decoration of their residences, and such personal gifts as jade, jewels and silks of all hues, exquisite embroideries and rare furs in profusion.

When the procession reached Kai-feng, in Honan, Their Majesties remained there for several weeks. Two important events occurred during this halt. The first was Old Buddha's sixty-sixth birthday. At Sian she had refused to allow any ostentatious celebration of her anniversary in view of the country's poverty, the desolation of war, and its tragic consequences. But now, news of the signing of the Peace Treaty having reached her, the Empress permitted her loyal subjects once again to offer the traditionally magnificent presents and entertainments, including several theatrical performances : for she never lost her delight in these, and even at Sian, actors had been sent for to provide them.

On 18 August in the previous year, Li Hung Chang, then in Tientsin, had written some moving lines in his Diary :

> A rest of a few days, and then I will proceed to Peking to stay the hand of the Powers as much as in me lies. Oh, if my own hand were not so weak and my cause so much weaker! The Court is in hiding and the people are distracted. There is no Government, and chaos reigns. I fear the task before me is too great for my strength and body, though I would do one thing more before I call the earthly battle over. I would have the foreigners believe in us once more, and would not deprive China of her national life; and I would like to bring Old Buddha back to the palace, and ask her if she had learned a lesson.

The Grand Old Man did indeed accomplish his task, but did not live to ask that interesting question of the Imperial Mistress whom he had so faithfully served for more than thirty years. He died at Peking, in his eightieth year, on 7 November 1901, almost two months to the day before Old Buddha's return there.

Li Hung Chang was the greatest Chinese statesman of the nineteenth century, and, according to his own Confucian code, high-principled. He was a masterly diplomat and bargainer; as Chester Tan excellently put it, 'to oppose what was impossible and to accept what was inevitable was his guiding principle in the peace negotiations'. In the Preface to his Memoirs, the Hon. John Foster described him as 'the greatest of Oriental statesmen and one of the most distinguished of the public men of the world'.

Li's devotion to Old Buddha was as unswerving as it was critical. Were there any doubt of this woman's intellectual brilliance, it would be eliminated by the personal respect in which he held her throughout his life. He made no concessions nor allowances for any of her weaknesses on grounds of femininity, and in their dealings with one another they were always on terms of intellectual parity. They frequently quarrelled. She blamed him unjustly for the disastrous defeat of China by Japan in 1894-5, and for some time he was in disgrace. He, driven to despair by her apocalyptic vision of the Boxers as the potential saviours of China, never minced his fervent denunciations of them.

Now, returning in triumph to her capital, Old Buddha, when at Kai-feng she learned of the death of Li Hung Chang, made the most honourable amend possible to his memory, ordering that a shrine be built to him at Peking: the highest honour ever bestowed on a Chinese subject by the Ching dynasty.

The Empress had learned her lesson and was now prepared 'to accept what was inevitable' : but as usual, after her own fashion.

The next stage on this triumphal progress was the crossing of the Yellow River by the Imperial party : a scene of the highest pageantry. Their Majesties, after making the ritual sacrifices to the River God, embarked in a splendid barge expressly built at enormous cost by the local officials in the shape of a dragon, its gilt and lacquer sparkling in the clear autumn sunshine. The barge and its richly dressed passengers—Their Majesties surrounded by Court ladies and 'musical maidens' dazzlingly pretty to tempt the eye and ear—attracted an enormous crowd to watch the scene from the banks, as the Empress Dowager and the Son of Heaven beamed graciously on their subjects.

Old Buddha now began her new campaign of benign affability by issuing a Decree ordering that on her entry into Peking, foreigners would be welcome to watch her arrival : cancelling the former stern rule that no one was ever allowed in the streets when an Imperial procession passed.

The terms of the Peace Protocol had laid down the procedure for future State visits of foreign envoys to Imperial audiences. Anticipating the inevitable, however, Old Buddha did not wait until these were forced on her, but announced in another welcoming Decree that the foreign Ministers would be received in the central Throne Hall of the Palace immediately following His Majesty's arrival, and that Her Majesty looked forward to renewing her former entertainment of their ladies.

On the last lap of her return, Old Buddha enjoyed a new thrill, for which she had longed ever since she had planned to visit Jung Lu at Tientsin with the Emperor, a visit that had to be postponed owing to the dramatic events of the Hundred Days. This was to ride in a railway train. An account of this remarkable journey was published in the *Times* on 2 March 1902 :

> The hour for leaving Cheng-ting fu was fixed by the Empress Dowager at 9.30 a.m. on January 3rd. It is significant of the character of this remarkable woman that she leaves nothing to chance . . . the long arm of her unquestioned authority reaches from the Throne literally to the servants' quarters . . . the master-mind which has guided the destinies of China for the last forty years by no means disdains to concern itself in minor matters of household commissariat and transport.

It was noticed by the great crowd that witnessed the Imperial train's departure that on the platform Her Majesty stood close beside Li Lien-ying as the Chief Eunuch and his assistants checked the unloading of the huge quantities of baggage containing tribute and treasure.

There were twenty-one carriages on the train. One of them was reserved for Jung Lu, Yuan Shi-kai and other high officials, and was between the Emperor's and the Empress Dowager's, which were ' . . . luxuriously furnished with costly curios and upholstered in Imperial yellow silk; each had its throne, divan, and reception-room. . . . '

At Pao-ting, the statesmen, finding themselves uncomfortably cramped in their shared carriage, complained to the railway officials, who thereupon obliged them with another first-class coach. But, 'Her Majesty immediately noticing this, called for explanations, which failed to meet with her approval. The extra carriage was removed forthwith, Yuan Shi-kai and his colleagues being reluctantly compelled to resume their uncomfortably crowded quarters; to these Her Majesty paid a visit of inspection before leaving the station, making inquiries as to the travellers' comfort, and expressing complete satisfaction at the arrangements generally. . . . '

It may be noted that the Chief Eunuch was provided with a first-class carriage all to himself, similar to those of the Imperial Princes.

' . . . a sign of the times . . . the Empress Dowager's sleeping compartment was furnished with a European bed. *Per contra*, it contained also materials for opium-smoking, of luxurious yet workmanlike appearance.'

This addiction of Old Buddha's was not, however, a sinister habit. After the day's work millions of her subjects, from the great and rich to the poorest coolies, took a small pipe or so without the slightest ill-effects. Opium, like nicotine or any other drug, is only harmful when it becomes an excessive and compulsive habit. The Empress's biographers, Bland and Backhouse, gave the following cosy account of her use of it :

Opium, like other luxuries, she took in strict moderation, but greatly enjoyed her pipe after the business of the day was done. It was her practice then to rest for an hour, smoking at intervals, a *siesta* which the Court knew better than to disturb. She fully realised the evils wrought by the abuse of the insidious drug, and approved of the laws, introduced by the initiative of Tang Shao-yi and other high officials, for its abolition. But her fellow-feeling for those who, like herself, could use it in moderation, and her experience of its soothing and stimulating effect on the mind, led her to insist that the Abolition Decree (November 22 1906) should not deprive persons over sixty years of age of their accustomed solace.

This was another instance of Old Buddha's flashes of insight. Nothing would have been simpler for the undisputed autocrat—who refused an additional railway carriage to her devoted servants Jung Lu, Yuan Shi-kai and their colleagues because she thought it presumptuous of them to have demanded it—than to have prohibited the use of opium to all her subjects whilst continuing secretly to smoke it herself. But by expressly excluding her own age-group from the general prohibition, she unashamedly identified her proclivities with those of her people.

Her Majesty took great pleasure in her first railway journey. It was, however, of capital importance to her that the train should arrive punctually—not according to any modern time-table, but to bring her into Peking at the exact hour the Imperial astrologers had appointed for her return. This having been accomplished, she took the same minute interest in the unloading of the precious baggage as she had done when it was entrained.

It was also considered necessary that the Imperial party should alight from the train and enter Peking with the traditional state : first into the Chinese City through the *Yung Tien Men,* then up the broad central road to the famous *Chien Men,* the great gate to the Tartar City, of which the tower had been destroyed by fire during the early days of the Boxer Rising and the siege. Over the gate, however, there remained a lunette, a kind of balcony with several deeply recessed windows.

Her Majesty had already let it be known that foreigners were to be permitted in future to gaze at her august person. Most of them had gathered on this high point of vantage for a sight of the Imperial procession. No doubt none of them ever forgot it, for no Caesar, returning to Rome in triumph from his victories, did so with greater pomp—or with greater audacity—than the defeated Empress who had fled from Peking in a common cart, disguised as an old peasant woman :

There was a strong wind and much dust. But all Peking had

collected on the top of the wall. . . . First to arrive were the
Manchu Bannermen on their fiery little horses. Next came a
group of Chinese officials in gala robes, and finally the
Imperial palanquins, which advanced at an almost incredible
speed between two lines of kneeling soldiers. The higher the
rank of the person carried in a palanquin, the faster he should
go. The Court chairs, on that memorable occasion seemed to
move as fast as the Tartar cavalry.

When they reached the enclosure between the wall and the
outer lunette, the chairs halted and the Emperor and Empress
stepped down, to carry out the ceremony, prescribed by the
Rites for a home-coming: that is to say, to burn incense and
recite some prayers in the tiny temple built up against the side
of the wall. In that temple there was a shrine to the tutelary
gods of the Manchus.

As she got out of her chair, the Empress glanced up at the
smoke-blackened walls and saw us; a row of foreigners, watching her arrival from behind the ramparts. The eunuchs
appeared to be trying to get her to move on, as it was not
seemly that she should remain there in full view of every-
body. . . .

This, however, was her deliberate new policy:

. . . the Empress was not to be hurried, and continued to
stand between two of her ladies, who held her up under the
arms on either side, not because she needed any support, but
because such is the custom in China, when a great personage
appears in public on a ceremonial occasion. The Emperor
stood and waited a little distance off. . . .

—knowing only too well who was the star in this superb performance.

At last she condescended to move, but before entering the
temple where the bonzes were all ready to begin the ceremony,
she stopped once more and, looking up at us, lifted her closed
hands under her chin, and made a series of little bows.

The effect of this gesture was astonishing. We had all gone

up on to the wall, in the hope of catching a glimpse, as she passed, of this terrible Empress, whom the West considered almost an enemy of the human race. But we had been impressed by the magnificence of the swiftly moving pageant, and by the beauty of the picturesque group, in palanquins of yellow satin, flashing with gold. Something told us that the return of the Court to Peking marked a turning-point in history, and in our breathless interest we forgot our resentment against the woman who was responsible for so much evil. That little bow, made to us who were watching her, and the graceful gesture of the closed hands, took us by surprise. From all along the wall there came an answering, spontaneous burst of applause. The Empress appeared pleased. She remained there for a few moments longer, looking up and smiling. Then she disappeared within the temple.

It was as simple as that. All was forgiven and forgotten.

By the magic of Old Buddha's gesture, East and West were once again all one happy family.

24   The New Look

Her Majesty's homecoming was not at first altogether joyful.
She had never forgotten nor forgiven the wrecking of the
Summer Palace in 1860. Forty years later, when she was obliged
again to leave the Forbidden City, she anticipated with bitter
hindsight that looting and plunder by the allied soldiery would
follow her departure. This time, therefore, she had taken certain
precautions to conceal her treasure-store.

In Sian the Empress learned with justified fury of the sacking
of the Imperial City and the second wrecking of the Summer
Palace. Even uglier than the looting was the vandalism, the wanton
destruction of irreplaceable works of art. In their search for the
Empress's hidden treasury, worth millions, the robbers destroyed
masterpieces of painting, pottery, cloisonné and carvings which
might have concealed gold and silver coins. Even so, for years
afterwards antique and curio dealers all over the world became
rich on the proceeds of the 1900 looting. A story was told at the
time illustrating the cynical greed with which the despoilers went
about their work:

'That is a fine sable coat! Bring it along.'

'But there is a Chinaman inside.'

'Give it a shake. He will fall out.'

'Which he did, only too pleased to escape with his life.'

Old Buddha, however, did partially succeed in beating the robbers. For on her return to Peking she found that the bundles of jewels and gold plate she had ordered the eunuchs to put down the wells were intact. Her private treasury was so cleverly bricked up that although hundreds of searchers must have passed it by time and time again, it was never discovered nor broken into.

An army of eunuchs was immediately set to work, rebuilding, restoring, repainting, regilding and replanting. The wrecked palaces were soon as splendid as ever, the weeds in the courtyards pulled up, and the ruined or stolen ornaments, screens, vases, thrones and carpets, replaced by those brought from Sian. One treasure among others that were irreplaceable was Her Majesty's personal great jade seal, which had vanished for ever in the confusion of her flight. And who would not sympathize with her disgust when Li Lien-ying showed her a photograph he had procured of a foreign devil, who had himself snapped sitting 'low on her throne, a leg across either arm of the yellow-cushioned chair, staring idiotically into the camera'?

The Old Buddha had undoubtedly, as Li Hung Chang hoped, learned her lesson. But as if to remind herself of it—and to nourish until the end of her life the hatred inspired in her by those who had forced it on her—there were two repairs that the Empress firmly refused to allow. The wheelmarks made by the allies' guns when they had been driven into the grounds of the Summer Palace were never obliterated, and the shell-hole in the wall of one of the buildings in the Winter Palace was never filled in.

Palaces might be restored, new treasures accumulated, gardens be brought into fresh flowering, as lovely as ever. But a little more than one year after Her Majesty's triumphal return to Peking she was faced with an irreparable loss.

Jung Lu continued to serve Yehonala as faithfully as ever. Since the death of Li Hung Chang he was her closest adviser and intermediary in diplomatic matters. But the foreigners had been and still were convinced that as former Commander-in-Chief

Jung Lu was the individual most responsible for the attack on the Legations, and he was obliged to accept so many slights from them that he finally attempted to resign. Her Majesty, as he might have anticipated, would not hear of it, and issued a Decree extolling him as the saviour of the Empire, whilst refusing his prayer.

Jung Lu died on 11 April 1903, at the age of sixty-seven. His death was a terrible blow to Yehonala, whom he had loved and served for so long and who, although very rarely showing any capacity for deep affection for another human being, almost certainly did love him as far as her ruthless ambition allowed. Der Ling claimed that she was 'at her side when word came that Jung Lu had passed away. For a moment she closed her eyes, and the hands on her lap clenched until the knuckles whitened with strain. There was pain in her face; but when she had conquered herself . . . the face which peered out at a suddenly darkened world was the face of a graven image, from which the sunlight of a strange companionship had vanished.'

Yehonala bestowed high posthumous honours on her faithful lover and servant, although the greatest was held in reserve until her own end was imminent. Her genuine sorrow at his death was clearly visible. Four days later Her Majesty went by train— usually a very gay occasion for her—to visit the magnificent tombs of her dynasty in the Western Hills. Her brother, Duke Kuei Hsiang, was kneeling on the platform to receive her. 'You,' she told him bitterly, 'have killed Jung Lu by recommending that useless doctor'—and without another word to him she entered her palanquin.

Although the Empress Dowager had lost her two wisest counsellors, Jung Lu and Li Hung Chang, she did her best to act according to their prayers and advice. Her most influential adviser was now Yuan Shi-kai, who although still only in his middle fifties became her Elder Statesman and foremost member of the Imperial Council.

In spite of sufficient reasons for continued hatred and bitterness, the Empress Dowager stuck to the new line she had laid down on her return to Peking. Her Majesty's affability towards the foreign diplomats and their wives redoubled. Her parties for these women were more splendid than ever, and she observed her social success with cynical amusement. The ladies simply fell over backwards in their admiration and praise of her graciousness and charm. One of them, Lady Susan Townley, wrote how difficult it was to realize that 'this friendly little woman with the brown face of a kindly Italian peasant was the mysterious and powerful autocrat who had deliberately debased and degraded the unfortunate Emperor sitting beside her; the fiend who had egged on the Boxers to nameless outrages'.

The Empress Dowager would not have been flattered by that patronizing description of herself. And the older she grew the more flattery she needed. Until the end of her life she remained wholly feminine at heart. Like other queens and most women, she fought an intense losing battle against advancing age : dyeing her hair black and covering her face with thick layers of make-up.

How Her Majesty wished to look—not a day over forty— could be seen in the portrait of her painted by Miss Katherine Carl, a protégée of Mrs Conger, the American Minister's energetic wife. According to Der Ling, it was difficult to persuade Old Buddha to sit for this work. After the first two sittings Her Majesty became bored and commanded her lady-in-waiting to deputize for her. This was unimportant, since the finished portrait bore no relation at all to the features of the sitter. She was pleased with it, however, since it gave her an appearance of eternal youthfulness and was a symbol of her sacred person. The picture was to be conveyed to America, for the St Louis Exhibition. Her Majesty decreed that it was never to be laid down, for this would have been a mark of disrespect to its subject. So it was carried upright, under a yellow silk canopy : a special miniature railway was built to carry it to the ship in this position. As it passed through the streets the people knelt in reverence, as they would have done had Her Majesty appeared in person. Before the portrait left the Palace the entire Court, led by the unfortunate Emperor, performed the ceremonial kowtows to it.

Her Majesty found Western art vastly inferior to Chinese painting, on which she had become an acknowledged authority. Yet there was another form of Western portraiture which Old Buddha discovered with the greatest pleasure : photography.

One of Der Ling's brothers, who was also a Court official, had a modern camera. He took many photographs of Her Majesty— formal and informal—sometimes alone, sometimes surrounded by her ladies and eunuchs in the gardens of the Summer Palace.

But Old Buddha was not satisfied merely to pose for them. She insisted on visiting the amateur's photographer's dark-room, where she sat for hours, minutely watching the entire process of development and printing, finally commenting, 'Well, one is never too old to learn.'

For, unlike her body, Yehonala's mind remained young, eager, and avid for new experiences.

Following her triumphant return from exile, neither the cares of office nor her dynastic problems affected Old Buddha's still formidable vitality for several years. The hot season was spent at the Summer Palace, where under her keen surveillance the grounds and gardens attained unparalleled splendour and beauty, and where the former rounds of water-picnics and theatrical entertainments were even more sumptuously staged than in the past. It was during a walk in those gardens that Miss Carl, to her amazement, saw Old Buddha charm a captive bird that had escaped into a tree down on to her hand, after all attempts by the eunuchs and others to retrieve it had failed :

The Chief Eunuch explained what they were doing and the Empress Dowager said : "I will call it down." I thought this was a vain boast and in my heart I pitied her. She was so accustomed to have the whole world bow to her, she fancied even a bird . . . would obey her mandate, and I watched to see how she would take her defeat. She had a long, wand-like stick . . . with a crook at the top. . . . Today she held the wand she carried aloft and made a low, bird-like sound with her lips, never taking her eyes off the bird. She had the most musical of voices, and its flute-like sound seemed like a magical magnet to the bird. He fluttered and began to descend from bough to bough until he lighted upon the crook of her wand, when she gently moved her other hand nearer and nearer, until it finally rested on her finger!

When in 1900 Old Buddha had taken a compulsory tour of her Empire, she acquired an appetite for travel which later she was able to gratify. She decided that after so many long years she would like to revisit Jehol, the scene of her first flight and triumphant return, and, having done so, to pay her respects to the ancestral palaces of the Great Pure Dynasty at Mukden. Der Ling accompanied her Imperial mistress on both these trips, and since she, too, was a Manchu of aristocratic descent, the visit to Mukden was a kind of pilgrimage for her as well. Kuang Hsu, whose health continued to deteriorate, was not excused on that ground from accompanying his aged jailer, who kept him as close to her person as in the past. On both occasions the huge travelling party included the Emperor, the young Empress and Princesses, ladies-in-waiting, maid-servants, the Chief Eunuch and a horde of lesser eunuchs. Her Majesty's railway-coach was of the greatest luxury and magnificence, and as the train whizzed through the stations on the way, out of the windows could be caught a brief glimpse of platforms filled with rows of kneeling officials dressed in their best clothes of many colours, none of whom, however, presumed to raise their eyes to the exalted passengers sweeping past them.

These fantastic tourists visited every one of the mausolea containing relics of the former Manchu Emperors. Their guide was Old Buddha, whose knowledge of her ancestral history was profound. In the glass cases containing the former possessions of Hsien Feng, 'the relics . . . were pitifully few. . . . '

'You know,' Her Majesty explained this away, 'Emperor Hsien Feng was not an artist. He did not care for beautiful things. He was really a lover of nature. He loved life, not inanimate things. He was a great ruler.' Der Ling took this obvious untruth with a grain of salt, as, probably, did she who made it. But face was saved.

Next they saw the 'gold bowl which had been the feeding-cup of the baby Tung Chih, his small stiff yellow coronation robe embroidered with dragons, and other souvenirs of his childhood, including 'two cases filled with his toys', one of which, a plaster rabbit, Old Buddha carried away with her.

All this time Kuang Hsu had been, as was generally the case, a silent witness of Her Majesty's proceedings. But later, when she was resting, he called Der Ling to him and said :

"There will never be anything here to remind the world of Emperor Kuang Hsu. He has nothing, nor will he ever have."

The American woman, Miss Katherine Carl, who painted the Empress's portrait, had many opportunities to observe her in private. In 1904 Miss Carl wrote that, 'Her Majesty was looking tired and anxious these days; her Audiences were unusually long and despatches were constantly arriving.' The Empress Dowager would take long and solitary walks in her gardens, and on one occasion 'she looked a pathetic figure. Her strong face looked tired and worn. Her arms hung listlessly by her side, and she seemed almost to have given up. I saw her furtively brush away a tear.'

The cause of Her Majesty's discouragement and grief was a renewed crisis in the Russo-Japanese conflict over Manchuria.

In 1902 the Russians had broken their agreement to vacate Manchuria by the following year. Once again the rivalry between the great Powers for Chinese territory flared up. Japan and Great Britain, alarmed by the Russian threat to Korea, signed an alliance on 30 January 1902. When neither these two Powers nor the United States succeeded in curbing the Russian aggression, Japan finally went to war against Russia, and in February 1904 was completely victorious. Once again the 'dwarf-men' had proved themselves the equals of any nation in successfully adapting to the demands of aggressive nineteenth-century colonialism. Once again China was obliged helplessly to watch the foreigners wrestling for possession of her territories. The bitterness of the situation was aggravated for Yehonala by the fact that those lands in dispute between Russia and Japan were the regions whence her ancestors had descended nearly four centuries previously to conquer China.

Der Ling claimed to have translated into Chinese and read to her daily the news of the Russo-Japanese conflict in Manchuria given in the foreign Press and by Reuter, and also to have been present at an audience the Empress gave to Yuan Shi-kai, who was then Viceroy of Chihli :

When the Empress asked Yuan Shi-kai his opinion of the probable result of the Russo-Japanese war, he told her that Japan would win it.

Her Majesty then spoke about the condition of things in China. She said that in case China were forced into war with another nation, we should be nowhere. We had nothing ready, no navy, no trained army, in fact nothing to enable us to protect ourselves. . . .

The indomitable Old Buddha was also disgusted by the obvious incompetence and ignorance of her military and naval 'advisers', who were 'of very little use to the country'.

Yet none of the other European Powers nor the United States wished to see Manchuria permanently under Russian domination. After Japan's smashing victory, some concessions to their young Asiatic rival had to be made. In 1905 the American President, Theodore Roosevelt, intervened. By the Treaty of Portsmouth the Russians were obliged to recognize Japan's interest in Korea, and transfer their so-called rights in the Liotang peninsula to Japan, as well as the southern half of Sakhalin and of the Manchurian railways. Both Russia and Japan undertook to withdraw their troops from Manchuria and to use the railways only for economic and industrial activities. Chinese interests were to be protected by a renewal of the 'Open Door' policy.

The Empress Dowager had never forgotten the bitter lesson of China's defeat by Japan in 1894. This new triumph against a much more powerful rival reinforced the lessons Li Hung Chang and Jung Lu had tried to teach her. In 1906 Her Majesty published a Decree in which the situation was recognized, but the remedies for it were still advocated in a somewhat half-hearted manner :

Yet even this 'Paper Tiger' was interpreted by the still influential reactionaries as a potential threat to their power and a challenge to their emoluments, licensed by centuries of Confucian tradition.

To Her Majesty's implacable opponents in south China, working more actively than ever for the overthrow of the Great Pure Dynasty and all it embodied, this Decree seemed no more than another proof of Old Buddha's duplicity and cunning.

Like her famous predecessor, the Chien Lung Emperor, Old Buddha never saw any incompatability between the power, wealth and glory of the Great Pure Dynasty and the progress and prosperity of the Middle Kingdom.

In the last years of her life the Empress issued a stream of edicts, most of which were almost certainly discussed with and possibly inspired by Jung Lu, and, after his death, Yuan Shi-kai. Among these edicts, however, was one that was accredited to Her Majesty and no one else.

Manchu women had never adopted the painful Chinese custom of binding the feet of little girls very tightly, so that their toes were permanently crippled, and they were left with the stumps, or 'lily feet', so much admired by their men. Whilst in her Decree the Manchu Empress did not command that this custom be abolished—for with her usual sensitivity to Chinese tradition she took care not to offend her male subjects by doing so—she urged that the educated classes should unite to oppose a custom so injurious to health and inhuman in practice.

Foot-binding did gradually die out, first amongst the cultured Chinese and more slowly among the 'stupid' people. There was always a keen latent feminism in Chinese women. Long before they began to take an active part in public life, the matriarch directed and controlled the family council and possessed absolute power over her descendants. The Manchu Empress was the supreme example of the embodiment of this Confucian tradition.

25 *The Emperor Mounts*
the Dragon

In August 1907 Old Buddha, then seventy-two, had a mild stroke. The signs of this—tightness of the facial muscles and a slight slant of the features—are plainly visible in the last photographs taken of her. Yet this attack did not appear to affect either her speech or her mental alertness, her mind and tongue remaining as sharp as ever. Nor did her appetite for power and despotic rule decline. In order to disperse the rumours that she was at the end of her tether, Her Majesty published another Decree referring to the promised Constitution. She also announced that she was looking forward to presiding at the opening meeting of the first Chinese Parliament.

Yet certain astute observers at Court such as the eunuchs in her close entourage noted that the Venerable Buddha was growing old, and began to think about the consequences of her ascending the Chariot.

The Emperor was still only in his late thirties. His apparent listlessness was partly due to ill-health, partly to mental depression; it might also have been a form of protective colouring, for even after his close confinement was ended Kuang Hsu felt his life to be in constant danger. He nursed a secret hope, how-

ever. In the diary that he kept during his imprisonment on Ying
Tai, the Emperor had written,

> I am ill, but I feel in my heart that I shall outlive the Old
> Buddha.

It was perhaps this optimistic feeling that sustained him during
his years of martyrdom. If that was the case, no one else shared
it. In the autumn of 1908 an event of great religious significance
occurred, when the Dalai Lama of Tibet travelled to Peking as a
tribute-bearer to the Throne.

The Dalai Lama was believed to be an incarnation of the
Buddha, and there was a widely held belief that it was unlucky
for two such incarnations—since the Son of Heaven was also one
—to be in the same place at the same time.

The Chief Eunuch begged Her Majesty to cancel the Dalai
Lama's visit on the grounds that if it took place 'the priest or the
sovereign would surely die'.

Li Lien-ying had originally nicknamed his mistress 'Old
Buddha'—but this was merely a complimentary title, with no
spiritual significance.

To his request Her Majesty replied that 'she had long since
decided that the Emperor's illness was incurable, and she saw no
reason, therefore, to stop the visit of the Dalai Lama, who, incidentally, was bringing rich presents and tribute from his far-
away dependency.

Whether or not the Empress was impatiently awaiting Kuang
Hsu's end, during the last years of his life she unbent slightly
towards him. She relieved him of certain dynastic duties, and
the eunuchs were ordered not to keep the Emperor waiting when
calling upon the Empress Dowager. At the meetings of the Grand
Council he was no longer obliged to remain on his knees whilst
awaiting Her Majesty's arrival and departure. According to a
Manchu official, Kuang Hsu was by then clearly aware of the
seriousness of his condition, and took refuge, when referring to it,
in bitter irony:

One morning, after perusal of a Censor's Memorial, which

contained several inaccurate statements, His Majesty observed to the Grand Council, "How little of truth there is in common rumour. For instance, I know myself to be really ill, yet here it is denied that there is anything the matter with me." The Empress Dowager here broke in: "Who has dared to utter such falsehoods? If caught, he will certainly be beheaded." Kuang Hsu then proceeded to say: "I am really getting weaker every day, and do not see my way to performing the necessary ceremonies on the occasion of Your Majesty's approaching birthday." Compassionately the Old Buddha replied: "It is more important to me that you should recover your health than that you should knock your head on the ground in my honour." The Emperor fell on his knees to thank her for these gracious words, but collapsed in a fainting fit.

Johnston reported that a member of the Imperial family described to him Kuang Hsu's 'last interview with his august jailoress':

One day in the autumn of 1908, he went to the Ning-Shou palace to prostrate himself, as he had done every day since his disgrace, before Her Majesty's throne. But his illness was entering its last stage, and he knew that he was dying. With drooping head and trembling limbs, supported by eunuchs, he tottered into the throne-hall, obviously on the verge of collapse. As he prepared to go down on his knees in the usual way, the Empress Dowager was struck by his extreme weakness and emaciation. The sight moved her, and the attendant eunuchs observed to their astonishment that there were tears in her eyes and on her cheeks. The ceremony of the Emperor's kowtow before the Empress Dowager was usually carried out in complete silence on both sides. On this occasion she suddenly broke the silence with these words: *pu yung hsing li*—"You need not kneel". But wearily the dying man sank to his knees, and as he did so he murmured in a scarcely audible voice, "I will kneel. It is for the last time."

Even Johnston allowed Old Buddha those tears of compassion.

Preparations were at their height for the two great but distinct occasions about to fall due : Her Majesty's seventy-third birthday and the audience she was going to give to the Dalai Lama. For the birthday celebrations the streets of the capital were gaily decorated with coloured lanterns, and in the Forbidden City there was to be a five-day drama festival.

Kuang Hsu was too ill to attend the reception for the Dalai Lama, but at eight o'clock on the morning of Her Majesty's birthday on 3 November, he staggered up from his sick-bed and went to pay his respects to Old Buddha. At the sight of him she immediately excused him from further ceremonial, and, in an apparently belated effort to prolong the Emperor's life, on the same afternoon she issued a special Decree, ordering the Dalai Lama to return forthwith to Tibet !

But so certain, apparently, was Old Buddha that the presence of the Dalai Lama in Peking did not threaten her own inexhaustible vitality that she spent the afternoon and evening of her seventy-third birthday picnicking on the lake. The whole Court was in fancy dress. Her Majesty herself, with supreme self-confidence, once again appeared in her favourite role or incarnation, as the Goddess of Mercy, Kuan Yin.

The party on the lake went on far into the evening; too far, since as the result of it Her Majesty caught a chill. Her condition was aggravated by another attack of dysentery from which she periodically suffered. This time it was caused by the fact that she most unwisely supped on a dish composed of crab-apples and clotted cream. The symptoms of this illness did not develop until two days later.

On 4 November the Empress attended as usual to State business : reading the many Memorials presented to her and presiding over the Council. But on the 5th neither the Empress Dowager nor the Emperor were able to leave their beds, and all matters of State were postponed for two days.

When he heard of Her Majesty's indisposition, the Dalai Lama, who was preparing for his departure from Peking, immediately sought an audience with her. He wished to present her with a particularly potent image of the Buddha, which, he told

her to her great relief, if carried at once to the Imperial
Mausoleum in the Eastern Hills, would obviate the unfortunate
conjunction of her stars and prolong her life for many more
years.

Her Majesty instructed Prince Ching to set out with it at once.
When he demurred, asking if it was wise for him to leave Peking
when both their Imperial Majesties were in poor health, as usual
Old Buddha would stand no nonsense from him or anyone else.

'I am not likely to die during the next few days,' she informed
him sharply. 'Already I feel much better. In any case you will
do as you are told.'

And indeed, her health did improve, whilst even the Emperor
rallied sufficiently to attend a Council meeting—together with
Her Majesty, who now seemed quite recovered—on Monday,
9 November.

Next morning, however, the condition of both the Imperial
patients had appreciably worsened: the Emperor was visibly
sinking. Prince Ching was sent an urgent message by the Grand
Council, begging him to return to Peking with all haste. Having
done so, the Prince arrived at the Palace early in the morning of
13 November. Old Buddha, indomitable as ever, received him
with the information that she was much better and would surely
be as well as ever very soon. Unquestionably, she believed this to
be the case. Moreover, now that Kuang Hsu's reign was so
rapidly and obviously coming to an end, she had business of
the greatest importance to attend to: the appointment of his heir
and successor, a matter on which her mind had long been made
up, but which she had not finalized because, according to her, a
new Emperor might not be nominated until his predecessor was
on his death-bed: a view she had not troubled about when she
had chosen the son of Prince Tuan as heir apparent.

The Empress had not forgotten the outcry at the time of her
own son's death, nor the fact that her neglect in appointing an
heir who might perform the necessary offices to propitiate his
ghost had resulted in the suicide of the patriotic Censor, Wu
Ko-tu, in a protesting gesture which had won him the lasting
admiration of all his compatriots. It was largely her fear that this

neglect on her part had called down the wrath of heaven on her
that had caused her to violate the dynastic laws a second time,
by appointing an heir apparent whilst the Emperor was still in
a condition to govern his country, had she allowed him to do so.
Certainly she was right in her opinion that not for a long time
had so many disasters befallen China as during her own tenure of
power.

Yet having broken her dynastic law on two occasions with such
tragic results, Old Buddha now did so a third time.

Whilst Kuang Hsu lay dying, and as soon as Prince Ching
arrived in the Forbidden City, Her Majesty summoned the
Grand Council in conclave. She herself rose from her sick-bed for
this memorable occasion and, in spite of the obvious indications
that she was still far from well, ascended the Throne and 'spoke
with all her wonted vehemence and lucidity'. A well-informed
member of the Grand Council, full of wonder at such an exhibition of strength of will, recorded the fact that she completely led
and dominated the Council, as usual allowing the members
present to state their views, and as usual, completely overriding
them.

Her mind had long been made up, so she informed the
assembled Imperial princes and statesmen, that 'in recognition
and reward of Jung Lu's lifelong devotion to her person, and his
paramount services to the Dynasty at the time of the Boxer
Rising, the new Emperor was to be his grandson, Pu Yi, the
infant son of his daughter and Prince Chun [the second] whom
at the same time she designated as Regent, with the title of Prince
co-operating in the Government'.

This decision of Her Majesty's was particularly unwelcome
to Yuan Shi-kai, since Prince Chun, Kuang Hsu's younger
brother, was that statesman's implacable enemy, and he therefore made another attempt to urge the claims of the Prince Pu
Lun. Whereupon Jung Lu's former love, Yehonala, the great
Empress Dowager, turned on him with a lightning flash of her
famous temper.

'You think,' she said, 'that I am old and in my dotage; but you
should have learned by now that when I make up my mind

nothing stops me from acting upon it. At a critical time in a nation's affairs a youthful sovereign is no doubt a source of danger to the State'—the Emperor designate was only two years old—'but do not forget,' Her Majesty emphasized, 'that I shall be here to direct and assist Prince Chun.' And there was no doubt in the minds of those who heard those words that Her Majesty was completely convinced that she would live for many more years to come.

The matter being settled, she then ordered two Decrees to be drafted, to be published in her name. By the first, Tsai-feng, Prince Chun, was to be given the title of Prince co-operating in the Government; by the second it was commanded that his baby son, Pu Yi, should be brought to the Palace immediately, to be educated within the Forbidden City.

And so for a second time an unfortunate infant was brought from his home to be presented by his father to the Empress Dowager and the Emperor as the future Son of Heaven. Prince Ching was given the delicate mission of informing the dying Kuang Hsu of these decrees.

Even on his death-bed Kuang Hsu knew no peace. Whilst he was still sufficiently conscious, he wrote out his testament. His Empress, Old Buddha's niece and protégée, whom he had always detested, later took possession of it. Yet the preface, containing some ominous lines, became known :

We were the second son of Prince Chun [the first] when the Empress Dowager selected Us for the Throne. She has always hated Us, but for Our misery of the past ten years Yuan Shi-kai is responsible, and one other.

The second name was said to have been illegible; it might be conjectured that it was the Chief Eunuch's.

When the time comes, I desire that Yuan be summarily beheaded.

Even when he was passing into semi-consciousness, Kuang Hsu still traced in the air with his forefinger the circular character composing the surname, Yuan, of his detested enemy, who had betrayed his schemes to the Empress Dowager and Jung Lu.

When he had a final lucid interval, he would not allow his attendants to dress him in the ceremonial Dragon Robes of longevity in which an Emperor was arrayed to begin his heavenward ride on the Dragon.

Her Majesty visited Kuang Hsu, but by then he had lapsed into coma. Eyewitnesses stated that Old Buddha showed no grief, but apparently relief, at the Emperor's demise.

There appeared to be no reliable proof that Kuang Hsu did not die a natural death from kidney disease. Even Johnston did not claim that Old Buddha murdered her nephew. Yet at the time it was very widely believed that she had committed this crime—or caused it to be committed—determined that Kuang Hsu should not outlive her. The story was revived in lurid detail by Der Ling. Although she was no longer at Court at the time, the Empress's former lady-in-waiting stated that the details of Kuang Hsu's last days were given to her by Chang Teh, a former principal eunuch and assistant of Li Lien-ying, who lived in retirement in Tientsin.

Der Ling began her account by referring to the diary Kuang Hsu had kept during his captivity, in which he had stated that 'immediately upon the death of Her Majesty' whom he hoped to outlive, 'Li Lien-ying be put to death' by beheading.

When the Chief Eunuch's spies informed him of this intention, he promptly reported to Her Majesty the Emperor's conviction that he would outlive her. Old Buddha's reaction, as he expected, was that this indicated another, future attempt by Kuang Hsu on her life. To which the Chief Eunuch, adviser and executioner, replied that, 'It would be beneficial to all concerned were His Majesty Kuang Hsu to die before Old Buddha.'

Thereupon, according to Der Ling, 'She took the bit in her teeth and gave the orders for which Li Lien-ying was waiting:

His Majesty is desperately ill. . . . Those to whom we have entrusted the task of preparing his medicines have perhaps been careless. . . . Hereafter, Li, you will have charge of ministering to Kuang Hsu.

Li Lien-ying thereupon began the task of systematically poisoning the Emperor, personally giving him his medicine. The Chief Eunuch and the Empress Dowager stood like two ghouls beside the dying Emperor's bed. Like Macbeth and Lady Macbeth, each tried to lay the blame for his death on the other. This, however, was a mere face-saving alibi, through which their helpless victim clearly saw.

Der Ling wrote that Kuang Hsu died in torment, and that according to her eunuch informant, Chang Teh, his death-chamber was a place of horror, where Li Lien-ying hovered over the dying Emperor 'like a bird of ill-omen'. Moreover, at Old Buddha's orders, the Chief Eunuch had the Emperor dressed in his burial clothes whilst he was still conscious.

The death of Kuang Hsu, whether a natural or an unnatural one, undoubtedly suited the plans of Her Majesty and of Li Lien-ying. He had lived too long: he should have died honorably, by his own hand, after his plot against her was frustrated, and the initiative taken by the British Minister compelled her at that time to depose him rather than to dispose of him. His continued existence was a constant threat to her own security, which she could only counter by keeping him at first in the closest confinement and later always in her immediate entourage. Like any convict on parole, obliged daily to visit the police, Kuang Hsu was obliged for ten years to perform the ritual of obeisance every day.

One slight posthumous satisfaction the shade of Kuang Hsu, however, did have. Almost the first official act of his younger brother, Prince Chun, who became Regent as the father of the infant Emperor, was to banish Yuan Shi-kai to his native province. That wily and wealthy politician betook himself there imperturbably, knowing that in due course he would return to fight another day.

The Kuang Hsu Emperor died on 14 November 1908, at the age of thirty-eight. There can hardly have been an unhappier or unluckier ruler anywhere.

26 Glory's End

By sheer determination and will-power the old Empress Dowager had apparently regained her health.

Immediately on the Kuang Hsu Emperor's death, she was at last able to rectify the dynastic misdeed which had called down upon her the wrath of the gods; which had led to the sacrificial suicide of Wu Ko-tu, and aroused the deep disapproval of her subjects, both Manchu and Chinese. She did this in the following Decree:

> The Emperor Tung Chih, having left no heir, was compelled to issue a Decree to the effect that, so soon as a child should be born to His Majesty Kuang Hsu, that child would be adopted as Heir to the Emperor Tung Chih. But now His Majesty Kuang Hsu has ascended on high, dragon-borne, and he also has left no heir. I am, therefore, now obliged to decree that Pu Yi, son of Tsai Feng, the Prince co-operating in the Government, should become heir by adoption to the Emperor Tung Chih, and that at the same time he should perform joint sacrifices at the shrine of His Majesty Kuang Hsu.

On 15 November Her Majesty arose early as usual, and by 6 a.m. she was presiding over the Imperial Council. Edicts were issued in the new Emperor's reign-name, which was Hsuan Tung, meaning Wide Control. Her Majesty would in future be known as Empress Grand Dowager, and would still retain the final authority : over the new Emperor, the Prince Regent, his father, and over the new Empress Dowager, Old Buddha's niece and widow of the late Emperor. Thus the continued supremacy of the Yehonala clan was ensured.

Plans were to be made for the picturesque ceremonies at which these titles would be inaugurated. All was thus in order for the beginning of the new reign, which, like its predecessor, was intended to confirm and continue Her Majesty's rulership for many years.

Suddenly, however, at her midday meal, the Empress Grand Dowager, as she had become, fainted away. In spite of the magical image presented to her by the Dalai Lama, which now awaited her at her tomb, she had not fully recovered her strength. The strain of her tremendous activities during the past twenty-four hours had been too great even for her robust constitution.

When Old Buddha regained consciousness she did so fully, still in command of all her faculties in spite of physical weakness. But she had a definite premonition of her approaching death.

Losing not a minute, Her Majesty immediately summoned the Grand Council, her niece, the new Empress Dowager, and Prince Chun, the Regent, to her palace. In their presence, un-hurriedly and quite calmly, she then dictated a Decree :

By command of the Empress Grand Dowager :

Yesterday I issued an Edict whereby Prince Chun was made Regent, and I commanded that the whole business of government should be in his hands, subject only to my instructions. Being seized of a mortal sickness, and being without hope of recovery, I now order that henceforward the government of the Empire shall be entirely in the hands of the Regent. Nevertheless, should there arise any question of vital importance, in regard to which an expression of the Empress Dowager's opinion is desirable, the Regent shall apply in person to her for instructions, and act accordingly.

By this last manoeuvre Her Majesty removed from Prince Chun any absolute power he might have tried to use to strengthen the hands of the Imperial clansmen against the Yehonala. Their proudest daughter was true to the last to the interests of her own kinsfolk.

Next, Old Buddha ordered the secretaries to draft her valedictory Decree. When they brought it to her, her mind was still quite clear. She carefully read it through several times, making various corrections to it, and commenting on her reasons for doing so as she wrote them.

The Decree was prefaced by all the titles that Yehonala had acquired (with the emoluments that went with them) during her long years of power :

The Valedictory Mandate of Her Majesty Tsu - Hsi - Tuan - Yu - K'ang - I - Chao - Yu - Chuang - Cheng - Shou - Kung - Ch'in - Hsien - Ch'ung - Hsi, the Empress Grand Dowager, declareth as follows : *

I, of humble virtue, did reverently receive the appointment of the late Emperor Hsien Feng, which prepared for me a place amongst his Consorts. When the late Emperor Tung Chih succeeded in early childhood to the Throne, there was rebellion still raging in the land, which was being vigorously suppressed. Not only did the Taiping and turbaned rebels engage in successive outbreaks, but disorder was spread by the Kuei-chou aborigines and by Mohammedan bandits. The provinces of the coast were in great distress, the people on the verge of ruin, widespread distress confronting us on all sides.

Co-operating then with the senior Consort of Hsien Feng, the Empress Dowager, of the Eastern Palace, I undertook the heavy duties of Government, toiling ever, day and night. Obeying the behests of His late Majesty, my husband, I urged on the metropolitan and provincial officials, as well as the

---

* The English transliteration of these titles, according to Sir James Stewart Lockhart, is as follows : 'the Loving-hearted and Fortunate, Upright and Aiding (the State), Happy and Careful (of her remaining years), Bright and Pleasant, Earnest and True, Long-lived and Serious, Reverent and Good, Exalted and Brilliant'.

military commanders, directing their policies, and striving for the restoration of peace. I employed virtuous officials and was ever ready to listen to wise counsel. I relieved my people's distress in times of flood and famine. By the goodwill and bounty of Heaven, I suppressed the rebellions and out of dire peril restored peace. Later, when the Emperor Tung Chih passed away and the Emperor Kuang Hsu, now just deceased, entered by adoption the great heritage, the crisis was even more dangerous and the condition of the people even more pitiable. Within the Empire calamities were rife, while from abroad we were confronted by repeated and increasing acts of aggression.

Once again it became my inevitable and bounden duty to assume the Regency. Two years ago I issued a Decree announcing the Throne's intention to grant a Constitution, and this present year I have promulgated the date at which it is to come into effect. Innumerable affairs of State have required direction at my hands, and I have laboured without ceasing and with all my might. Fortunately my constitution was naturally strong, and I have been able to face my duties with undiminished vigour. During the summer and autumn of this year, however, I have frequently been in bad health, at a time when pressing affairs of State allowed me no repose. I lost my sleep and appetite, and gradually my strength failed me. Yet even then I took no rest, not for a single day. And yesterday saw the death of His Majesty Kuang Hsu; whereat my grief overwhelmed me. I can bear no more, and so am I come to the pass where no possible hope of recovery remains.

Looking back upon the memories of these last fifty years, I perceive how calamities from within and aggression from without have come upon us in relentless succession, and that my life has never enjoyed a moment's respite from anxiety. But today definite progress has been made towards necessary reforms. The new Emperor is but an infant, just reaching the age when wise instruction is of the highest importance. The Prince Regent and all our officials must henceforth work loyally together to strengthen the foundations of the Empire.

His Majesty must devote himself to studying the interests of the country and so refrain from giving way to personal grief. That he may diligently pursue his studies, and hereafter add fresh lustre to the glorious achievements of his ancestors, is now my earnest prayer.

Mourning to be worn for only twenty-seven days.
Cause this to be known everywhere!
Tenth Moon, 23rd day [15 November 1908].

This nobly-worded document was drawn up, according to custom, by the best scribes. But when Her Majesty read it over, she made several corrections to it, of which the most interesting was the paragraph beginning with the sentence, 'Once again it became my inevitable and bounden duty to assume the Regency,' which referred to her *coup d'état* after the Hundred Days, and was clearly an attempt to justify it. To those around her death-bed the Empress, in fact, said as much, explaining to them that it was not merely from personal ambition, as her enemies claimed, that she had returned to power, but because the State required her guidance. Undoubtedly she by then believed this to be the case. Yet that her conscience was troubling her, and that she did have qualms, was made plain shortly afterwards, when she spoke her famous last words.

'Never again,' she commanded them, 'allow any woman to hold the supreme power in the State. It is against the house-law of our Dynasty, and should be strictly forbidden. Be careful not to permit eunuchs to meddle in Government matters. The Ming Dynasty was brought to ruin by eunuchs, and its fate should be a warning to my people.'

Yet only a few hours previously she had decreed that her niece, now the reigning Empress Dowager, should in an emergency have the last word in matters of policy.

But if, like so many lesser women, Old Buddha was occasionally inconsistent, and although she had certainly not always lived in accordance with the high principles she proclaimed on her death-bed, at the last moment she was calm, courageous, and sincere. Having clutched at power with all her might, suddenly she seemed quite reconciled to renouncing it, and her self-control and majesty deeply impressed the weeping relatives and waiting-women who were standing beside her.

Since Old Buddha had only been taken fatally ill at her mid-day meal, her suffering must have been very slight, for, having signed her final Decree and pronounced her last words, and remaining conscious almost to the ultimate moment of her life, she died three hours later, at 3 p.m., according to the account given to Bland and Backhouse by those then present. They said that 'her mouth remained fixedly open, which the Chinese interpret as a sign that the spirit of the deceased is unwilling to leave the body and take its departure for the place of the Nine Springs'.

It was probably true that this ardent spirit was unwilling to renounce the supreme power to which it had so tenaciously clung for nearly half a century. It was the spirit of a born leader, of a great dictator, in a female body, not of Imperial descent, like those of Catherine the Great and Catherine de Medici : pre-destined to rule over greater Empires than theirs and a nation of more than four hundred million human beings. Yehonala, as she mentioned in her valedictory Memorial, had been exception-ally lucky in possessing, like those two queens also, enormous natural vitality and a tremendously strong constitution. In due course age worked its corrosion even in that proud flesh. There is little doubt that in the last three years of her life Old Buddha knew this, fought with her usual tenacity a terrific rear-guard action against advancing Death, and when she felt herself beaten surrendered with such courage, such realistic intelligence, as she had shown all her life when threatened with defeat. Whether she was as pious a Buddhist as her Christian admirers claimed, she was certainly a natural Stoic.

Her obsequies were as superlatively impressive and gorgeous as even she could have wished. Her body was conveyed to the mausoleum in the Eastern hills.

This had been 'originally built by the faithful Jung Lu for his Imperial Mistress' at a cost of more than one million pounds.

The Empress Grand Dowager's funeral was the costliest in

living memory, the expenses amounting to more than another one million pounds. But, according to usage, it did not take place until nearly a year after her death, nor before ample provision had been made for her comfort and convenience 'on the other side'.

The ritual method for ensuring this was to prepare figures of attendants, soldiers, eunuchs and handwomen made of paper, with the necessary appurtenances, which were then ceremonially burnt. In addition to all the usual luxuries to which Her Majesty had been used in this world, and with which she must be provided in the other—at the 'Yellow Springs'—a marvellous barge was erected outside the Forbidden City, more than one hundred and fifty feet long, fitted out exactly as her marble barge at the Summer Palace had been, manned by life-sized paper eunuchs and waiting-women, dressed in gossamer silk, floating on an artificial lake on which swam lotus-plants; and after the Regent had performed the necessary sacrifices in the Emperor's name, it was set alight and burnt, wafting it over to the regions where it was to await the moment when Her Majesty's shade would seat itself on the gilt paper throne provided for it. No less than three thousand paper effigies of attendants, officials, musicians, actors, chair-bearers, horses, camels and carriages were provided separately.

Old Buddha's enemies accused her of avarice as well as extravagance. At her death her personal fortune was roughly estimated to be around sixteen millions pounds. About half of this, in bullion, gold Buddhas and ritual vessels, was buried in the palace grounds before her flight in 1900. The basis for this solid fortune was said to be the hoard which the young Western Empress had acquired when she confiscated all the property of the treacherous Su Shun after the death of Hsien Feng and her return to Peking in 1861.

It was generally known that Her Majesty's tomb contained such rich treasure. Yet it remained undisturbed until July 1928, when a kind of combined assault by a group of looters was perpetrated on the Imperial mausolea. According to Johnston, 'the mausolea were immensely strong, and it required dynamite to burst them open. Coffins were broken open and the bodies flung out on the floor. The remains of one of the greatest sovereigns who ever occupied the Chinese throne—Kao Tsung [Chien Lung]—and also the body of the Empress Dowager, Tzu Hsi, "the Venerable Buddha", were hacked to pieces and their bones scattered. The scene, when it was afterwards visited by the Emperor's messengers, was indescribably hideous. . . .

'A special court was set up to try a few of the minor offenders, but they were only lightly punished, if at all. No serious attempt was made to arrest the ringleaders, who included military officers of high rank. They escaped all punishment, and were even allowed to retain possession of their loot, much of which has since been dispersed throughout the world. . . . '

The fact that the tombs were not broken into until then can be accounted for by the tremendous reverence felt by the Chinese for the dead, and the fear of awful retribution should their graves be disturbed. But by 1928 northern China was in a state of turmoil, and the Hsuan Tung Emperor was so only in name. Johnston no doubt rightly thought that the principal motive for the looting was plunder, yet this does not explain the outrage on the bodies of the great Ching rulers. Was it done casually, although brutally; or deliberately, as a mark of contempt for the then almost extinct Manchu dynasty, which, after a glorious beginning, had ended in disaster, both for itself and for the Middle Kingdom?

27 The Words of the Empress!

Long ago it had been prophesied that a Yehonala woman would cause the downfall of the Great Pure dynasty, and Old Buddha still remembered this ancient prediction on her death-bed.

Johnston's statement that she was a woman of no intelligence was contrary to all the evidence provided by her tenure of power. But in regard to the libels on her sexual life current throughout the second half of the nineteenth century, he made an interesting and reasonable suggestion, that, instead of being a woman of appalling sexual depravity, she was quite the reverse and was in fact sex-starved.

It seems indeed probable that Yehonala never felt love or passion for any man except Jung Lu : that she sublimated her sexual instincts successfully in the achievement of her tremendous ambition, in becoming the greatest female autocrat the world has ever known. Nevertheless, her thwarted physical desires found outlets which her enemies correctly denounced : immense greed for wealth as well as power, insensate extravagance, and fiendish cruelty towards the unfortunates who aroused her hatred and gave her the opportunities to gratify it. These were all sublimation-activities.

Her most notorious crimes were said to be the poisoning of her

dynastic sister, the Eastern Empress, Tzu An; the elimination of
A-lu-te; conniving at the debauching of her son, the Tung Chih
Emperor; the drowning of the Pearl Concubine of Kuang Hsu;
and her attempted, although thwarted, murder of that luckless
Emperor himself.

On the evidence, it seems fairly clear that the Empress
Dowager was responsible for the deaths of those three unfortunate
females, not out of personal spite so much as because each of them
in their different ways represented a threat to her own continued
tenure of power. Tzu An was conspiring with Prince Kung, or
so it appeared to Tzu Hsi, to deprive the Western Empress of her
dominant position. Had A-lu-te and her unborn child (if a male)
survived, Tzu Hsi would have been relegated to a position of
political impotence : an impossible situation from her point of
view. The Pearl Concubine had been Kuang Hsu's ally in his
abortive attempt to depose and—in her view—murder Her
Imperial Majesty, in 1898.

It must never be forgotten, also, that in the Imperial City the
law of the jungle—'Eat or be eaten', 'Kill or be killed'—prevailed
as simply and naturally as in the great forests where the tigers
lurked. On several occasions, from the death of the Hsien Feng
Emperor at Jehol until the Hundred Days, Yehonala was fighting
for her life as well as her power. Perhaps her greatest virtue was
her indomitable courage.

For nearly fifty years, from 1861 to 1908, the Empress
Dowager was the Governess of China. During most of that time
she endeavoured to keep face—or faith—with her ancestors and
people. Behind the imperturbable Imperial façade, as was
occasionally glimpsed by Li Hung Chang, who was a critical
judge of feminine behaviour, was a woman often secretly
worried, acutely anxious, and on rare occasions even panic-
stricken. When, as happened at such moments of tension and
crisis, she lost her temper, she would hit out at the first unfortunate available on whom to vent her irrepressible anger. But
afterwards she would regret it. Her obvious sincerity then, when
her rage abated, bound her administrators and statesmen even
more closely to her service.

Almost certainly, the troubles that befell the Middle Kingdom in the second half of the nineteenth century were *not* brought about by the Empress Dowager. They were the result of circumstances at that time beyond the control of the wisest Chinese statesmen, as well as the stupidest, most incompetent and venal. It is not even certain that, in spite of her physical seclusion within her palaces, the Empress was as ill-informed on the rapacity and intrigues of the foreign Powers as such critics as Johnston claimed.

The Empress Dowager was not the direct cause of the downfall and disintegration that had already begun to set in before the reign of her husband, the Hsien Feng Emperor, and for a time she even succeeded—with the assistance of the foreign Powers, anxious to keep the Ching dynasty going as a bulwark against complete anarchy and revolution—in maintaining an uneasy equilibrium between all the conflicting forces within and on the periphery of her realm. After 1900, apart from the Russo-Japanese conflict in Manchuria, matters remained relatively peaceful until her death eight years later. But when she did die, the last of the outstanding Manchu rulers left the scene. Not until forty years later did a new and powerful régime restore the vast country to unity, fulfilling the Empress Dowager's life-long ambition once and for ever to rid the Chinese nation of foreign invaders and aggressors.

The Motherly and Auspicious Empress's rule was a glorious failure; her tenure of power a long and bitter rear-guard action to defer defeat by the march of time and the ineluctable process of history. This does not, however, justify the exaggerated panegyrics bestowed on the Empress Dowager after her death by her British and American admirers.

Towards the end of her life Old Buddha became more and more popular with her subjects :

> To the great mass of her people, who had never seen her . . . the Old Buddha stood for the embodiment of courage, liberality and kindness of heart. If, as they knew, she was subject to

fierce outbursts of sudden rage, the fact did her no injury in the eyes of a race which believes that wrath-matter undischarged is a virulent poison in the system

—a belief born out by modern endocrinology, since in rage or fear the adrenal glands tend to overwork, with unpleasant physiological results.

To them she was a great ruler and a *bon enfant*. In a country where merciless officials and torture are a part of the long-accepted order of things, no more stress was laid on her numerous acts of cold-blooded tyranny than, shall we say, was laid on the beheading of Earls at the close of the fifteenth century in England.

One of the writers had the good fortune once to see the Empress when proceeding in her palanquin to the Eastern tombs. . . . As her chair passed along a line of kneeling peasantry, the curtains were open and it was seen that the Old Buddha was asleep. The good country people were delighted. "Look," they cried, "the Old Buddha is sleeping. Really, she has far too much work to do! A rare woman—what a pleasure to see her thus!"

The 'stupid' people also firmly believed that when she passed over to 'the other side' their Empress would continue to watch over their welfare. If that were the case, Old Buddha could hardly help a smug smile of satisfaction at seeing how completely and literally the present Chinese régime, including so many of her descendants, has fulfilled and vindicated her patriotic ambition to free Chinese territory from foreign domination and to reclaim every scrap of it that was torn from the motherland. Her own abortive attempt to achieve this was foredoomed to failure for lack of powerful weapons, well-trained and regularly paid armies, and honest incorruptible officials. The Boxer Rising, the one offensive effort of her reign, ended in ignominious defeat and the infliction of still more crushing financial burdens on the Chinese people by the foreigners.

In a few years' time the Dragon's Teeth may well constitute

the greatest menace the Western world—Russia, Europe, the United States—has ever had to face, unless we can learn our lesson at last and accept the great Chinese nation with respect, on a basis of complete equality, as the Russian nation has already been accepted by Europe and the United States. In that case the Yellow Peril may recede from our frontiers. It is, after all, a peril that, through our ancestors' rapacity and our own lack of sympathy and goodwill towards the Chinese people and their great and glorious culture, we have brought on ourselves.

Perhaps, if we listen very carefully, from the 'other side' of the Bamboo Curtain we may discern, faintly but clearly, the voice of Old Buddha :

The Words of the Empress!

28   *Full Circle*

During the peace negotiations after the Boxer Rising, Sir Robert Hart resumed his role as unofficial intermediary between the Chinese plenipotentiaries, Li Hung Chang and his colleagues, and the incensed foreigners. For the modern world, however, Hart's importance does not rest on his career activities so much as on the astounding prophecies contained in his own account and interpretation of this event.

'This episode of today,' wrote Hart, 'is not meaningless—it is the prelude to a century of change and the keynote of the future history of the Far East; the China of the year 2000 will be very different from the China of 1900!'

'But what,' Hart asked, in no rhetorical sense, 'is this Yellow Peril?'

And he answered that,

> . . . this race, after thousands of years of haughty seclusion and exclusiveness, has been pushed by the force of circumstances and by the superior strength of assailants into treaty relations with the rest of the world, but regards that as a humiliation, sees no benefits accruing from it, and is looking

forward to the day when it in turn will be strong enough to
. . . do away with foreign intercourse, interference, and in-
trusion . . . its every member is tingling with Chinese feeling—
"China for the Chinese and out with the foreigners!" The
Boxer movement is doubtless the product of official inspiration,
but it has taken hold of the popular imagination, and will
spread like wildfire . . . it is, in short, a purely patriotic volun-
teer movement, and its object is to strengthen China—and
for a Chinese programme. . . . The Boxer patriot of the future
will possess the best weapons that money can buy, and then the
'Yellow Peril' will be beyond ignoring.

Twenty millions or more of Boxers, armed, drilled, disci-
plined, and animated by patriotic, if mistaken motives, will
make residence in China impossible for foreigners, will take
back from foreigners everything foreigners have taken from
China, will pay off old grudges with interest, and will carry
the Chinese flag and Chinese armies into many a place that
even fancy will not suggest today, thus preparing for the future
upheavals and disasters never dreamed of. In fifty years' time
there will be millions of Boxers in serried ranks and war's
panoply at the call of the Chinese Government; there is not the
slightest doubt of that!

It took almost exactly fifty years for that prophecy to come
true. 'In 1960,' according to a recent authority, 'indications were
that there were some 650 million Chinese in mainland China . . .
continuing to increase by some fifteen million a year, or some
two thousand an hour.'

That is modern China's problem—and the world's.

The Chinese Revolution began within four years of the death
of the Empress Dowager. Any doubts as to the powerful stabiliz-
ing influence exercised by Old Buddha until almost her last
moment vanish in consequence. When that influence ceased, the
tottering Manchu dynasty and Confucian régime were doomed.

In desperation, the Regent, Prince Chun, recalled his former
enemy Yuan Shi-kai, who still believed in the dynastic tradition.

The Abdication Decree of the last Emperor on 12 February 1912, ended the Great Pure Dynasty of the Aisin Giorro.

Meanwhile, in the south, Sun Yat Sen, had founded his new Republican party.

The Empress Dowager and her Government had long pursued Dr Sun Yat Sen with as much vindictiveness as Kang Yu-weh. He was kidnapped and imprisoned in the Chinese Embassy in London in 1896, but managed to smuggle out a note to the famous Scottish surgeon, Sir James Cantlie, and was rescued. Only a month before the abdication of the last Emperor he returned from exile and became provisional President of the new Republic at Nanking, its capital at that time. But in order to unite north and south Dr Sun offered Yuan Shi-kai the Presidency. Yuan accepted the offer but had no intention of co-operating with the southern revolutionaries. His aim was a China united under his own rule, and he even aspired to found a new dynasty, with himself as Emperor. The monarchy was actually proclaimed in 1915, but Yuan never succeeded in his wild ambition. He died on 6 June 1916, the last of the great Viceroys.

After the death of Yuan Shi-kai, north China became a chaotic battlefield for the troops of contending warlords and generals.

At Canton, meanwhile, the traditional republican stronghold, Dr Sun reorganized his party during the 1920s under the title of Kuomintang, National People's Party, which in due course became the ruling Chinese political organization, until overthrown by the Communists in 1948.

After Dr Sun Yat Sen's death in 1925, in Peking, where he had gone to confer with three northern leaders with a view to uniting the country at last, the leadership of the Kuomintang passed to a brilliant young military man called Chiang Kai-shek, who, although a republican, had a traditional Confucian upbringing.

Dr Sun had married the elder daughter, Soong Ching-ling, of a Shanghai printer; Chiang Kai-shek in due course became the husband of her younger sister, Mai-ling.

These two exceptionally intelligent and lovely girls were the new figureheads of the Chinese women's increasingly successful struggle for equality and independence : the first women leaders nationally known since the death of Old Buddha. But whereas Madame Chiang Kai-shek became an ardent Methodist, the President's widow found herself increasingly drawn towards Communism. Mai-ling became the First Lady of Formosa; Soong Ching-ling (having reassumed her maiden name) a Vice-President of the Chinese People's Republic.

The Chinese Communist Party was founded on 1 July 1921, only four years after the seizure of power by the Russian Communist Party under Lenin.

Dr Sun had been strongly attracted by Lenin's personality and success. He reorganized his party in 1921 with the help of Soviet 'advisers', but their intervention in Chinese affairs was a failure and they were soon withdrawn.

Very quickly after the President's death, his successor, Chiang Kai-shek, fell out with the orthodox Communist leadership. His own strong Confucianist leanings and his wife's equally enthusiastic Christian outlook made any further collaboration between the extreme Leftists and the Kuomintang impossible. Chiang, realizing at this early stage that China could not exist under two such deeply incompatible régimes as his own and the Communists', attempted to suppress them before they could become strong enough to challenge his leadership.

But the Chinese Communists were led by a triumvirate of dedicated revolutionaries : the theoretician and politician, Mao Tse Tung; the Red general, Chu Teh; and the young diplomat Chou En Lai, a member of one of the most distinguished mandarin families, who as a student had joined the Communist Party. Pursued by Kuomintang forces, this small but fanatically dedicated Party undertook the famous Long March from south-eastern China to the fastness of Yennan in the far north-west. This epic trek lasted an entire year, from October 1934 until the same month in 1935. They established themselves in the cave-dwellings among the barren loess wilderness, beginning their propaganda amongst the poorest peasantry, and organizing their first guerrilla army, later known as the Eighth Route Army.

Whilst the rest of the major Powers had ceased to attempt to 'carve up the Chinese melon', only still holding on to the enclaves they had won in the nineteenth century, Japan took advantage of the collapse of the northern governments to consolidate her hold on Manchuria.

On 18 September 1931 the Japanese invaded north-east China.

Chiang Kai-shek's and the Kuomintang's vendetta against the Chinese Communists was interrupted by the Generalissimo's heroic resistance to Japanese aggression, in which, on the Comintern's instructions, the Chinese Communists offered him their aid. An uneasy truce was negotiated between Chiang and Mao Tse Tung. The Communist armies, which had developed great skill at guerrilla warfare, loyally joined with those of the Kuomintang to repel the invader. In 1938, Chou En Lai was sent as his party's representative to Hankow, where the Generalissimo had then established his headquarters. But had it not been for the outbreak of the Second World War, and Pearl Harbour, the Chinese might never have dislodged the Japanese from their conquests on the mainland.

By 1944, however, the Kuomintang, which had started out with such high ideals and so much promise, was disintegrating, largely owing to the traditional vice or disease of all previous Chinese governments: the corruption of its officials. As soon as the World War ended, the Communists seized the advantage over their former rivals and short-lived allies. Bitter civil war lasted for another four years, until 1948, when Chiang Kai-shek and the remnants of his loyal forces were driven from the mainland to Taiwan, which the Japanese had once occupied as Formosa.

On 1 October 1949 the Communists came to power, proclaiming the People's Republic of China at Peking, under the leadership of Mao Tse Tung.

Among all the melancholy stories of deposed monarchs since the murder of the Tsar, Tsarina, and their family in the Ekaterinburg cellar, none is stranger nor more dramatic than that of the child who, only shortly before her death, the Empress Dowager appointed as the last Manchu Emperor of China. His personal name was Pu Yi. Under the influence of his British tutor, Mr R. F. Johnston, he chose and, during his boyhood, used for a time a European-Christian prefix to it : Henry. Very soon the boy Emperor was ousted by Yuan Shi-kai. For a brief period he was allowed to remain in the Forbidden City as head of his dynasty, later with a pension from the Republican Government, which, however, was irregularly and infrequently paid. The unfortunate young Emperor remained the Son of Heaven, occupant of the Dragon Throne, but his rule was non-existent, and the ritualistic gestures symbolizing his vanished authority were mere shadow-play. In 1928 he was obliged to take refuge in Tientsin, where he learned in July of the desecration of his ancestors' mausolea in the Eastern Hills. The Japanese, finding him, as they thought, a useful tool, then invited him to become Emperor of their new dominion, Manchukuo.

In accepting this Japanese offer Henry Pu Yi had visions of some day,　' their help, returning to rule again over the vast lands of China that his barbaric but mighty forebears had conquered three hundred years previously. But he had none of their genius, their ruthlessness, nor any followers of his own. This is how he told his story :

> I was made the Emperor of the Ching dynasty at the age of two. Three years later, in 1911, the revolution led by Sun Yat Sen overthrew the monarchy. Though the Ching court gave up its political power, the Republicans agreed to let me retain my title, palace abode, and retinue, and appropriated an annual sum of four million taels, or 125,000 kilograms of silver, for my expenses. So I continued the ritual of sitting on the throne inside the thick vermilion-coloured walls of the Forbidden City. I was attended by one thousand eunuchs, more than one hundred physicians, some two hundred chefs and cooks, and protected by several hundred guards.

To Pu Yi's credit, however, it was he who abolished the centuries-old power of the eunuchs. Johnston described how this occurred.

In 1923, after 'a somewhat painful interview' between the

young Emperor and his father, Prince Chun, the Regent, 'Prince Chun, in a state bordering on hysteria, gave way. . . . Under the eyes of General Wang's soldiers the eunuchs assembled to learn their fate. They received the news of their dismissal in silence. In less than an hour they had all passed through the Gate of Spiritual Valour, and the Forbidden City knew them as permanent residents no more.'

But if you have tears, forbear to shed them now. Most of the eunuchs had done well for themselves, even if they were not all multi-millionaires like their dreaded chief, Li Lien-ying.

'For three or four days,' Johnston continues, 'the Pekingese populace enjoyed the unwonted spectacle of palace-eunuchs sitting in disconsolate groups on the parade-ground between the northern wall of the Forbidden City and Prospect Hill, awaiting their turn to return to the palace in twos and threes to collect their personal property and to receive the grants of money which each one received according to his age and seniority.'

'This mentality of " I am above all," ' Pu Yi wrote further, 'instilled in me since childhood, gave birth to the most reactionary political ambition. I could not reconcile myself to the downfall of the Ching dynasty. I was determined to restore the rule of the Aisin Giorro.'

After describing in harrowing terms the oppression of Japanese rule in Manchukuo under his alleged reign and with his concurrence at the time, Pu Yi continued :

I was arrested together with my retinue and other officials of the puppet state by the Soviet army which helped to free the north-east. We were taken to the Soviet Union and held under detention for five years. In 1950 we were sent back to China.

In the train, poor Pu Yi 'almost went crazy with fear thinking of the unbearable humiliations and bloody revenge awaiting me. . . . '

To his immense surprise and relief, the new Chinese authorities treated him kindly, fed him well : 'No one ever insulted or abused us; beatings and scoldings were simply non-existent.'

Instead, he was given intensive courses in the new way of life, training in manual labour, and a treatment that in the West is known as brain-washing.

On 4 December 1959, 'after ten years of re-education, I was granted a special pardon and released by the People's Government. Since then I have become an ordinary citizen of China, one who lives by his own labour.'

At the age of fifty-seven, Pu Yi married a modern Chinese girl, a nurse. After working first as an horticulturist and later on historical research, he was promoted to the Committee for the Collection and Compilation of Historical Materials, under the National Committee of the People's Political Consultative Conference, of which he was also elected a member.

Had Yehonala not become an Imperial Concubine in 1853, she would have been married to Jung Lu. In that event Comrade Pu Yi Aisin Giorro would have been her grandson. Although this was not to be, nevertheless he ranks as such according to the Ching dynastic house-law, since the Matriarch, the Holy Mother, was the Emperor's titular parent. When Her Majesty chose Jung Lu's baby grandson as heir to the Kuang Hsu Emperor, she herself in her last dynastic Decree assumed the title of Empress Grand Dowager, symbolically Imperial Grandmother.

And that is China, where, in the course of thousands of years of turbulent history, threaded by golden strands of wisdom and compromise, the wheel has again and again turned full circle.

Acknowledgement of Sources and brief Bibliography

At an early stage in my research it became clear how few were the reliable sources on the life of the Empress Dowager Tzu Hsi. The Annals of the Ching dynasty are in several instances as unreliable as the libels published by the Empress's enemies. Very few of her subjects came into direct contact with Her Majesty. With the exception of the American painter Miss Katherine Carl, almost none of the foreigners who wrote about the Empress Dowager did so, and then only after 1900. I therefore endeavoured as far as possible to use as sources only those who, like Der Ling, Li Hung Chang, and Sir Robert Hart, were in her personal or political service, and the works listed below by other biographers and historians who approached the problem of her mysterious personality and existence without accepting, even if referring to, the many legends about her. An exception had to be made in the case of R. F. Johnston, who, although violently prejudiced against the Empress Dowager, did have an intimate and scholarly knowledge of the Forbidden City and its administration.

I am greatly indebted to the authors, trustees and publishers of these works for permission to quote from them:

Bland and Backhouse, *China Under the Empress Dowager* (Heinemann, 1911), and *Annals of the Court of Peking* (Heinemann, 1914).

Juliet Bredon, *Sir Robert Hart* [Hutchinson, 1909].

Mrs Conger, *Letters from China* (cf. P. W. Sergeant, *The Great Empress Dowager of China* (Hutchinson, 1910).

Der Ling (Princess), *Two Years in the Forbidden City* (T. Fisher Unwin, 1912), *Old Buddha* (John Lane, 1919), and *Imperial Incense* (Stanley Paul, 1934).

Peter Fleming, *The Siege at Peking* (Rupert Hart-Davis, 1959).

Herbert A. Giles, *China and the Manchus* (C.U.P., 1912).

Sir Robert Hart, *'These from the Land of Sinim'* (Chapman and Hall, 1901).

Charles O. Hucker, *China, Asia in the Modern World* (New American Library, 1963).

R. F. Johnston, *Twilight in the Forbidden City* (Victor Gollancz, 1934).

Li Hung Chang, *Memoirs* (Constable, 1913).

Sir Claude Macdonald, cf. *Blue Book,* China, No. 1, 1899, quoted by Bland and Backhouse, op. cit.

Victor Purcell, *The Boxer Uprising* (C.U.P., 1963).

Pu Yi Aisin Giorro, 'From Emperor to Ordinary Citizen' (*China Reconstructs,* Vol. XIII, No. 1, January 1964).

P. W. Sergeant, *The Great Empress Dowager of China* (Hutchinson, 1910).

Chester C. Tan, *The Boxer Catastrophe* (Columbia University Press, 1955).

Daniele Varè, *The Last of the Empresses* (John Murray, 1938).

Wilhelm II, *The Kaiser's Letters to the Tsar* (Hodder and Stoughton, 1920).

Mary Clabaugh Wright, *The Last Stand of Chinese Conservatism* (Stanford University Press, 1957).

Wu Yung, *The Flight of an Empress* (Faber and Faber, 1937).

Notes

Chapter 1

There are many descriptions and maps of Peking and the Forbidden City under the Manchu régime. Two of the most detailed are in *China Under the Empress Dowager* and *Twilight in the Forbidden City*.

The peacock (or phoenix) was the avian emblem of the Emperor as the eagle was of the Emperors of Austria and Germany.

The central government consisted of six Boards or Ministries administered jointly by Manchus and Chinese. His Majesty was personally advised by his Grand Council, consisting of Imperial Princes and high officials.

The Censorate was an autonomous body, the members of which had the widest powers to criticize or denounce officials or practices of which they disapproved. They might even call the Son of Heaven to order in their memorials to the Throne. This they frequently did, with outstanding moral courage, at the risk of severe punishment, disgrace, or even the loss of their lives.

All Chinese histories and chronicles contain denunciations of the eunuchs and their crimes; none, however, appear to give the point of view of these unfortunate men. Most Chinese rulers and their Courts regarded them as a necessary evil.

Chapter 2

There appears to be no certainty as to the Empress Dowager's birthplace, nor about the precise date when she arrived in Peking as a child; either with both or one of her parents.

'Princess' Der Ling—she claimed that the Empress Dowager had given her this title—was a Manchu, daughter of a nobleman and a secret Christian, partly educated in France. In 1903, when the old Empress wished to learn more about Western customs, institutions, and women, she summoned her to Court, with her mother and sister. Der Ling remained there for a little more than two years. She claimed that the Empress confided in her in order that Der Ling might write her life-story. In many ways Der Ling's descriptions of the Empress Dowager's character and life have the ring of truth; they have therefore been frequently quoted here. But in other respects they conflict with evidence or reports from reliable sources. They must, therefore, be accepted with a certain reserve.

According to Bland and Backhouse, the legend that Yehonala was already nubile when travelling with her mother to Peking, and the tale of the loan of money to the widow was invented by the Imperial Prince Tun, in order that the Empress Dowager and the Yehonala clan might lose face by this account of her early poverty.

Chapter 3

There are very many sources regarding the Taiping Rising. A recent account, which I have briefly followed, is in Victor Purcell's authoritative work, *The Boxer Rising*. Chinese Communist historians, re-interpreting their country's history, regard it as a combined peasant-proletarian rebellion against Manchu Imperialism, and foreign aggression.

When the Manchus conquered China they decreed that all male Chinese must shave their frontal hair and wear their back-hair in a queue as a token of submission. The Taipings refused to do so and were contemptuously referred to by the Manchus and their supporters as 'the long-haired rebels'.

According to Mary Clabaugh Wright, Marquis Teng Kuo-fan was both 'the greatest philosopher of the age' and its 'harshest disciplinarian'. The Communists list him and Li Hung Chang, his lieutenant, as the villains of the period. But for them and the assistance given by the foreign Powers, notably Great Britain, to their armies, the Manchu régime might well then have collapsed.

Matteo Ricci (1552-1610) was the most famous Jesuit missionary to China. He was a sinophile who learned the language and adopted Chinese dress. He arrived at the Court of the last Ming Emperor with presents of clocks, globes, books of European maps and engravings, which were eagerly received. After the overthrow of the Ming the first Manchu Emperor, Shun Chih, retained Ricci in Peking, where he died.

A full translation of the delightful Mandates addressed to King George III by the Chien Lung Emperor after receiving his envoys at Jehol, and that of the Mandate from the Chia Chin Emperor on Lord Amhert's abortive embassy to his Court, are in *Annals of the Court of Peking*.

Chapter 4
A detailed description of Hsien Feng's funeral procession from Jehol to Peking is given in Varè's *The Last of the Empresses*.

Chapter 5
The Western Empress's Decrees—the first in the child Emperor's name, the second in her own—are fully translated in *China Under the Empress Dowager*.

Chapter 6
Charles George Gordon (1833–85) was the famous British com-

mander known first as 'Chinese' Gordon and later as 'Gordon of Khartoum', where he was killed. At the time of the Taiping Rebellion Gordon was seconded by his superior officer, General Staveley, to the command of the 'Ever Victorious Army' at the request of Li Hung Chang, with whom, however, he quarrelled bitterly when that Chinese leader executed certain prisoners whose lives Gordon had promised to spare if they surrendered. Gordon was given the Yellow Jacket—the highest decoration—by the Throne, but as a British officer refused the large sum of money also offered to him.

Chapter 7

Slanderous gossip about Yehonala is quoted in detail in *Annals of the Court of Peking,* in which Bland and Backhouse gave four extracts from writers which they headed with the caution that all these accusations were 'the work of men who set out with the avowed purpose of vilifying the Manchus in general and Old Buddha in particular'. They also differed 'very materially on important details of evidence, and also . . . suggested constructive memory developed to a very high degree of elasticity'.

The Edict by the Co-Empresses on assuming the Regency is given in full in *China Under the Empress Dowager;* also the Decree of 1864. The dialogue between Her Majesty and Tseng Kuo-fan was quoted in full in the same work from a contemporary Chinese document.

Extracts from Wo Ko-tu's Memorial on the foreign devils and the reply to it of the Co-Empresses are quoted from *China Under the Empress Dowager.* This Memorial refers to the five cardinal tenets of Confucianism, which for centuries governed all Chinese family and social relationships.

Chapter 8

The excerpts from Tzu An's Decrees on An-te-hai are quoted from *China Under the Empress Dowager.*

The excerpts from the Co-Empress's Decree are from the same source.

Chapter 9
The theory that the Tung Chih Emperor was put to death by the
use of a face-towel infected with virulent smallpox was advanced
by Daniel Varè in *The Last of the Empresses,* where he gave
another instance of such an alleged murder in 1929, of a German
Colonel Bauer.

Chapter 10
The Empress Dowager's words at the Council meeting to appoint
a successor to the Tung Chih Emperor and her Decrees on the
subject are quoted from *China Under the Empress Dowager.*

There is little doubt that the Empress had some responsibility,
whether directly or indirectly, for the death of A-lu-te. The
Annals claim that on his death-bed Tung Chih tried to safeguard
the throne from the Holy Mother's machinations, but unsuccess-
fully. The story told there of A-lu-te's suicide is horrifying but
plausible. According to this, her father Chung Chi, the Imperial
tutor, who wished to remain in Tzu Hsi's favour, gave his
daughter the opium with which she killed herself. He remained
at Court, a loyal and appreciated servant of Her Majesty, until
after the Boxer Rising when he also committed suicide.

Chapter 11
In his valedictory Memorial, translated in full in *China Under
the Empress Dowager,* Jung Lu referred as follows to his
disgrace : 'While acting as Captain-General of the Peking
Gendarmerie, I incurred Your Majesty's displeasure; thereafter
for seven years I awaited, without incurring, the fitting penalty
for my offence.'

Chapter 12
The excerpts from the Decree dismissing Prince Kung are quoted
from *China Under the Empress Dowager*; the reply to the
Memorialists is from the same source.

Kuang Hsu's Consort, the Empress Lung Yu, succeeded Tzu Hsi
as Empress Dowager. During the minority of the last Manchu

Emperor Hsuan Tung (better known as Pu Yi) she modelled her
conduct on that of her illustrious predecessor, but without much
success. Her favourite eunuch became nearly as notorious as
Li Lien-ying. Cf. *Twilight in the Forbidden City.*

The description of Kuang Hsu's marriage and his vain protests
against being forced into it were given by Der Ling, who was
not then at Court but claimed to have known the Emperor
intimately later.

Chapter 13
Der Ling was in the Empress Dowager's service after her return
to the Summer Palace in 1902; her descriptions of Her Majesty's
life there may therefore be regarded as first-hand. There is also
a vivid account of the various ritual festivals in Varè's *The Last
of the Empresses,* from which the names of some of these occasions have been quoted. The excerpts from the Edicts are quoted
from *China Under the Empress Dowager.*

Chapter 14
The following works contain the lines quoted here on the foreign
aggression in the nineteenth century: *The Siege at Peking*; *The
Boxer Catastrophe*; *The Boxer Uprising,* from which the lines
on Li Hung Chang's innovations are also quoted. Li Hung
Chang's own accounts of his visit to Paris and dealings with the
Empress Dowager are from his *Memoirs.* His pawnbroking and
other business transactions and his acceptance of bribes, although
quite in accordance with Confucian tradition, made him very
unpopular with many later critics, including of course the Communist historians.

Chapter 15
Excerpts from the Memorial by the Censor An Wei-chun are
quoted from *China Under the Empress Dowager*; also excerpts
from the Emperor's reply, dictated by the Empress Dowager;
the Edict on educational reform and the Vermilion Rescript
handed to Weng Tung-ho.

Chapter 16

The differing versions of Kuang Hsu's plot against Old Buddha are to be found in *Twilight in the Forbidden City* on the one hand and *China Under the Empress Dowager* on the other. The differences are partly due to the fact that Johnston's book was not published until 1934, whilst Bland and Backhouse's authoritative work appeared in 1912, and partly to the sympathies of their respective authors. Bland and Backhouse admired the Empress Dowager almost to veneration; Johnston, who was a fervent admirer of Kang Yu-wei, detested her. Der Ling's account seems as close to the truth as one is likely to get, since it is not improbable that Kuang Hsu did confide in her as she claimed.

The account of Jung Lu's visit to Old Buddha and Kuang Hsu's message to Kang Yu-wei are cited from *China Under the Empress Dowager*; Kuang Hsu's own account from *Old Buddha*. Kuang Hsu's Decree is quoted from *China Under the Empress Dowager*. The same work contains the *Times* report on the visit of the Chinese physician to the Emperor in full. Kuang Hsu's prison at the Summer Palace is described in detail in *Twilight in the Forbidden City*.

Chapter 17

Li Hung Chang's two-hour session with the Empress Dowager is described in his *Memoirs*.

Excerpt from the Empress Dowager's Decree quoted from *China Under the Empress Dowager*.

Chapter 18

Sir Claude Macdonald, the British Minister, reported to his Government on Her Majesty's reception of the Legation ladies in a letter (*Blue Book*, China, No. 1, 1899) quoted in *China Under the Empress Dowager*.

The excerpt from the Empress's Decree is quoted from Chester Tan's *The Boxer Catastrophe*.

Chapter 19

A most interesting account of magical practices in the Western hemisphere, which closely resemble those of the Boxers and other Chinese mediums, is contained in Patrick Leigh Fermor's *The Traveller's Tree*. Undoubtedly such invocatory rites were and still are common to primitive peoples all over the world.

In view of the Empress Dowager's alliance with the Boxers, the most important point was that raised by Victor Purcell in *The Boxer Uprising* as to whether the movement was or was not originally an anti-Ching and a proletarian-nationalist one. After consulting several other sources, I concluded that Purcell had made out a conclusive claim for his interpretation of the situation, and therefore accepted his view. Another definitive work is Chester Tan's *The Boxer Catastrophe,* from which I have quoted the lines from Li Ping-heng's Memorial on the Big Sword Society. Mr Conger's dispatch is quoted in part from *The Boxer Uprising.*

Jung Lu's letter to the Viceroy of Fukien is given in full in *China Under the Empress Dowager,* from which my excerpts are quoted.

Sir Robert Hart's comments on the Boxers are quoted from 'These from the Land of Sinim'.

Chapter 20

The telegram from Jung Lu to General Nieh Shi-cheng is quoted from *The Boxer Catastrophe.*

The anecdote regarding the British Minister and the race-course is quoted from *The Siege at Peking.*

Sir Robert Hart's accounts are quoted from 'These from the Land of Sinim'.

Dr G. E. Morison's report is given in detail in *The Siege at Peking.*

The stories about Prince Tuan, the heir apparent, and Her Majesty's displeasure with them and with the Kansu general, are from 'The Diary of His Excellency Ching Shan' in *China Under*

the Empress Dowager. Certain authorities, notably Purcell, considered this document to be a fabrication, primarily to justify Jung Lu. Yet it has such an unmistakable flavour of the chaotic conditions at Court at that crisis that it seemed to me worth quoting.

It seems a little odd that after devoting a whole scholarly work to *The Boxer Uprising* Purcell should have dismissed it as a mere incident in Chinese history.

The 'Yellow Lotus Holy Mother' anecdote is quoted from the *Annals*.

Li Ping-heng's claim was quoted in *The Boxer Catastrophe*.

Prince Ching's and Jung Lu's telegrams are quoted from *China Under the Empress Dowager*.

F. W. Sutterlee's report to the *Daily Mail* is discussed in detail by Peter Fleming in *The Siege at Peking*. The Kaiser's cartoon on the 'Yellow Peril' is reproduced in *The Siege at Peking*. Cf. also *The Kaiser's Letters to the Tsar*.

Chapter 21

According to the *Annals* it was the eunuch Tsui who helped Li Lien-ying to drown the Pearl Concubine. This eunuch was also one of Kuang Hsu's chief tormentors. On the day of the Emperor's death this eunuch was—at his last request to Her Majesty—driven from the Palace. Bland and Backhouse dryly commented that 'his fortune was probably an important factor in this decision', since it reverted to the privy purse. Bearing in mind the Empress's death so soon afterwards, she may have had secret misgivings that Tsui was about to attempt her own murder. Wu Lung told the story of his reception of the fleeing Imperial family and his services to Old Buddha to Liu Kun in 1919. This was later adapted and edited by Ida Pruitt in *The Flight of an Empress*. Certain authorities have queried its genuineness in some particulars. Yet Wu Lung's descriptions of Old Buddha and her moods—from gracious imperturbability to sudden blazing fury— ring true.

The Soochow official's letter is quoted in full in *China Under the Empress Dowager* and also in *The Boxer Catastrophe*.

Chapter 22
The telegram from the Empress Dowager to Li Hung Chang is quoted from his *Memoirs*.

The Decrees issued at Sianfu from which excerpts have been quoted here are given in full in *China Under the Empress Dowager*.

The summary of the Articles of the Allies' Joint Note is quoted from *The Boxer Catastrophe*.

The comment on Article 6 is quoted from Purcell; Count Witte's cynical remark to his colleague is from the same source.

Chapter 23
Detailed descriptions of the Court's triumphal return to Peking are given in *China Under the Empress Dowager* and several other sources already mentioned.

Li Hung Chang's entry in his diary is quoted from his *Memoirs*.

The *Times* account of the railway journey to Peking is given in full in *China Under the Empress Dowager*.

Excerpts from the account of Her Majesty's use of opium are quoted from the same source.

Don Rodolfo Borghese's delightful description of Her Majesty's triumphal entry into Peking is quoted from Daniele Varè's *The Last of the Empresses*.

Chapter 24
The anecdote about the theft of the sable coat is quoted from the above work.

According to the *Annals*, one of Her Majesty's greatest treasures was a solid rock of jade, carved and engraved with poems by the Ming Emperor, Yung Lo, and by Chien Lung, about eight feet long. It 'was stolen from Tzu Hsi's apartments at the Summer Palace by an officer of the allied forces . . . and sold by him to an American connoisseur and diplomat'. According to this source, in due course it found its way to the Metropolitan Museum of Art. The Empress was 'very fond of this curio and much distressed at its loss'.

Der Ling, in *Old Buddha,* described the snapshot of the foreign devil seated on the Imperial throne; she also stated that Her Majesty refused to have the wheel-marks removed or the shell-hole filled in. Der Ling's description of Old Buddha's grief at Jung Lu's death, partly quoted here, is very moving; so is the curt expression of it by the Empress to her brother, quoted from *China Under the Empress Dowager.*

Lady Susan Townley's naive description of Her Majesty is quoted from Sergeant's *The Great Empress Dowager of China.*

The story of the bird-charming by Her Majesty is partly quoted from Miss Carl's *Memoirs* as quoted more fully by Varè. The Empress Dowager was very fond of birds. According to the *Annals* she would periodically release those in the palaces from their cages; the eunuchs caught them again, however, and sold them to dealers who resold them to the palace officials, a petty instance of their rapacity.

Der Ling's charming descriptions of the Imperial pilgrimages to Jehol and Mukden are partly quoted from *Imperial Incense.*

Madame Chiang Kai-shek informed the present writer that the Empress Dowager was directly responsible for the abolition of the painful custom of the foot-binding of young Chinese girls.

Chapter 25
For a detailed description of the Dalai Lama's visit to Peking cf. Johnston's *Twilight in the Forbidden City.* But he was in error in stating that the Dalai Lama's presence was a menace to the Empress Dowager. 'Old Buddha' was only a nickname flatteringly given her by Li Lien-ying and did not mean that she also was an incarnation of that divinity, as the Emperor—the Son

of Heaven—was assumed to be. The version given in *China Under the Empress Dowager* seems nearer the facts and certainly to Her Majesty's own interpretation of them. Kuang Hsu's remarks on his illness are quoted from this source also.

Johnston's account of the Emperor's last official interview with Her Majesty, quoted here, is almost the only non-derogatory reference to her in *Twilight in the Forbidden City.*

The Empress's sharp rebuke to Prince Ching is quoted from *China Under the Empress Dowager,* as is the account of her information to the Grand Council that she intended to appoint Jung Lu's grandson as Emperor designate; also the preface to Kuang Hsu's testament.

Der Ling's sensational claim that the Empress and Li Lien-ying poisoned Kuang Hsu is quoted here because the eunuch Chang Teh, who allegedly told her of it, might have been speaking the truth. But all 'evidence' based on eunuch's gossip must be treated with great reserve.

China Under the Empress Dowager contains a reproduction of the photograph of Her Majesty as the Boddhisatva Kuan Yin, with Li Lien-ying in attendance.

Chapter 26

The Empress's Decree on the appointment as Emperor of Pu-yi is quoted in part, and her Valedictory Decree in full, from *China Under the Empress Dowager.* The list of her honorific titles, with their transliteration, is from Sergeant's *The Great Empress Dowager of China.*

A full description of Her Majesty's obsequies was quoted from *The Times* in *China Under the Empress Dowager.* A detailed inventory of the treasure buried with her, according to Li Lien-ying, was given in the *Illustrated London News,* quoted by Varè.

The looting of the tombs of the Ching dynasty was described in detail by Johnston in *Twilight in the Forbidden City.*

Chapter 27

Excerpts from the charming description of Old Buddha by the country folk are quoted from *China Under the Empress Dowager.*

I have not quoted the large number of opinions on the Empress Dowager, whether in exaggerated praise or blame, in many works I have read which did not appear to me sufficiently reliable sources. It may, however, be of interest to refer to 'Wen Ching', who wrote one of the most vituperative accounts of her, which is still quoted by Her Majesty's posthumous enemies and those who prefer legend to fact. This account 'issued from the safe asylum of a British Colony . . . so obviously distorted by hatred . . . and so recklessly inaccurate on matters of verifiable detail as to be useless,' according to Bland and Backhouse in the *Annals,* was written under that pseudonym by Dr Lim Boon Keng, a Chinese scholar, contemporary, and intimate friend of Kang Yu-wei and Dr Sun Yat Sen. In 1938 the present writer met Dr Lim, then a delightful old gentleman, in Singapore. He was the father of Dr Robert K. Lim, who had studied medicine in Britain and was the founder of the Chinese Army Medical Service during the Kuomintang régime and war of resistance to the Japanese.

Chapter 28

Sir Robert Hart's sensational prophecy is partly quoted from '*These from the Land of Sinim*'. The figures given are from an essay on China by Charles O. Hucker in *Asia in the Modern World.*

Excerpts from Pu Yi's own story are quoted from *China Reconstructs* (January 1964).

Index of Chinese Names

General Index